PENGUIN BOOKS

Fleecing the Lamb

David Cruise and Alison Griffiths are a successful writing team whose work has appeared in most Canadian national magazines and earned them three national writing awards. In addition to the best-selling *Fleecing the Lamb*, they are the authors of *Lords of the Line*, which was both a critical and commercial success, as was David's first book, *The Money Rustlers*, cowritten with Paul Grescoe. David and Alison live on the Gorge in Victoria with their two daughters.

David Cruise & Alison Griffiths

FLEECING THE LAMB

The Inside Story of the Vancouver Stock Exchange

Penguin Books

PENGUIN BOOKS
Published by the Penguin Group
Penguin Books Canada Ltd, 10 Alcorn Avenue, Toronto, Ontario,
Canada M4V 1E4
Penguin Books Ltd, 27 Wrights Lane, London W8 5TZ, England
Penguin Books USA Inc., 375 Hudson Street, New York, New York 10014, U.S.A.
Penguin Books Australia Ltd, Ringwood, Victoria, Australia
Penguin Books (NZ) Ltd, 182-190 Wairau Road, Auckland 10, New Zealand

Penguin Books Ltd, Registered Offices: Harmondsworth, Middlesex, England

First published by Douglas & McIntyre Ltd., 1987

Published in Penguin Books, 1991

10 9 8 7 6 5 4 3 2 1

Manufactured in Canada

Canadian Cataloguing in Publication Data
Cruise, David, 1950—
    Fleecing the lamb : the inside story of the
Vancouver Stock Exchange

ISBN 0-14-014585-0

1. Vancouver Stock Exchange. I. Griffiths,
Alison, 1953— II. Title.

HG5160.V3C8 1991   332.64'271133   C90-095502-3

Contents

Acknowledgements

To Mum and Dad who always told me to try. AG
To Jack for his steadfast belief in us. DC

Many people devoted their time to making this book possible. We want to thank all the policemen, civil servants, exchange employees, exchange ex-employees, securities lawyers, accountants, brokers, investors and promoters who took the time to answer our questions. Particular appreciation goes out to Bob Mullock, Bill Irwin, Bob Scott, Rupert Bullock, Ted Affleck and Al Dilworth for their patience and valuable information.

Critical to the writing of this book was the time given to us by Peter Brown, Brian Harwood, Ted Turton, the Keevils, Murray Pezim, Egil Lorntzsen, Bruce McDonald, Terry Podolski, Ken Hanna, Ray Cottrell, Brian Graves, David Reesor, Stanley Burke, Michael Brown, Ron Truesdale, George Cross and John Woods.

Also, without the assistance of K. C. Black, Jeffrey Black, Bernie Nayman and John Black, the chapter on Morris Black the promoter would be far less than it is. In the same vein Margaret Newcombe and Bodo von Alvensleben provided priceless memories of their father, as did Robert McGraw of his father. Cecil Clark, an amateur historian, provided key insights into Alvo von Alvensleben's career.

The paper research was aided by Shirley Mooney, librarian at the Vancouver *Sun*, the staff of the periodical section at the University of British Columbia UBC library, the staff of the City of Vancouver Archives, the State of Washington archives, the Northwest Room of the

Vancouver Public Library and the Provincial Archives of British Columbia. We also extend thanks to Joyce Courtney, in charge of public relations at the Vancouver Stock Exchange.

In particular we wish to thank Sandy Ross, who generously allowed us to use the research and transcripts from his excellent book *The Traders*. His insight and encouragement were much appreciated.

Our former agent, David Colbert, provided a sympathetic and knowledgeable ear.

Perhaps the greatest debt of gratitude goes to Kathleen Mentzos and her husband, Bob, who provided a loving second home to our youngest daughter, Quinn, born during the writing of this book.

Finally, we would like to thank the dozens of people who are breathing a sigh of relief because their names appear nowhere in this book.

Shortly after the Vancouver Stock Exchange (VSE) opened its doors in August 1907, C. D. Rand, the first president, received three small, individually wrapped parcels. The first contained a bull, the second a bear and the third a lamb—shorn to the quick. Rand pretended to be puzzled, joking that he understood lambs to gambol on the green and brokers more often on the red and black. But Rand, a hard-nosed trader who had previously worked on the New York Stock Exchange, well understood the significance of the three figures. The bull refers to a rising market, the bear to a plunging one and the lamb to the hapless investor who gets fleeced whatever direction the market is taking. Whoever sent the parcels knew that in order to profit, the VSE would need a steady supply of lambs willing to be shorn and shorn again. What the anonymous donor couldn't have foreseen was the fine art the VSE was to make of the shearing.

Introduction

"If you have a faint heart or slow wits, steer clear of the Vancouver exchange. It's that simple." FORBES, April 27, 1981.

The Vancouver Stock Exchange is the largest exchange in the world dealing almost exclusively in speculative stocks. It is also one of the most profitable business entities on the face of the earth, owned and operated by the forty-eight brokerage firms that trade there. In 1986, 3.5 billion shares valued at $4.5 billion were traded on the VSE and over $700 million worth of financing was completed that year. The average daily trading volume was 12.2 million shares worth $13.4 million, or approximately $1.10 a share. The figures don't begin to hint at the real story of where the money goes and for whom it makes a profit.

Nearly half of every dollar invested in the VSE does not reach the companies in which it is invested but finds its way directly into the pockets of brokers, promoters and insiders. It's as if you went into a bank and gave the teller $1,000, half of which was passed to owners of the bank as a kind of unofficial surcharge. If your bank account was a listed company, as little as 21 per cent of the remaining $500, or $150, might end up on the deposit slip.* This is all great news for those who service the VSE in one way or another. But for the investor—or lamb —this means that little over 10 per cent of their original $1,000 investment is working to provide a return. In fact, VSE investors lose some of their money 84 per cent of the time and all of it 40 per cent of the time.

These startling facts and figures come from an exhaustive 1979 study, *Public Financing of Junior Resource Securities in British Columbia*, by Michael J. Brown, J. Haig deB. Farris and Jack R. Jefferson. The authors are unimpeachable sources. Aside from their legal and market background, they are the founders of Ventures West Management Inc., the leading venture capital company in western Canada. Some say Ventures West is everything the VSE should be and isn't. The report covered the most favourable time period possible for the exchange since the analysis spans the years from 1965 to 1978, over a decade of extraordinary mine finding. The study carefully examined every single company listed on the VSE during the thirteen years in question. During the study period, $1,239,691,000, including commissions, was raised on the VSE through the purchase, by investors, of primary and secondary issues. Of the total money raised, only $635,575,000, or 51.3 per cent, was received by the companies for which it was collected. The property vendors received 7.9 per cent ($97,977,000), the promoters 13.8 per cent ($170,527,000) and the brokerage firms 27 per cent ($335,612,000) of the total. The study did not investigate trading profits.

The authors' conclusions were damning:

> The real organizers of the market are the brokers, promoters and property vendors—all of which groups benefit from it. New issues are their lifeblood, for, as can be seen from the distributions of average gain, their trading commissions would tend to atrophy as companies fall by the wayside. Yet it is the brokers who hold twelve of the fifteen governorships of the VSE. The conflict with the public interest seems obvious. . . . As an interesting aside, these sub-groups, who are organizers of the marketplace and not members of the public, seem able to make much higher returns than the public compared to their investment.

*The matter of exactly how much money invested in junior stocks actually gets put into the ground or directly applied to a company is hotly debated. The Ontario Securities Commission staff has estimated that the figure is as low as 21 per cent. At times, none of the investors' money is directly applied to its intended purpose.

> This suggests (in normal economic theory) that they are taking much higher risks. However, such seems not really to be the case for a variety of reasons concerned with the manner in which the marketplace is organized.

This statement is the key to the whole thing. Even if investors accept unfavourable odds and a high degree of risk as inherent to the speculative market, it would all be fair and equitable so long as they are playing the same game as everyone else. But they are not. The market is often compared to a card game, lottery or racetrack gamble. The comparison is a masterful piece of disinformation. In a horse race, you know that the jockeys, trainers and racetrack touts aren't making the rules, and the odds are clearly posted. Comparing what happens on the exchange with a game of chance implies the element of fairness that the flip of dice or shuffle of cards guarantees. There is none of this randomness or fairness about the dealings of the speculative market. The simple fact is that those who know more—who have inside information—make the money. Those with less information—the general public—invariably lose. The best comparison for the speculative market is with carnival games complete with barkers and shills. One in particular comes to mind, the game where you try to throw a ring over a circle that's too big for it. Add a blindfold and a few spins around, and you have a rough analogy to the chances the average investor has of making a profit on the VSE.

The Brown Farris & Jefferson study has never been replicated, debated or even contradicted for the simple reason that the minute the B.C. Ministry of Economic Development received it, the report was buried. Few even know it exists, much less what it contains, even though some of its findings were leaked in 1980. The profitability the report alludes to is found in the financial statements of VSE members. For instance, Canarim Investment Corporation Ltd. of Vancouver, the dominant firm dealing with VSE underwriting and trading, and one of the few local houses to publish statistics, had 1980 pretax profits of more than $30 million. That same year, the much larger Toronto firm of Midland Doherty reported only $16 million in profit. In 1984, after a two-year recession which devastated the West, Canarim still had a net income of $16 million. Since then, Canarim has decided to keep its financial details to itself.

The Vancouver Stock Exchange has tightened up its rules somewhat in recent years but with little effect on those attracted to the money or to the overall profitability of the exchange. In 1974 the Co-ordinated Law Enforcement Unit estimated that 20 to 30 per cent of VSE trading was manipulated and that twenty-five to fifty people with criminal records were involved with the exchange in some way. Police market specialists privately admit that the situation has become far worse, not better, as the recession and changing government priorities have seriously weakened their capabilities. Virtually every brokerage house on the street, even some of the national firms that do their best to avoid direct association with the VSE, employ a fixer or paper me-chanic whose specialty is getting around the exchange's rules. "Some deals come through that don't have the fundamentals we look for; le-gitimate assets, earning potential, proper management etc.," says a broker with a highly respected local brokerage house. "Sexy little deals. Interesting, profitable. We can't put our stamp on them, of course, so we hire a promoter and give him some seed stock. He lets a broker from another house down the street take down [buy] 25-cent stock to ensure a market. The lawyers who register the company have no idea who's behind it. It opens at $1 [per share], we make a bundle, and no one's the wiser."

This is the story behind the evolution of the Vancouver Stock Ex-change from a self-conscious little exchange in 1907 into the money machine it is today. It is the story of the men, and some women, who have built the exchange and profited from it. Some were saints, many were sinners, and on the fringes existed the biggest collection of grifters, con artists and rogues anywhere. It is also the story of the handful of mines, oil and gas wells, and industrial companies that have been discovered or developed, often serendipitously, as a result of their association with the Vancouver Stock Exchange. Love it or hate it, the VSE is never dull.

PART I

The Early Years

The formative years of the Vancouver Stock Exchange, from its inception in 1907 through two world wars until the early 1960s, saw the establishment of a cycle of boom, bust and scandal that has characterized the VSE ever since.

The Vancouver Stock Exchange had undeniably humble beginnings, but what it lacks in stature it has more than made up for in colourful characters and their antics. Alvo von Alvensleben was the VSE's first promoter and one of the most compelling figures to emerge during its entire history. The quality and cleverness of his promotions coupled with his understanding of investors' vagaries were phenomenal and extremely sophisticated for the time.

Another character, more self-contained but even more successful, was John McGraw, owner of Continental Securities. Singular in his utter domination of the exchange and the western speculative market, McGraw disdained bombast, preferring to make his market killings quietly. He ruled in a placid time, but his era laid the foundation for the turbulence and the profitability of the 1960s.

CHAPTER 1

The Birth of the
Vancouver Stock Exchange

"They were happy enough days, but profitless, largely." VSE MEMBER C. M. OLIVER, commenting on the exchange's early years.

B ritish Columbia's early history is pockmarked by a frenzied boom/bust pattern of gold discovery and exploitation. Waves of gold diggers and settlers descended on the colony in the nearly forty years between the first gold discovery on the Fraser River in 1858 to the great Rossland stampede of '98. The attitude of many gold diggers toward the West was little better than "Get in, get yer gold, and get out." Their legacy remains behind in the hundreds of ghost towns that haunt the interior of B.C. The scattered shells of dilapidated, rust-roofed, grey buildings, rank with damp and moss, bear witness to the enormous physical and financial activity once created by the pursuit of gold.

The character of B.C. gold rushes was exemplified by the prospectors, the grubstakers, the dreamers and the opportunists who hoped to dig, pan or blast their way into a fortune. The boom/bust cycles they fuelled, in turn, fed another more parasitical activity—the sale of common stocks. The gold rush securities salesmen, using all the high-pressure techniques of the patent medicine trade, were the spiritual forefathers of today's stock promoters. Fast talking, fast thinking and faster moving, they descended on a town, waving certificates they promised were the next best thing to the nuggets themselves. Sometimes the mine names on the heavily and ornately engraved paper were real, sometimes the mines and names were just fanciful products of their own minds.

The success of these stock salesmen prompted other citizens to capitalize on the public's interest in buying largely worthless bits of paper. They all realized that if there was a market in selling these stocks to the public, there was also a market in buying them back and selling them again, at a higher price, to someone else. A stock exchange was the answer. It would, the proponents argued, protect the public and also enhance the economic activity of the province as an altruistic side benefit. Better yet, an exchange would direct some of the money being paid to stock hustlers into more legitimate pockets. Unfortunately, many of the people behind these early exchanges were little better than those they sought to replace. Most of them came from the East to feed on what they believed would be short-lived western prosperity. All they hoped for was a few years of easy riches. So compelling was the notion of a stock exchange that between 1877 and 1907 at least a dozen institutions of varying respectability came and went.

Finally, in 1906, Donald Von Cramer (he later dropped the Von), a respected banker, began convening informal discussions with the goal of forming a stock exchange devoted exclusively to mining issues. Von Cramer, like most Vancouverites, was new to the city. He had arrived in 1898 as manager of the Royal Bank's new West Coast branch, and later he organized the Vancouver Trust Company. Over the years, he had become an influential resident, serving on the Board of Trade and as the founding president of the Vancouver-Canadian Club in 1912. The Rossland gold rush in 1898 had largely profited Spokane, thanks to the stock exchange in that city, and Von Cramer thought that Vancouver should have one of its own. He found a willing ally in C. D. Rand, a real estate dealer and a mining broker who had financed many mine ventures. Von Cramer, Rand and ten others* met week after week at their various clubs to thrash out their vision of

---

*Attendees came and went, but the final twelve listed on the incorporation documents were J. R. Waghorn, Ewen W. MacLean, Donald Von Cramer, Charles D. Rand, R. Byron-Johnson, A. B. Diplock, W. L. Germaine, John Kendall, Charles J. Loewen, J. F. Maguire, F. J. Procter and Herbert E. A. Robertson.

an exchange that would "roust the eastern bankers from their lethargy" by providing a place for the hard-driven prospector to finance his work.

By March 1907, plans for the new exchange were complete. Bill 55, a private member's bill, was introduced in the British Columbia legislature for the purpose of incorporating the Vancouver Stock Exchange. Opposition to the bill was expected because, a year earlier, a joint-stock company had been incorporated calling itself the Vancouver Stock Exchange, precisely the name coveted by the twelve founders. "I was called up by telephone, and also received some letters. But I see no one here," said house chairman Mr. Bowser in the legislature. "What will you do about the name? There may be some conflict."

"Oh we're not afraid of them," retorted Harold Robertson, a lawyer who appeared for the founders. "It is not a question of you being afraid of them," responded MLA Stuart Henderson. "It is the interest of the public we are concerned with. No doubt they will be confused by the similarity of names." The debate continued with a dozen facetious suggestions for new names. "Why not call it the Rainy Hollow Stock Exchange? " suggested the member for Nanaimo. "Or Rainy without the Hollow," joked another member, playing on the fact that Victoria had a drier, more pleasant climate than the ever-damp Vancouver.

Finally, with no one to speak for the other company, the second Vancouver Stock Exchange was allowed to take the name. The only discussion concerned the liability of the exchange members. The founders' proposal to limit their financial responsibility to their annual dues met no opposition. The bill passed through two readings with no amendments and was given royal assent on April 25, 1907, together with acts to protect horse-breeders and to regulate the hours during which children of tender years may be on the streets. The creation of the VSE was a psychological coup de grâce to Victoria, once the premier city on the Pacific coast outside of San Francisco. It had already lost its control over trade, communications and industry in B.C. and, with the failure of the Victoria-based Bank of B.C. in the late 1890s and its absorption by the Canadian Bank of Commerce in 1900, lost its grip on finance as well.

Of the twelve Vancouver businessmen who signed their names to the VSE charter, only one, C. D. Rand (who had worked briefly for a brokerage firm in New York), had any real experience in common stocks. Despite Von Cramer's sponsorship of the original meetings,

Rand was the power and became the exchange's first president. In his speech at the opening of the VSE, Rand spoke bitterly of the role played by British Columbia in Spokane's current prosperity as the largest exchange in the West outside of San Francisco:

> When the mining districts of Slocan, Rossland and Boundary were discovered, prospectors endeavored to interest business men of the British Columbia coast cities in the different properties but received practically no encouragement and the result was that prospectors went to Spokane and the businessmen of that city grasped the opportunity. . . . The millions which were paid into the coffers of the Spokane citizens were reinvested by them in the purchase of real estate and the erection of magnificent buildings and Spokane today owes a very large proportion of its prosperity to the mines of British Columbia.

Rand's authority was so unquestioned that long after he left the position of president he still was the exclusive public spokesman for the VSE. He remained one of the most powerful figures on the exchange until his death in 1914. The VSE, in honour of his contribution, closed on January 9th, the day of his funeral.

The other founders were a mix of financial men, merchants, real estate brokers, entrepreneurs and opportunists. Charles Loewen had begun his real estate firm, Loewen, Harvey & Humble Ltd., in 1893. J. R. Waghorn was also a real estate man whose firm, Waghorn, Gwynn & Company, advertised heavily using a large handwritten X as their symbol. Before coming to Vancouver, Waghorn had founded the *Waghorn Guide*, a Winnipeg financial magazine. A. B. Diplock had arrived in 1887 and by 1899 had a thriving importing and wholesale business that dealt in "Crockery, Lamps and Fancy Goods." Taciturn, pipe-smoking C. M. Oliver, whose firm still exists, was a mine broker who'd actually worked in the first gold camp at Rossland. Oliver was convinced that silver would eventually become the standard of the world currencies, long before the Hunt brothers tried to buy it all.

One of the most successful of the early members was A. E. "Johnny" Jukes. In 1909, at the age of twenty-two, he bought a VSE seat in the name of his firm, A. E. Jukes and Company.* Johnny Jukes had attended Trinity College in Port Hope, Ontario, and University

*There is some discrepancy in historical records. Jukes was associated with the VSE in 1907 when he was underage, but his role is unclear.

School in Victoria. His father, Andrew Jukes, the local manager of the Imperial Bank of Canada, was credited with bringing the sport of cricket to Vancouver when the family moved there in 1895.

An aggressive, astute man nicknamed John Bull, Jukes financed many B.C. mines including Bralorne, a huge gold discovery in the 1930s, and a number of others in the Bridge River–Sheep Creek region during the Depression. Like many financial pioneers, Jukes was as tough as a frontier sheriff, and he abhorred layabouts and union men. During the July 1946 hearing before a Department of Mines special committee investigating the possibility of legislating a forty-four-hour week for B.C.'s 7,500 metalliferous miners, Jukes and Harvey Murphy, the international representative of the Union of Mine, Mill and Smelter Workers, nearly came to blows. "You're one of the most hostile employers in B.C.," vilified Murphy, who went on to accuse Jukes of dumping a load of food rather than feed it to striking workers. Jukes was president of the vsE in 1933, '34 and '35 and again in 1939, '40 and '41. He died in 1954.

The vsE members were enthusiastic and eager, but 1907 was a bad year to begin trading. Not only was the world in the midst of a severe recession, but the public was still simmering over their losses to "bucket-shop brokers" during the Rossland and Klondike gold rushes. The fly-by-night exchanges of those days had made the words stockbroker and highway robber synonymous. Even well-meaning brokers were derided in editorials from the Rockies to the coast as "sharpies with gilt edged tongues and junk securities." So bad was the memory of early exchanges that C. D. Rand took pains in his 1907 opening speech to reassure the public that the vsE was an entirely different animal:

> These brokers were posing as philanthropists, and were taking much credit to themselves for the great part they were taking in the development of British Columbia, but when the bubble burst, and the wildcats dropped out of sight these same brokers, instead of taking their share of the responsibility, endeavored to place the blame for the wildcatting upon the brokers of British Columbia.

To make the vsE's life more difficult, the banking community was frankly derisive of the new exchange and offered little help to brokers seeking loans.

Since most stock trading outside Toronto and New York was in unlisted securities, the thrust of all the VSE's promotion was designed to persuade investors to deal only with VSE members and listed companies. Rand set the tone in his opening address:

> Let the buyers of privately exploited unlisted stocks seek out the persuasive men who sold them and demand that they give as well as take — to the extent of even one-fourth of their holdings—and they will be treated to an exhibition of "welshing" and "quitting" which would be a spectacle for both gods and men.

The public wasn't easily convinced. Hawkers flogging miracle cures off the back of horse-drawn carts were, if anything, more respected than the men who spent their lives selling opportunities to get in on the ground floor of Glad Tidings Mine. At least a bottle of Malaise-Be-Gone Emulsion was something the buyer could hold and drink—even if it gave him nothing more than a rousing bout of flatulence or some pleasant, opium-induced dreams. Stockbrokers, on the other hand, had recently made a name for themselves by not even bothering to deliver the certificates of the securities they sold. Nonetheless, eighteen of the thirty seats had been sold by the time the first trade was made on August 1, 1907. When these pipe-smoking, black-booted gentlemen witnessed the first VSE trade—1000 shares of Alberta Coal at 43 cents*—they were confident they had inaugurated a new era for the West. It was to be an era that would be free from or at least inconvenient for the fast-buck artists who had given the stock market a bad name.

The VSE also had to win over the mining community and convince companies to list on the exchange, an even more difficult task. At the end of 1908 only fourteen companies had paid the required $50 fee and were officially listed on the VSE's board. The exchange's first employee, John Kendall, who was also a seat holder, complained of the situation to other members, saying that some kind of promotional campaign was necessary. The VSE's executive committee met and formulated a plan to put companies on the board, whether they needed it or not. Kendall hastily put together a form letter with an underlined blank space for the name of the appropriate company. The letter read:

---

*C. D. Rand purchased the 1000 Alberta Coal and he immediately turned around and tried to sell it again at 45 cents. There were no takers.

Dear Sir, *re Vancouver Stock Exchange*

I am instructed by the Committee to notify you of their intention to enlarge the trading list of stocks quoted on the Exchange and to include ----------- as an "Unlisted" stock, the committee find more or less outside trading in same and a desire on the part of some shareholders to see a staple [*sic*] market quotation for the shares and sales reported. The Committee would be glad to see your stock regularly listed on the Exchange and they invite you to fill up the enclosed form with full particulars for their consideration. A listed stock indicates that the Exchange has been furnished with full information of the Company's affairs and financial position and have passed the investigating committee, whereas an unlisted stock has no such standing. In any event the Company will be pleased to receive a copy of your prospectus and last Annual Report for filing.

The official listing Fee is $50.00, which should accompany the application.

Yours faithfully,
John Kendall, Secretary.

Dozens of these letters were sent out with mixed results. The agent for Beaver Valley Oil Company took exception to the insinuation that an unlisted stock had no standing and claimed that Beaver Valley had no business being listed on an exchange because it was a purely speculative venture. He wrote that the exploration was "a good clean gamble," but added: "If oil is not struck the stock will be valueless and it would be a crime to offer it for sale." He went on to point out that even if a strike was made the company would have no need of the exchange, since the find would speak for itself and "draw interest on its merits."

The gentlemen founders of the VSE took considerable pains to demonstrate the serious and conservative nature of their business. It didn't much matter that the shares of Mother Lode Ltd. represented at best a piece of bush and at worst some fancy paper, as long as the stock was traded courteously and the members scrupulously avoided taking any responsibility for the fortunes of the various companies. The mechanics of trading consumed far more time than any other aspect of the VSE's business. Initially, an exchange member was assigned to chair the call for a period of time. Everyone took a turn. The call itself consisted of an auctionlike system where the listed stocks were announced one after the other alphabetically. On each call, the chair would ask if there were any bids or offers from the floor. A broker who wanted to buy or sell would yell or raise his hand. In the 1920s, when trading volumes escalated, the call sometimes made it only halfway through the alphabet in one day. Anyone with business to transact in an un-called stock had to wait for the next day.

No such problem existed during the calm trading days of the VSE's first three years. Volume was so light that on many days only a few thousand shares exchanged hands. Only four of the thirty-two listed and unlisted companies traded on July 14, 1910; and on thirty-seven other days in the first six months of that year, all the trading was done between two men in less than four stocks. For most members the stock market was a sideline, a pleasant diversion. In the first few years, all of them earned the bulk of their income elsewhere, and for some, membership in the exchange made for incongruous letterheads. John S. Rankin, one of the first eighteen members, was also an auctioneer, real estate and mining agent who offered "high class furniture sales."

The money that early members made came largely from buying and selling stock for themselves. Since a stock could be listed only with the sponsorship of a member, most of the companies on the board were those in which members or their friends had an interest. Some-times stocks would be dropped from the board with no warning and for no obvious reason save for the fact that the interested member no longer held any shares. Other times stocks would remain listed, but after trading had ceased and a suitable period of time had passed, the member in charge of the trading simply stopped bothering to call for bids and offers.

While the VSE took little responsibility for the companies it listed, membership in the exchange was a very different matter. When some-one applied for a seat, the management committee, comprised of the exchange secretary and four others, conducted a search for judge-ments, chattel mortgages or conditional sales registered against the applicant. Far more important than financial standing, however, was the matter of good name, determined almost exclusively from letters of reference. Any hint of scandal in a man's past disqualified him in-stantly. Conversely, members of good families were easily admitted regardless of experience or situation.

In 1908, for example, the youngest son of a wealthy Scottish family applied for a seat. He was being farmed out to the colonies as neither position nor fortune awaited him in Edinburgh, but his business experience was limited to less than a year with a failed shipping company. As the exchange executive debated his merits, they spent no time on his lack of knowledge in the securities industry or in business generally. All they were concerned about was his reputation and social standing. A letter from the young man's banker in Edinburgh vouched for his character, saying he was a "good and steady young chap" with nothing to besmirch his family's old name save a small bank account and a bit of bad luck in business. The executive voted unanimously to let him into the exchange. Another application in 1910 was accompanied by a recommendation from an Irish stockbroker, Josias Cunningham & Company. The firm's owner noted sadly that the prospective member had no business experience and was the son of a Dublin broker whose firm had come to grief. But he hoped that the vse would not be swayed "toward rejection of same young gentleman" because he had "good social position" and "his character is well thought of in important circles." The young man was admitted forthwith.

The point of all this exclusivity was to warn undesirables working the vse territory that the exchange meant business and that its members were men to be reckoned with. Unfortunately, the presence of sons of good families did little to frighten off the crooks and sharp operators. In fact, it almost seemed to attract them. On August 1, 1907, the day the vse opened for business, the lengthy front-page article in the Vancouver *Daily World*, covering the address by C. D. Rand, was dwarfed by a three-quarter-page ad taken out by a notorious stock promoter from Kansas City, by the name of Dobbin. In it he promoted a scheme that promised "a fortune in 5 years" if investors would only entrust their savings to his expertise.

A 1908 English newspaper story also caused considerable embarrassment at the exchange:

Proceedings are pending in the Irish courts for the compulsory winding-up of the Fish Oil and Guano Company, Ltd. This was a promotion of one J. C. W. Stanley, who will be remembered in connection with other fishy ventures, such as the Irish Fish and Ice Company, Limited, the Irish Fisheries Development Syndicate, Limited, the Irish Fish Oil and Guano Company, Limited, and the Newfoundland Fish Industries, Limited, all defunct. Mr. Stanley is now turning from fish to paper, for I learn that he is a director and consulting engineer of the British Canadian Wood Pulp and Paper Company, Limited [briefly listed on the vse], and he has submitted to the board a process of his own, by which he not only extracts soda, but also gas and turpentine from wood. Some years ago Mr. Stanley had an invention by which he was to convert the refuse of the dustbin into paper. The only thing this company did in this line was issue shares, and I venture to think that the only gas which this new process is likely to emit is that which emanates from Mr. Stanley himself.

Stanley's schemes sound remarkably similar to many of the industrial ventures launched on the VSE in later years.

Hoping to thwart scoundrels like Dobbin and Stanley, the VSE offered itself to the public as a clearing-house for mining activities, and in every advertisement and article written about it, Rand stated the exchange's willingness to provide information to investors. His magnanimity backfired. Letters from the West Indies, Scotland, India and other parts of the empire flooded the VSE with enquiries about stock. Many of the requests were based on dog-eared press releases that had been passed from one hand to another, and rarely did they have anything to do with VSE-listed stocks. An Austrian count wintering in Mexico wrote to the exchange executive in 1910, complaining that he couldn't get any information "as to the state of things" in Vancouver. In the same year, the writer of a letter on Bank of Bengal letterhead politely asked the VSE to submit to him a list of recommended B.C. investments. There also must have been a core of curious investors residing in the Waldorf Hotel in Fernie, B.C., because several letters from the hotel landed on the desk of John Kendall. Below the ornate letterhead, promising WHITE HELP THROUGHOUT, came requests for information about mining companies, most of which were not listed on the VSE.

If the VSE's greatest irritation was those who saw it as a combination library and investment counsellor, its biggest public relations headache was the always optimistic, usually irregular and rarely accurate information released by listed companies. The VSE members were attempting to emulate the respectable image and gentlemanly racetrack lingo of more established exchanges and brokerage firms. They wanted to be able to issue the kind of reports that came from London and New York firms, reports such as: "Cream of Tartar after a spurt has eased, Prussiate of Soda is dull, Creosote has good enquiry." Yet, the VSE was plagued by statements like "It is a sinche [sic] that we have an ore shoot," and "Untold Wealth is shortly expected," and "Results are so promising your good directors have been rendered spechless [*sic*]," which lowered the tone of daily business.

Amusing, inflammatory and ungrammatical as these "promotional statements" were, there was nothing illegal in them. Although C. D. Rand promised to ensure the merit of listed companies, it was quickly apparent that the exchange members were out of their league when it came to vetting stock. They, like everyone else, relied primarily on word of mouth about mineral discoveries. So, despite endless proclamations warning the public of "speculations which might have the effect of discrediting British Columbia," the VSE contented itself with ensuring that trading in listed stocks went according to bylaws and left the companies to their own devices.

Although trading was still sporadic throughout the first half of 1910, interest in the VSE began to quicken that year. The first seats had sold for $125 and by April 21, 1910, all thirty were taken. The VSE increased the number of available seats to thirty-five and within a few months sold them as well, the last one for the astronomical sum of $3,250. As the year progressed, so did trading, which more than doubled between 1909 and 1910 from 847,665 shares valued at $290,683 to over 1.8 million shares valued at $673,342.

The VSE members, who had been content with their narrow, cramped quarters in the back of a store on West Pender Street, began to talk about needing more space. The rent of $50 a month gave them the use of the Pender Street room for only half a day but that didn't matter because the entire list of stocks could be called several times in the first hour. One of the members was deputized to seek new quarters, which he found in the McLean building (owned by another VSE member), also the home of the *Daily Province* newspaper. Delighted with their rising trading figures, the executive optimistically rented rooms for a full day at $100 month and established a second session on weekdays from 3:30 to 4:30 P.M., thereby giving members an adequate lunch break of three hours. These rooms were palatial in comparison to the old ones: the board was well lit and visible from every corner of the floor, comfortable oak chairs replaced the previous rickety seats and there was even a fine brass railing against which the members could lean and kibitz with onlookers during the session.

Except for Alvo von Alvensleben, John Kendall was the busiest member of the exchange. In addition to his VSE administrative duties and his position on the management committee, Kendall had a rapidly growing brokerage firm, which he ran single-handedly. When the VSE opened, underwriting was infrequent, but as the short years of prewar prosperity crept west, it began to take its place in the business of VSE members.

When a firm agrees to underwrite a company, it makes a commitment to sell a certain amount of stock. In those days, brokers usually bought the stock themselves and then resold it for whatever they could get, pocketing the difference. Today a "best efforts" underwriting is common, whereby the firm simply agrees to do its best to sell the issue. Any stock that is not sold returns to the company's treasury.

Kendall was one of the first VSE members to underwrite companies, then called sponsorship, in any systematic manner. In 1910 he posted a letter on the VSE bulletin board, informing all that he had sponsored Green Lake Mining and Milling Company Ltd. by underwriting 150,000 shares. He intended to maintain the market by bidding "up to 10 cents every day to keep the stock up as protection for the general public." He showed that he was serious about keeping the stock liquid by offering a 5 per cent commission. With the 5 per cent as an incentive, bidding on Green Lake was lively for several weeks, after which Kendall must have sold all the cheap stock* he had received or bought because there were no further bids. Three months after he posted his letter, the stock was unobtrusively dropped from the call. This was the VSE's first case of a promoter making a market, blowing off his stock and then letting the company disappear.

Kendall was so busy with his brokerage firm that his VSE paperwork suffered, and in 1911 D. Whiteside, registrar of joint-stock companies for British Columbia, sent the exchange a stern warning: "You are hereby notified that you have failed for a period of two years preceding the date of this notice to send to or to file such documents as are by law required to be made." Whiteside added insult to injury by asking if the stock exchange was still in business. Kendall also had trouble paying the VSE's bills on time, and that same year received a letter from Dominion Rating & Mercantile Agency, a firm specializing in the collection of delinquent accounts, informing the exchange that it owed $25.00 to Angell Engraving Company. The collection com-

---

*Cheap stock (sometimes called founder's, seed capital or preprospectus shares) is the stock usually received by an underwriting firm, promoter, or other insider as part of the agreement to finance a company with a public offering or private placement. In 1910 an underwriter could be given stock free in return for his sponsorship and attempts to place the shares. In 1980, in an attempt to limit abuses by firms that bought huge amounts of cheap stock to sell to their clients at inflated prices, the cost of cheap stock was increased to 15 cents. It was increased again in 1985 to 25 cents.

pany's letterhead put any recipient firmly in his place: OUR SYSTEM
GETS THE MONEY ANY OLD PLACE. NO COLLECTION NO CHARGE.
WE FURNISH LISTS OF DEAD BEATS AND LOCATE NON-PAYING
DEBTORS WHO HAVE ABSCONDED.

The VSE has always retained the distinct atmosphere of a private
club, whose members close ranks in adversity. But in practice they lost
no sentiment in viciously groin-kicking each other beneath the table.
The increasing profitability only made this nasty character trait worse,
and VSE members developed passionate opinions about matters such
as the delivery of stock. It took two days to deliver certificates to
buyers in Victoria, three to four days to investors in Seattle and most
centres in the Pacific Northwest, and sometimes a week to some of the
small, remote towns in British Columbia's interior and the Rockies.
Now, computerized transfers have virtually relegated stock certificates
to the archives, but sellers still have three days to deliver stock.

William F. Irwin, who took over the stock and bond brokers Sharp
& Irvine Company Ltd. in 1909, was one of the exchange's resident
complainers about the issue of stock delivery. In 1910 he accused a fellow broker, J. Boyd Young, of "sharp practice" because Young refused
to accept stock certificates on Monday when they had been due two
days before. Young had good reason since the price had declined by 3
cents; by holding out, he could buy the same stock for $75 less. Irwin
appealed and lost.

Another malcontent was A. N. Wolverton, a brusque, sarcastic
man who took delight in uncovering transgressions by fellow members. He was usually in the right, which didn't endear him to the various management committees that had to deal with his complaints. In
1911 he wrote a letter to VSE president H. J. Thorne about Lucky Jim
Zinc Mines Ltd., one of the hot stocks of that year. The company
promised to send Wolverton the stock by messenger, if he would wire
the money for its purchase to the Alexandra Hotel in Winnipeg where
the company president was staying. The money was wired, but the
messenger sent to pick up the stock was turned away from the hotel.
The company avoided further contact simply by refusing to answer letters from Wolverton, who, in a fury at having the considerable sum of
$4000 tied up, demanded that the exchange suspend Lucky Jim. Wol-
verton finally got his stock, and the company remained on the board.

The VSE's first bull market slowed in the latter part of 1913 as talk
of war became more prevalent. The boom had turned to bust by July
31, 1914, when the management committee resolved to "close until

further notice" because of uncertainties in the market caused by rumours of war in Europe.* The vse members were actually protecting their positions since a great many of them, as well as their attorneys and partners, had taken huge positions in many of the listed companies during the recent prosperous times, and they feared a run on the stocks. The vse remained closed for two months until October 1st, when it reopened for a morning session only from 10:30 until 12:15; in the afternoons the office was handed over to the spca for meetings and general business. The exchange was not to experience another boom until the pre-Depression hysteria of 1927, '28 and '29.

*Today it is one of the vse's proudest boasts that the exchange has never been closed in all its years of operation. This was only one instance. There are at least three others, including closing on the day of C. D. Rand's funeral.

CHAPTER 2

Alvo von Alvensleben, the First Promoter

"People will be interested in this dumbkopf [sic] German who doesn't know much English but who sees opportunities" VON ALVENSLEBEN explaining why he wanted spelling and grammatical mistakes left in his promotional copy (from an article in *The Daily Colonist*, May 10, 1964, written by Cecil Clark).

A lthough the founding fathers of the Vancouver Stock Exchange took considerable pains to cultivate a sober image, among their members was one of the most colourful stock promoters who ever lived. Constantine Gustav Alvo von Alvensleben, the VSE's first full-fledged stock promoter, was a forerunner of the Morris Blacks, the Murray Pezims and the Bruce McDonalds who have epitomized the exchange in recent years. So successful was he during the period from 1907 to 1913 that, on his death in October 1965, forty-one years after his empire had crumbled, the Vancouver *Province* proclaimed: "Von Alvensleben built one of the largest fortunes in the history of B.C."

His personal wealth, some estimate as high as $25 million in 1912, was staggering. Even more impressive was the fact that he made and lost it all in less than a decade. Aside from his accomplishments, von Alvensleben carried with him an aura of mystery, which became the foundation of his legend. It was widely believed that he was Kaiser Wilhelm's personal agent in the New World. When von Alvensleben built the luxurious Wigwam Inn on 155 secluded acres along the shores of Indian Arm outside Vancouver, it was rumoured to be the Kaiser's hunting lodge. Once the war started, it was said that Wilhelm intended to use it as his summer palace as soon as he had dispatched his enemies and had a little more free time. Von Alvensleben was also reputed to be a German spy, and during the war many believed that his sumptuous second home in Victoria was ringed with secret gun emplacements.

Like many stock promoters, von Alvensleben was destined to have only a brief moment in the sun. The moment was intense enough for its memory to live for decades. In six short years, he became a multi-millionaire, owning and controlling a complex network of businesses, land and vse-listed companies. At the same time, he lived with the frantic zeal of Zelda and F. Scott Fitzgerald, charming, titillating and outraging the Vancouver gentry. He speculated with an almost wrathful obsession in anything that could be bought, and he brought to the somnolent Vancouver stock market flamboyance and excitement.

Von Alvensleben was born into the German nobility in 1880, the third son of Baroness Anna Veltheim and Count Werner Alvo von Alvensleben, former ambassador to the court of the tsar of Russia. The massive family estate in Neu Gattersleben (now in East Germany) included some of the richest lands of Lower Saxony but, with two older brothers, Alvo's hopes of succeeding to the title were slender. In 1898, the count decided that Alvo, then eighteen, should enter military college to prepare for life as a soldier. He also prayed that the army would straighten out his young son, who was already showing signs of becoming a wastrel. The count had the means to buy him a commission but insisted that Alvo bear the ignominy of the lower ranks for nearly a year before receiving his commission as a second-lieutenant in the artillery.

Von Alvensleben, a man of considerable energy, dissipated it on anything but work. Ambition was only an irritant, and he spent five years at the same rank with no hint of promotion. If anything, his appetite for self-indulgence grew. Sometimes he would spend the 150

---

*Alvo's younger brother Bodo succeeded to the title when the count died, since neither Alvo nor his elder brother Werner were interested in running the family estate and the oldest brother had died during the First World War. In all, Alvo had four brothers and two sisters.

marks a month from his commission, as well as the 500-mark allowance from his father, in a single bout of drinking and gambling on the horses. After that money was gone, he simply borrowed as much as he could get. "He has absolutely no conception of the value of money," complained an increasingly irate count. Once, on learning of his son's indebtedness, he threatened to have him posted to an isolated Polish garrison town, so small that even Alvo couldn't spend money.

By 1904, father and son were fed up with each other. The two of them agreed that if the count paid for a steamer ticket across the Atlantic, Alvo would never come begging for money again. Alvo boarded a ship in Hamburg and set out to join his brother Joachim, a coffee grower in El Salvador. When he arrived he took up his life much as he had left it in Germany. "Uncle Joachim was so exasperated with him that he finally said, 'Money doesn't grow on trees you know. You have to earn it,' " says Alvo's daughter, Margaret Newcombe. "This was a new idea to Daddy." It happened that Joachim's annoyance with his brother coincided with a coffee glut that eroded world prices and virtually ruined him. Alvo's easy life disappeared almost overnight.

Fortunately, young von Alvensleben had other plans anyway. He had been hearing rumours about gold in Alaska and decided to try his hand as a prospector. By the time he arrived in British Columbia the gold excitement was over and he was nearly broke. Like many other turn-of-the-century immigrants, he expected to find Canada a rough, lawless place with cowboys and Indians chasing each other through buffalo herds. Accordingly, he had left six steamer trunks full of clothing in El Salvador and arrived in the New World with only two suits and his hunting rifle.

Von Alvensleben made his way to Vancouver in the summer of 1904 and was surprised to discover a raw but quickly developing city. There wasn't a cowboy in sight. With no plans, no inkling of how to make his way and few skills other than gambling and spending money, he took a hotel room and waited for something to happen. The room, at a dollar a day, was his first-ever gesture to economy. Still, his money lasted only two weeks, and as no one in Vancouver had taken much notice of him, he sold his rifle and outfitted himself to explore the Fraser Valley and look for work. Decked out in a Tyrolean hat, an African safari-type hunting jacket, whipcord breeches and stockings, he was the perfect caricature of the German nobleman. He was quite a sight trudging along the muddy roads of the valley, begging for food

and sleeping in haystacks. After several days of walking, he was offered work pitching hay (he called it making haycakes) for two dollars
a day, including sleeping accommodations in the barn. It was a tough,
physical job for a young man accustomed to noble ease. He left within
a few weeks for an even more demanding position as a $4-a-day boat
puller in the Fraser River salmon fleet, handling the oars, nets and
sails on a two-man fishboat. The owner of the boat got two-thirds of
the take. They grossed 10 cents a fish, primarily sockeye, and could
catch, on average, 120 fish a day. He laboured all that summer and in
the fall was taken on at the nearby Brunswick cannery as the winter
night watchman.

During his year here he met his bride-to-be, Edith Mary Westcott, a
teacher in Ladner, a small farm community near Vancouver. Being a
watchman was a good job and not too taxing, but von Alvensleben
was beginning to feel the unfamiliar stirrings of ambition and turned
to moonlighting during the day. He shot game (he got 35 cents for
mallards and 45 cents a brace for pigeon and teal) for Vancouver restaurants and exclusive city clubs, several of which would soon admit
him as a member. Once he had made these contacts, he bought a
small cart and horse and began to sell fresh produce in addition to the
game. No one would have been more astonished at his transformation
than the count. The spoiled, pampered aristocrat thrived on privation
and challenge. The New World, where everyone was busy making his
own way, turned the wastrel into a survivor, and then something
much more.

By 1905 von Alvensleben had saved enough to buy his own boat,
and he benefited from one of the best salmon runs the Fraser ha⌣ ever
seen. So many fish were caught that the overwhelmed cannery had to
place a limit of 150 fish per boat per day. Within two years von
Alvensleben had stashed away $1,500. It was the seed of his empire.

He was already something of an entrepreneur in 1907 and, looking
around him, saw a prosperous future in business. Western Canada was
on the verge of explosive growth, and its promise of resources, land
and riches was luring an increasing number of people away from
Europe and the more established cities of eastern Canada. The first
thing he did was use some of his capital to rent a small office on Granville Street in Vancouver and to order a considerable quantity of impressive letterhead lithoed with the title: "Alvensleben Finance and
General Investment Co." He then marched into the office of the editor of the Vancouver *Sun* newspaper and imperiously demanded an

open-ended account. "Credit?" asked the bemused editor. "For how long, and to what limit?" "Forever," shouted Alvo. "And no limit." The editor, taken with his foreign charm, brass and fervent belief in the future of Vancouver, granted him ninety days of credit. In the following Saturday's paper, his first two-page ad appeared. The advertising department begged him to clean up his convoluted grammar, but Alvo was adamant. He, like every good promoter before or since, knew his mark. "The very things you want to straighten out are the points that give it appeal," he told the disbelieving admen. "Why, people will be interested in this dumbkopf [sic] German who doesn't know much English but who sees opportunities." The next day, customers dropped into his office just to point out his mistakes, and before they knew it, were buying land.

Von Alvensleben's personal correspondence in English shows no sign of the tortured phrasing or grammatical and spelling errors that characterized his advertisements. He obviously used his English at whatever level he believed would have the most impact. There was much of the actor about von Alvensleben. Like his written English, his speech varied with the circumstances, becoming increasingly broken and flawed when it suited his purpose to appear the dummkopf. He also used his noble connection mercilessly. Those he chose to charm were immediately taken with his fine manners and sophisticated air, and the rest couldn't help but be impressed by his palpably aristocratic presence. He was a strikingly handsome man: unusually tall, 6′ 2″, slim and muscular, his sharp, angular face with its full moustache was dominated by cool, penetrating eyes. His moods could shift in moments from effusive and charming to aloof and threatening. And, when he chose to be threatening, he could be very threatening indeed. Once, just before the war, he, his wife and his brother Bodo were going home from the Vancouver Opera House on the interurban tram. A gang of men, returning to their land-clearing camp on the outskirts of the city after a night on the town, were brawling and cursing in the smoking compartment. When the conductor was unable to stop the ruckus, von Alvensleben told them he would personally throw them off the tram if they didn't stop. Jeering, they set upon him, but he and the 6′ 8″ Bodo, who apparently hadn't stood up until this point, pummeled them and tossed them into the street.

Shortly after opening his Granville Street office, von Alvensleben bought one of the first seats offered by the VSE. He was a market natural and took to the penny stock game with a flourish. On many days his personal trading accounted for more than half the total VSE volume and an unknown portion of the unlisted trading. Within a year, von Alvensleben moved to new and larger offices to accommodate the three salesmen who now worked for him. At the same time, he made his first voyage back to Europe to re-establish family connections in Germany, London and Holland and to begin developing the network of aristocratic investors who were to funnel millions into Canada through him. Von Alvensleben was in a perfect position to tap the vast fortunes of Europe: he was of the nobility yet had one foot in the promising and exotic New World. Even educated Europeans believed the frontier gold-rush mythology of fabulous wealth awaiting everyone. This trip established von Alvensleben as the first pipeline of European money into the VSE.

When he returned from Europe with his younger brother Bodo, having patched up his differences with the count, he married Edith Westcott. Despite Alvensleben's free-spirited past, the love between the two of them was deep and enduring. He affectionately called her Pussy, and his children remember that when they were together von Alvensleben seldom paid attention to anyone else. Like the rest of his life, his marriage flew in the face of accepted tradition: his wife came from a respectable family, but she was *nichtsgeboren* — a commoner. Edith's elder sister, seventeen years her senior, opposed the marriage vehemently. Finally, despairing of receiving family approval, the two of them, like starry-eyed teen-agers, eloped at the age of thirty. They had three children, a daughter Margaret and two sons, Bodo and Gero. Sadly, none of the children were to profit from his fortunes.

Von Alvensleben's first recorded stock promotion was the Canadian-American Oil Company, formed to drill for oil in Alberta's Athabasca Tar Sands. In his newspaper advertising he showed admirable restraint, emphasizing the risky nature of the enterprise and bluntly warning those who couldn't afford to lose the money not to buy shares. Of course, his caution only inflamed interest, and investors snapped up the underwriting. Although the Canadian-American Oil Company, like many others of its kind, hit a series of dry holes, von Alvensleben had established his remarkable ability to raise money.

His promotions could be sober and reserved or as dramatic as his personality. He developed a masterly talent for writing tout sheets, then primly called sales letters, that were full of flash and verve. He sent out hundreds of them to the German elite. His techniques were advanced and very systematic for the time: some of his letters were even accompanied by professional photographs of the property or mine in question and were reinforced by full-page ads in the German newspapers. The results were immediate and stunningly successful. In just over four years he brought between $7 and $10 million in German capital to British Columbia, seducing investment out of Reichschancellor Theobald von Bethmann Hollweg, Field Marshall August von Mackensen, Emma Mumm of Mumm's champagne and Frau Bertha Krupp von Bohlen und Halbach, a steel millionairess. The VSE frowned on advertising stocks and prices but studiously avoided tackling his letter campaigns that were drawing so much investment into the exchange.

Von Alvensleben's reputation and tout sheets spread across North America, and even New York financiers became aware of the noble promoter. As he became more successful, he spent more and more time travelling, inspecting properties and raising capital. Wherever he went he was dogged by idea men, prospectors, inventors, cranks and anyone who had anything to sell. One man intercepted him as he was rushing from his office: "Mr. von Alvensleben, I have been sitting on that chair waiting to see you all afternoon!" Alvo grabbed the chair and thrust it at him. "In that case, my dear sir, you may keep the chair. Take it, it's yours." And he rushed off.

Although von Alvensleben's reputation rested on his stock market accomplishments, the foundation of his empire was land. Fortuitously, his era coincided with one of the great real estate booms in the history of the West. Between 1908 and 1912, speculators bought land with heedless frenzy.* Property was bought and flipped for a profit so quickly, sometimes within hours or days of the original purchase, that people didn't even bother to get title. After a few years of this, tracing ownership became a laborious and confusing task. Land from choice downtown sites to bits of bog no one had ever seen were traded on margin, like stocks. Speculators even took options on property and then sold the options overnight. Everyone from tram conductors to school teachers was a real estate investor.

Von Alvensleben's quick mind and willingness to take risks made him one of the most successful flippers, and word that he was bidding

---

*Today people talk about the 1979–81 real estate boom as if it were the most significant in the country's history. But there were at least three earlier ones, in 1898, 1911 and 1929, that rivalled or surpassed the speculative excess of 1979–81 and the subsequent and spectacular crash.

on something was sufficient to cause a stampede of competitive bidders. Von Alvensleben was seldom the loser, but he didn't really like the ephemeral world of real estate speculation where nothing was produced except paper. "It's no good," he would emphasize, "just swapping corner lots with one another. You've got to build on them. Better to buy an expensive lot in the heart of town and build on it." He often said that his real estate dream was to erect a fifty-storey building adjacent to the Bank of England in London. The very absurdity and extravagance of the notion prompted much laughter over port and cigars about von A's eccentricities. He did, however, make a start on his dream in 1912 with the construction of the seven-storey Dominion Trust Building (also known as the West Pender Building), the highest in Vancouver at the time.

By 1910, von Alvensleben was a respected member of the Vancouver business elite and hosted the first-ever annual VSE dinner at his newly completed Wigwam Inn, which was already making an international name for itself with guests like John Jacob Astor and John D. Rockefeller. The dinner was an important affair attended by pillars of the financial community who, for the first time, publicly admitted that the VSE might be more than a passing thing. Even though many of the exchange members were successful businessmen in their own right, they were still stained by the scallywag reputation that followed stockbrokers around like a persistent germ. Von Alvensleben was a perfect foil for such opinions. Despite his proclivity for high living, he dazzled the guests with his aristocratic demeanour and demonstrated an enviable flair for entertaining. The report of the evening in the *Daily Province* was really a rave review:

> The steamer Tarter had been chartered for the trip. And a party, numbering in all about sixty persons, made the lovely voyage up the North Arm [now Indian Arm] through the majestic scenery offered by the mountains looming blue through the opalescent haze. Dinner followed amid surroundings of luxury and comfort and the spectacular proceedings were closed by a fine display of fireworks.

The lengthy report continued:

> Mr. Alvo von Alvensleben delighted the diners with a flowing speech full of witty sayings. He first discovered the baby exchange in the arms of its father C. D. Rand. "To become a father," he proclaimed, "is not

difficult. To be one, there's the rub." Soon the public became sponsors of the babe, and its future was secured.

In his speech von Alvensleben chided bankers, likening them to oysters who closed up at the approach of anything ticklish. "They just hate the word loan. They have substituted overdraft in its place." But he admitted that the bankers had given valuable support to the exchange "when they found its policy steady. In the future we feel sure of their support."

With a staff of fifty employees in 1912, von Alvensleben was at his peak. He owned fishing boats, logging companies, mining camps, mines, a trust company, hotels, oil wells, subdivisions, a whaling fleet, ranches and, of course, publicly listed companies.* Among his holdings were Standard Fish and Fertilizer, Standard Fisheries and Whaling, Vancouver Timber and Trading, Vancouver-Nanaimo Coal Mining, Issaquah & Superior Mining Company, Queen Charlotte Island Fisheries, Indian River Park (operators of the Wigwam Inn), and the German-Canadian Trust Company of Victoria.

Unlike many of his successors in the promotion game, von Alvensleben saw himself as a developer. Many of his companies were thriving producers of one sort or another, and even his VSE investments occasionally led to the development of a mine. He didn't confine himself to Canadian investments, and his fame as the man who brought German millions to British Columbia prompted hundreds of business opportunities all over North America. It didn't hurt that he was seen as the man with a direct link to Kaiser Wilhelm.

There is no question that some of his work was as an agent for German industry. During one of his trips to Europe, von Alvensleben learned that German chemical plants desperately needed high-quality carbon because most of the known European sources were near the point of depletion. He began to search for a carbon source in North America and in 1912 settled on the tiny, moribund town of Issaquah, Washington, a community paralyzed from eight years of labour strikes and a mine closure. When tests confirmed that the Issaquah coal was the highest quality carbon, he announced he would reopen the mine. If that weren't enough, von Alvensleben proclaimed that a $1 million

*It was a common and expected practice for stock exchange members to own majority positions in listed companies. Many brokers also received directorships in return for sponsoring or underwriting a company and for encouraging investors to buy its stock.

chemical plant would be built with German funds. More homes were built in Issaquah in 1913 and 1914 than in the previous twenty years as the mine payroll ballooned from nothing to $30,000 a month. Washington State newspaper accounts at the time recorded that "The Count," as the Americans called him, was working directly for the Kaiser. One report even mentioned that the chemical plant was critical to a possible German war effort, but there was no evidence of concern over this. Even today, twenty years after his death and seventy-five years after the events in question, von Alvensleben is hailed as "The Savior of Issaquah."

As von Alvensleben's fortune soared, so did his display of it. He had two houses in 1912, one in Victoria and a mansion (now the exclusive Crofton School for Girls) on Forty-First Avenue in Vancouver. With its meticulously manicured lawns, twenty acres of grounds, thirteen servants and string of thoroughbreds, the estate was the centre of Vancouver gay life. Von Alvensleben had not lost his appetite for excess, and everything he did from entertaining to driving was at full speed. He would often send his chauffeur into the back seat and race his Packard Tourer along the unpaved roads in the city, collecting a scrapbook full of speeding tickets. Frustrated at the endless court appearances to pay the fines, he offered one judge $100 and asked the court to let him know when it was used up. He also loved to dwell on his recent poverty-stricken past, especially if he could shock or embarrass someone at the same time. At a dinner in the Vancouver Club with a visiting baron, he noticed the waiter gawking at him. "Yes, dammit," he shouted so the whole room could hear, "I'm the man who used to sell eggs and butter at the back door. Now stop your staring at me and get on with your serving!"

Compared to von Alvensleben, the rest of the VSE members seemed dry and insipid. But "The Count" had many other acquaintances, some of whom rivalled him in their eccentricities. It was a rich time and place for unusual characters. One such was Warburton Mayer Pike. Although educated at Rugby and Oxford and from a distinguished West Country family, Pike was a grand adventurer in the Victorian tradition with a distinct "penchant for slumming." By the time he arrived in Victoria in 1884 at the age of twenty-three, he had hunted in Scandinavia, Iceland and the U.S., and had tried his hand at wrangling as a cowboy in Texas and Oregon. Later he also became an author, and *The Barren Ground of Northern Canada* (1892) details a twenty-month ordeal in which Pike hiked from Edmonton to Great

Slave Lake. His most famous expedition was a canoe trip along the Pelling and Yukon rivers through Alaska, which he wrote about in *Through The Sub-Arctic Forest* (1896).

Warburton Pike also had a head for business and rapidly became one of the wealthiest men in British Columbia through his ownership of large tracts of property in Victoria and the Gulf Islands, and a variety of other business enterprises. He lived in the Union Club adjacent to the Empress Hotel in Victoria. Then, as now, the club was the hub of power in the city and, when the legislature was sitting, in the province as well. Despite the club's legendary stuffiness, it was an era when adventurers, especially those well born, were admired. The Union gentlemen had no problem with Pikey's ways, though he habitually went barefoot in the club, dressed in ragged clothes and carried an even more ragged rucksack. Pike was a millionaire but rarely carried money with him, and he was frequently thrown off trains for not having the fare. His amusement value to a man like von Alvensleben was high—he was rich and clever yet he was often mistaken for a bum. It was the kind of joke Alvo enjoyed.

During von Alvensleben's association with Pike in 1912 and 1913, the German was at the pinnacle of his success. But the sands of his empire were already shifting beneath his feet. When the real estate boom slowed and reversed into a general recession in 1913, the land von Alvensleben used to secure his mortgages and loans dropped by as much as 50 per cent in value and ceased to provide the ready cash his relentless investments required. To complicate matters, interest rates began rising, and Vancouver bankers became less willing to float the large loans von Alvensleben had used to keep his empire expanding. He began using the treasuries of one company to support another, and all were accumulating more debt against increasingly less equity. Von Alvensleben was aware of the seriousness of his situation as early as 1912. Between then and 1914 he made at least four trips to Europe and several to New York. At first he had little trouble finding investors, but the amounts they were willing to risk was less than in the past and even that dried up as the threat of war escalated. In 1914 he set off for a final desperate fund-raising trip for the $2 million he needed to keep the shaky pyramid of his enterprises from toppling.

Von Alvensleben's decline is charted by the correspondence between two friends, Warburton Pike and Marshall Bond. These two and Lord Osborne de Vere Beauclerc (twelfth Duke of St. Albans) were seeking to interest von Alvensleben's promoting genius in their coal mining properties in northern B.C., where von Alvensleben also owned forty claims. "Von A- is working on a flotation in Europe. I fortunately learned this afternoon, and also learned that Von A- will be here tomorrow or Friday," Bond wrote to Pike at the Union Club in Victoria on November 20, 1912. Pike replied, "I came out here yesterday and happened to meet von Alvensleben in the street. . . . He is a very good fellow I think you will like him when you meet him and he seems quite willing to let us join him or to join us in any deal you may get up."

Pike and Bond spent weeks trying to talk to von Alvensleben, who, unknown to them, was beginning his own search for capital and was spending virtually all his time travelling from one property to another and from one potential investor to another. Finally, Bond grabbed a few hurried minutes of his time. Von Alvensleben agreed to find buyers for their adjoining claims during his forthcoming trip to England. Impatiently, they waited for news, but as time wore on, their confidence dwindled. "Alvensleben is not a very prompt man," wrote Bond in January 1913. "I wish I felt really sure that he would go to England on that business."

Pike responded, "Von A seems so jumpy and unavailable that it is hard to say what he may do. . . . He has certainly done big things, but whether through business acumen or from being a plunger on a rising market I can't make up my mind. But as he holds the sine qua non of a big promotion . . . we can't well do other than be the tail of the kite that must follow his evolutions."

The trip to England never materialized, but von Alvensleben promised he would attempt to sell the claims in New York. By now his partners were openly worried; they already had passed up an opportunity to sell the claims to someone else, and the prospect of profit on the land began to appear bleak. Pike wondered if Alvo would be "a bit too rapid man" for the New York investors. The eastern trip was made, but he went straight to Germany, bypassing New York.

Bond and Pike were at first furious and then deeply concerned when rumours about von Alvensleben reached them. "I hear conflicting reports about Alvensleben," wrote Bond on April 2, 1913. "A fellow who has an office in the Pacific Building told me that he heard A intended giving up his office there and moving to the old Dominion Trust Building way down Hasting St. 'Why is that?' I asked. 'Cheaper rent I suppose,' he replied." But news from Europe appeared good: "Von Ettinger told me Alvensleben had sent out $500,000 and had raised $3 million more which he would get in May. Another fellow told me that Alvo had raised his money and was now going to have a good time before returning," Bond penned hopefully.

Von Alvensleben returned in August 1913 with nothing to show for his trip. The trio gave up on him. While von Alvensleben had been dashing around Europe, his brokerage business, long neglected and left in the hands of inexperienced juniors, had fallen into a shambles, and the VSE was threatening to sell his seat unless he cleared up his arrears of fees and dues. He patched up things for a few months and in the spring of 1914 left on a last desperate trip to Germany. He frantically shuttled between London and Berlin, trying to coax something more from the once eager aristocracy and business community. On August 2nd, dispirited and empty-handed, he left Europe via Copenhagen. Two days later, Britain declared war on Germany.

When his ship arrived in Seattle, he was greeted by the news that all his holdings had been confiscated by the Custodian of Enemy Aliens' Property and that if he set foot in Canada he would be arrested. The only thing von Alvensleben was able to salvage was his considerable wine cellar. He wrote to his wife, instructing her to join him in Seattle, and told her to gather up their household goods and to pack their wines in large crates. The crates were delayed at the border, waiting a clearance from the military authorities. Von Alvensleben's lawyer urged him to create an international incident, but he decided to handle it himself. He wrote to the officer commanding the B.C. Military District and ended the letter with:

> If on further consideration, you find it impossible to release my wines, I shall accept your decision and make no more fuss about it. I shall also be pleased to donate the wines, with my compliments, to the officers' mess of whatever unit you may designate. But upon one condition— that the first toast to be drunk from the wines shall be to the health of His Imperial Majesty the Emperor of Germany.

The wines arrived within the week.

Von Alvensleben sent for his family and watched bleakly as his estate was liquidated. To make matters worse, he was still being hounded by rumours tagging him as a spy for the Kaiser; some stories even called him the Kaiser's illegitimate son. Then a message, allegedly between German agents, was intercepted sometime during the early war years and leaked to the press: "Von Alvensleben will also present another plan with reference to the purchase of the Wright aeroplane factory in Dayton, Ohio. We would thereby probably be placed in the position of being able to prevent the greatest part of the export of flying machines from the United States." When the U.S. joined the war, the Americans took no chances and imprisoned von Alvensleben with other unfortunates at Fort Douglas in Utah. He showed a bit of his old fire when he led a nearly successful attempt to tunnel to freedom later that year. So persistent was the mystique surrounding him, even after he was interned, that numerous reports circulated about his being spotted in disguise in Vancouver or Victoria. Even today some believe that he managed to hide a large chunk of his fortune. His children wish it were true. "My first memory of him was when I was five years old. I remember seeing this guy with a big beard walking up the path to our house and mother running down to embrace him," recalls Bodo of his father's release after the war. "We were always a very poor family."

Von Alvensleben was not released until 1921, and his family had been living on $100 a month donated to them by the Swiss Red Cross. After the war, von Alvensleben remained in Seattle and became an American citizen in 1939. He continued to dabble in real estate and began Normandy Park, a Seattle suburb. He also kept his hand in the stock market in a small way and opened a modest placer mine in northern B.C., which he and his wife managed during the summer even though they were in their seventies at the time. Their daughter Margaret recalls her mother writing that von Alvensleben was swimming in the nearby glacial lake and that she was sunbathing naked while she penned the letter. Von Alvensleben's fortunes were gone, but not his zest for life.

Curiously, the vse, which had been the first to threaten him, was the last to sell him out. As if longing for the heady days von Alvensleben had brought to it, the exchange hung on to his seat until 1918 when it was seized and sold to pay his debts.

CHAPTER 3

The Great War and the Great Crash

"To the Boys on the Exchange. Goodbye. I am off on the Great Adventure. I did the best I could." Deathbed note penned in 1917 by VSE PRESIDENT DONALD M. MACGREGOR.

During the war, the calm and generally pleasant trading days disintegrated into a dullness that paralyzed the exchange. Days passed without a single trade being made. The 1915 annual general meeting consumed a mere nine lines in the minute book, and only the faithful John Kendall was present. Many of the VSE members, like von Alvensleben, had abandoned caution during the real estate fever and, consequently, were so overextended by 1915 that there were more members in arrears for dues than were paid up. Some, like Johnny Jukes and Victor Odlum, solved the problem by going off to fight the war. Fees for the appointment of attorneys (now called floor traders) were suspended, and the exchange began to accept promissory notes in lieu of cash. Even the strict vetting of character for membership was relaxed since there were so many vacant seats that no one wanted to buy.

Desperate for activity, the members eliminated some rules just to give the exchange the appearance of doing business. In 1916 members were urged to carry out all dealings in local stocks on the floor, even if the stocks were not listed, so "passers-by and men of business might see the exchange is doing its best for the country." It was a sad time for the group of men who had seen themselves a decade ago chasing the stock markets of New York, Toronto and Montreal with pioneer zeal. In the last years of the war, virtually all the remaining members were in arrears with fees. So listless were they that when fines were levied, no one bothered to pay and no one bothered to collect. About the only excitement during the dreary four war years was the death of vse president Donald M. MacGregor. The vse closed for the day of his funeral.

In those days selling short, or selling for a decline as it was then called, was an acceptable but uncommon practice. Short selling has changed little over the years. Basically, it involves the sale of a stock that the seller does not own. The seller hopes the price will decline so he can buy the stock at a lower price than he sold it for, to cover the sale and make a profit.

During the war, however, short selling was prohibited or tightly controlled on the Montreal and Toronto exchanges because authorities feared it could trigger a run on the market if news from the front was bad. In Vancouver, liquidity was so poor and buyers so scarce that the shorters were left alone. Winter was always the best time to short a stock. Brokers could find ready excuses for not delivering certificates because "deep troughs of snow," "broken sled wheels" or "ailing motor cars" kept them away from the exchange. A succession of such explanations allowed them to wait longer than normal for the price of the stock to drop, when they would buy it back to make good the initial sale.

The vse lost no time, however, in censuring violators of the rule against advertising. In 1919 C. M. Oliver and H. J. Thorne charged A. N. Wolverton with advertising the 10-cent-a-share price of New Hazelton Gold—Cobalt in a market letter. Wolverton immediately retaliated by accusing Oliver and Thorne of calling for bids and offerings of stocks not listed on the vse board. Wolverton's claim was dismissed and his wrist slapped. N. T. Burdick, another member, was fined $25 a few months later for advertising both stock prices and his brokerage fees in the Daily Province. Many brokers evaded the rules by running "blind ads," which encouraged prospective investors to write to a box number for details of various tantalizing mining prospects. Dragnet campaigns, called junk mail today, were also used. These household blitzes, usually aimed at the housewife, were not spoken of but tolerated by the vse so long as members forebore to keep their prices out of print.

V-day released a small bout of financial hysteria that injected lethargic markets around the continent with some badly needed activity. By 1920, though many vse members were still in debt, the treasury purse still flaccid and the listings meagre, some signs of life emerged as the exchange resolved to "crack the whip" over those who had been deliberately skirting the rules, those very rules the vse had earlier decided to relax. The records of that year show the first ever trading halts of both listed and unlisted or "miscellaneous" companies. Usually at issue was a financial deal pending, information about exploration results or disputes over titles of land. Not so different from today, with the exception that now many trading halts also result from a company's failure to file financial reports. In those days, however, there were no filing requirements once the listing fee had been paid.

Trading halts were purely subjective and usually meant that one of the members owned stock in that company and was frightened by a rapidly declining price. Sometimes, too, shouts from the gallery, suggesting a company was in trouble and "why didn't the 'change do something about it" were sufficient for whoever was calling the stocks to "refuse to publish prices" for that particular stock until the furor died down.

As part of the postwar whip cracking, the vse took a hard look at the rules themselves. Even rules of order were changed. W. F. Irwin was appointed deputy chairman responsible for calling the stocks early in 1921. On January 18th, before the morning session began, Irwin decided to change the order of the call after two members who dealt only in bonds complained they were tired of having to wait until the end of the day to do their trading. Halfway through the rearranged morning call, vse president C. M. Oliver wandered in with Johnny Jukes. Oliver made a bid for Victory Bonds, only to be told by Irwin that the order had been changed and the bonds had already been cleared up. Oliver protested vigorously, and Irwin hotly called him an "interfering so and so." The ensuing interchange gave both brokers and audience considerably more stimulation than any trading had for years.

G. T. Webster, the exchange secretary, sent Irwin a letter sternly taking him to task. "In the opinion of the Board of Management, your action in the matter of addressing the President during the Call was reprehensible and they request that you retract remarks referred to, at the next session following." Irwin flatly refused, retorting that, on the contrary, Oliver should be fined for disrupting the call. A series of claims and counterclaims was made, but in the end Irwin was fined $100, by far the largest amount levied to that point.

Other faithful seat holders were dealt with even more harshly as the pall of war began to fade. Late in 1921, John Kendall and former VSE president J. W. Nanson were struck off the list of members for being in arrears.

The orgy of enforcement suited A. N. Wolverton perfectly. Between 1919 and 1921, he launched numerous complaints against fellow members for noncompletion of sales, nondelivery of stock and "jiggery-pokery" when bids were being called for. He maintained several times that he had been done out of sales or purchases because official recognition of a deal had not been quick enough to prevent someone else from jumping in with a better offer. It is hard to see how this could have happened, since before moving on to the next stock, the caller often waited for members to clean and relight their pipes. Wolverton was the VSE's president in 1915, '17, '18, '23 and '40. He was an excellent though conservative administrator, and when he died, was considered to be the grand old man of the exchange.

The VSE also decided it needed more control over listed companies, and in 1922 a bylaw amendment gave the exchange the right to raise margins as an emergency measure. Margins normally stood at 33⅓ per cent, meaning the purchase of stock had to be accompanied by at least 33⅓ per cent of the value in cash or some other negotiable security. A margin is the percentage of a transaction paid by an investor when he purchases securities on credit. The more credit a firm extends to a client, and the lower the margin, the more risk the broker assumes. By raising the margin of a suspicious stock, the VSE could force an investor to put more cash into it, thus decreasing the risk for the broker and consequently the exchange.

During 1922 and '23, several companies were called before the management committee for an explanation of their company affairs. The VSE had never shown such interest before, though when wild fluctuation in the price of Boundary Red Mountain in 1923 prompted such a move, the event proved to be more social than analytical. "Resolved that a hearty vote of thanks be sent to Mr. Valentine expressing appreciation of report," is the notation in the minutes following his appearance as the company representative to justify the activity. Valentine's explanation for the price swings was simple: "I think someone's doing some gambling with our stock. It has nothing to do with us I'm sure."

So many requests for information about the merits of such and such a company were clogging the desk of the VSE president that the exchange decided, in 1925, to make a book available to the public, complete with data on the various listings. The information often consisted of enlightening bulletins such as: "a gang of men leave tomorrow night to begin work on Red Cliff mine" and "the company has settled complaints by the mine men about insufficiencies of food and drink."

During the VSE's first decade, stock promotion was a simple affair, though not always a straightforward one. Prospectors promoted themselves and whatever piece of dirt had caught their fancy. They would stake a few claims, sometimes within sight of a working mine or a big find, sometimes on a piece of rough ground that looked, smelled, tasted or just plain felt right. Test holes were dug by hand and pieces of rock laboriously hauled over difficult terrain to a larger centre for analysis, though sometimes that part was left out. Prospectors developed a keen eye for ore concentration, and frequently, when it came time to raise money, their opinion was as bankable as any scientific analysis. They often had a group of people they would regularly solicit for a grubstake. Most of the time they were only after enough to money to get them back out to the bush for another round of banging rocks.

As the VSE established itself as an enduring marketplace, prospectors began to approach brokers for funds. Out of this alliance often came a listed company. In return for organizing and selling the underwriting, the broker would receive some shares. The prospector, in return for selling his claims to the company, would also receive shares, which were usually escrowed, meaning the shares could not be sold until the property proved itself or until enough time had passed to make the venture appear legitimate. (Today, escrowed shares may not be bought or sold without permission from the superintendent of brokers or the VSE.) Both the promoter and the broker also had the opportunity to buy a certain number of "cheap shares," often at a penny apiece, before the company was actually listed. These shares could be sold at any time. Either the broker or the prospector or both acted as the company promoter, depending on which one had the most at stake. Since there were no rules against brokers owning the listed companies themselves, they frequently acted as promoters.

As time passed, the roles began to shift. Brokers tried to give the appearance of greater objectivity and less involvement with specific companies, so it was left once more to the prospector to hype his stock. Many prospectors did all their own promoting in the initial stages of setting up a mining company for exploration and, hopefully, development. Brokers, betting both ends against the middle, would agree to push the shares once the company was listed. Then they sat back and waited to see how well the prospector did before jumping in and getting involved.

A second kind of promoter emerged during the 1920s, the licensed broker-dealers, who were an odd combination of broker and promoter. The only real restriction in their licences was that they could not trade directly on the vse floor; they had to use the services of a seat holder. Broker-dealers were mongrels: part promoter, part broker and part snake-oil salesman. The vse treated them apologetically, but members were quick to blame their less savoury cousins when anything went wrong. Most of the broker-dealers operated out of back rooms selling unlisted stocks to anyone, using phone blitzes, door-to-door campaigns and sales letters to snare the gullible. Often the hapless buyer discovered, too late, that the certificates he or she purchased had been issued by a long-defunct company. Policing them was difficult because broker-dealers were virtually unregulated and because few individuals actually complained of having been mulcted, probably out of embarrassment for their naiveté. In 1922 a woman investor, one of the few who did complain, said she had bought $3,500 worth of stock in a mining company that the promoter claimed had developed a technique for enhancing silver. It was a variation on the old alchemy gambit: the technique supposedly enabled miners to take ore with a very low concentration of silver in it and increase the amount present by "purifying" it. "You believed that? " a policeman queried with a barely suppressed smile when he took her name. The woman told the police that the promoter and the company had disappeared. "We'll do what we can," she was told as her complaint was shelved.

In 1923, the first recorded police investigation of the vse was spurred by a letter from A. J. Henley of Saskatoon, claiming he had been swindled out of $10,000 in a vse transaction. The minutes intimate that a vse member was involved, but the case was never raised again in the press or in the board room. If these or any other similar issues had reached the public eye, the vse had a convenient scapegoat to explain such irregularities: broker-dealers. The exchange and the broker-dealers developed an uncomfortable yet symbiotic relationship that was to last until 1973, when their role was eliminated by the Securities Act. As disreputable as the broker-dealers sometimes were, they represented an important source of income to the VSE brokers. They conducted a considerable amount of trading on the VSE through the member brokers, and more importantly, companies started or sponsored by them occasionally ended up on the board. As well, broker-dealers sometimes did the dirty work for VSE members: when the placement of an underwriting got into trouble, brokers turned to their less reputable counterparts to get rid of the stock any way they could. Officially, however, the VSE frowned on any contact between the two groups and winced when broker-dealers took out flashy ads exhorting the public to "Buy Lucky Leaf Mines and Give Your Children Happier Lives."

As trading charged up toward the zenith of pre-Crash market hysteria, broker-dealers increasingly flogged their wares in the daily papers. The exchange had never been busier, but as VSE brokers saw the pie getting bigger, they wanted more of it. Fearing that the broker-dealers' business was growing even faster than their own, the exchange members fought back by ignoring many VSE rules entirely. By summer 1929, advertising was as common as if it were a requirement of VSE membership. Respectable, established firms were placing "notices" little different from those of the broker-dealers: "YUKON GOLD Selling 4 weeks ago 25 cents, Selling last week 35 cents, Selling Monday 40 cents, Selling Thursday 50 cents, Selling Soon $1.00," ran one C. M. Oliver ad.

The bull market, which was leading so many brokers along the crass route of advertising, had begun in 1926 when the value of shares trading on the VSE was $1.9 million. In 1927 it increased almost 300 per cent to $5.2 million. Over 2.4 million shares of mining stocks alone, with a value of $844,000, changed hands in December 1927, almost double that of any previous month. The number of listings only increased by a fraction in comparison. That meant the market was doing little to finance new ventures, either speculative or otherwise. There were simply many more people panting for their share of what seemed to be ridiculously easy profits. Seats on the VSE were selling for $12,000 to $15,000 compared to the low of $100 bid for a seat in 1921 (the exchange voted to reject that offer, pegging the minimum price at $150). Then, in 1929, a Vancouver businessman paid $55,000 for one of the coveted seats.

Share prices were escalating at the same pace. Companies like Coast Copper shot from $7.14 to to $40 in a few months in 1927, and then up to $60 in 1928. When Coast Copper waned, Pend Oreille jumped in, climbing from $1 to $25 in a matter of months in early 1929. A newspaper account bluntly described the trading pattern: "Just as in the case of Coast Copper the original shareholders took their profits on the upward movement and sold out." In other words, aside from any mining potential the companies might have had, the market was being run by canny promoters.

A third stock that fuelled market excitement was Home Oil. When Home Oil issued its first 800,000 shares in early 1928 for $2 apiece, the indifference was overwhelming. The public was leery of oil stocks after a wave of instant companies with location bets had cashed in on the first discovery of naptha in Turner Valley in 1911.* Companies with location or proximity bets have property in the vicinity of a real discovery and hope to find something themselves, but generally they are after a vicarious share price boost.† Although gas started to flow from Turner's Royalite No. 4 in 1925, producing attractive profits for Imperial Oil, the public was shy. They were suspicious of oil, which did not have the cachet of gold, copper or other known minerals. Even when Home Oil began drilling in the vicinity of No. 4, the share price hung around $2 and most of the shareholders were still the original subscribers. Then, in March 1929, a Home Oil well gushed in with a flow of five hundred to six hundred barrels a day. Public reluctance was abandoned as the stock immediately shot to $26.

Interest in mining stocks was kindled by the huge profits made from Consolidated Mining and Smelting, which took over the moribund Rossland gold properties and successfully developed them with the new technology available in the late 1920s. Shares in Consolidated were trading at $240 in Toronto and Montreal, and the VSE pointed proudly to the Consolidated listing on its own board, even though only seven shares were traded in all of 1927. Stock markets were soaring everywhere, but the still young West retained the allure of frontier days and the venerable *Financial Times* of London singled out British

---

*Date from Ed Gould's book, *Oil: The History of Canada's Oil and Gas Industry*, published by Hancock House in 1976.
†Even today, location bets are a well-used promoting strategy, and not always in the resource area. When computers were a hot item in the late 1970s and early 1980s, dozens of "computer" companies appeared on the VSE with promises of hardware, software and distribution rights.

Columbia for special attention: "A province which is producing over $60,000,000 worth of metals and paying not far short of $10,000,000 is obviously not to be despised."

Never had VSE stocks risen so quickly and so high. Some members joked that the phrase "penny dreadful," used to refer to VSE issues, would have to be changed to "dollar dreadful." The exchange tried to cope with it all by hiring extra staff, sometimes right off the street. In 1927 its employees numbered five, including the dour-faced, dedicated secretary Bert Sprange, and two years later multiplied to thirty. Brokerage houses trebled their staffs, competing viciously for anyone with any expertise.

Playing the market was becoming such a popular public pastime that the largest brokerage houses set up their own duplicate boards, complete with markers, so investors could watch the action first hand. The public had been banned from the exchange in 1924, except by invitation, because the noise, catcalls and "excessive expectoration" disrupted the daily sessions. New high-speed tickers were installed in most of the houses after an 8-million-share day in New York kept them running an hour and a half behind schedule. And some houses purchased a trans-lux, which projected the ticker tape results onto a screen. Trading even in speculative securities seemed to be acquiring a skin of respectability and was beginning to be seen as integral to the civilized progression of humankind. "Just as the Indians and the white settlers had common meeting grounds for barter and trade, so the people meet on the floors of an exchange through their brokers," read one solemn Vancouver *Sun* editorial.

Prosperity always seems to bring out the worst in the VSE, and the first prolonged bull market was tainted by the great bucketing scandals of 1928–29. Although the bucketing scandals involved all the Canadian exchanges, they were rampant on the VSE and on the Standard Stock Exchange (SSE). The SSE was so disgraced by these scandals that it was forced to merge with the Toronto Stock Exchange in 1934. The Montreal and Toronto exchanges and the newspapers in both cities denigrated anyone having anything to do with speculative stocks. "Mining brokers, looked upon as members of a very junior and somewhat unstable exchange, found themselves rolling in clover—and big new motor cars," ran a *Financial Post* editorial referring to the VSE and the SSE. The mining brokers were despised by the blue-chip and bond traders in Toronto, Montreal and Vancouver as they hired miles of telegraph wire, decorated fancy new offices and insinuated themselves into the business of other brokers. The *Financial Post* likened them to apple maggots:

> They "cleaned up" because Canadians went into mining as a crowd of boys run to a new-found orchard from the trees of which are hanging clusters of luscious red pippins. And Canadians found many rich and juicy apples in the mining orchard. For a time they feasted to their hearts' desires. But they also found, as the first intoxication died, that the pest and the worm and the parasite had entered the orchard.

The *Financial Post* called the frenzy in mine stock trading, "a monstrous betrayal of the confidence of the Canadian people" and "a cynical exploitation of public confidence."

What the *Financial Post* and others objected to was the fact that investors had little or no control over how their money was spent once it was handed over to a broker. Even so, the indignant outrage seems a little excessive, since junior stocks had always been the black sheep of the securities business. What really sparked the moralistic vilification was the fact that the crooked trading was happening on stock exchanges themselves. Bucketing had been around ever since the first share certificate, but everyone assumed that the stock exchanges were free from it. Even the VSE, a poor cousin to the MSE and TSE, was still a stock exchange, an institution with rules and regulations. The bucket-shop rabble was supposed to inhabit the alleyways of a city, not its exchange floor. The other factor behind the acrimonious attacks was the belief that the laxity of the VSE was reflecting badly on the senior exchanges.

The bucketing that pervaded the industry was of the simplest variety. Brokers were taking money for the purchase of stocks, then hanging onto the cash, hoping or knowing the price would go down so that they could pocket the difference. What they were doing was more correctly called "fraudulent conversion," but the market has always been more comfortable with chummy, clublike terms, so the term "bucketing" stuck. Bucketing was inordinately difficult to prove since the more canny brokers concurrently made small legitimate transactions, in order to have buy or sell slips to show nosy clients should they ask for proof an order had gone through.

As the extent of crooked trading became known, reporters and politicians and the public forgot all their earlier high-minded talk about the importance of a speculative stock market to the development of a young, wealthy country. When the Vancouver police finally admitted that "bucketing has reached considerable proportions in the city," the public turned on stock exchanges generally, and the VSE in particular, with the righteous fervour of a lynch mob. A letter from J. Wallwork to the Vancouver *Daily Province,* sums up the general sentiment:

> It is only a short time ago that the brokers in this city occupied very small offices and board rooms were practically non-existent. Then the public started to get interested, commissions began to roll in, offices and staffs were enlarged, fine buildings went up and all from what? Surely not from the little deals the brokers made between themselves when they used to sit in a semi-circle and call a 200-share day a good one. No the goose—in more ways than one—that laid the nice eggs was the public, and if the executive of the Vancouver Stock Exchange is going to allow its "rigid rules" to be scorned and the public deliberately robbed then it won't be long before its members will be back into obscurity.

The VSE stoutly maintained that none of its members was involved and publicly offered to help investigate the sordid mess. "No such process of trading is possible in the Stock Exchange, where all members are under the severe discipline of the management committee," stated a VSE press release. As proof, the exchange pointed out that eighteen months earlier it had conducted a "searching investigation into alleged bucketing" and that "rigid rules" had been put in place. It was the first mention of such an investigation and, fortunately for the VSE, the public and press were already so inflamed by the revelations that no one thought to ask why a searching investigation was conducted and why rigid rules were developed if no exchange members were involved. "These rules are most stringent," VSE president S. W. Miller told the press, "and the slightest suspicion that any member has infringed any of these regulations renders that member liable to immediate suspension pending thorough investigation of the charges." The public was not informed that Miller himself had been fined three times in 1926 and 1927, twice for failing to deliver stock on time and once for buying stock with a client's money but not his permission. In all three cases, the "stringent rules" resulted in the imposition of the minimum $5 fine.

The attorney general of British Columbia, R. H. Pooley, washed his hands of the bucketing probe. "Vancouver is not on my beat," he said. "This is a matter for the city police to attend to." By the time Pooley made this statement in late September 1929, the charges had gone far beyond mere bucketing to include stock manipulation and fraud. There were allegations that rings of operators were acquiring large blocks of stock, in some cases as much as 70 per cent of the shares issued, buying and selling to themselves to drive the price up and then selling out quickly. Brokers were commonly urging clients to buy stock that they were selling short. And the brokers who were not involved in these things were busy using the highly efficient mining rumour mill to control stock prices.

Into the fracas waded the well-meaning but clearly overmatched Vancouver chief of police, W. J. Bingham. He and Mayor W. H. Malkin held a hurried morning meeting on September 17, 1929, to see what could be done to end the various illegal and unethical activities and to salvage the reputation of the VSE, which was being blackened by the grimy shadow of "hole-in-wall" operators. Headlines that day made little distinction between VSE members and other brokers, announcing: "Bucket Probe Is Started." The story in the *Daily Province* began: "The drive on Vancouver bucketeers begins today," and reported that Bingham was "in possession of certain specific information and is unwilling to reveal his hand." The next day the chief grandly announced that he was embarking upon a secret probe to investigate all the brokerage houses in the city. The VSE member firms were enraged at the imputation of wrongdoing and the press equally so at the chief's naive tactics. "Bingham Bungles Bucketing Investigation" was one headline. The story said:

> Undoubtedly, the chief of Police and the Police commission have reasonable grounds for their belief that "bucketing" is being practised by some brokers in the city. Unfortunately, the announcement of their determination to investigate and punish will have an effect entirely opposite to the one desired. Warning a suspect of your intention is a poor way to go about catching him.

The same paper that accused Bingham of bungling and criticized the government for not stepping in to clean up the exchange, exhibited the general confusion about securities regulation when the editor later wrote: "The matter would be dealt with more efficiently by the Stock Exchange authorities than it could possibly be by the police.

for the Stock Exchange has the power to deal with unethical practices, which are usually just outside the province of the law courts." No explanation was given of how the VSE could possibly deal with the problem if none of its members was implicated.

The most miserable month in Chief Bingham's career came to an abrupt end on October 24, 1929, with Black Thursday and the great Crash. That appalling stock market catastrophe brought a merciful and premature end to the VSE's first major scandal.

CHAPTER 4

Depression, Gold and War Again

"A broker who is trading both for himself and a customer is in a position to accept a purchase for himself if it is beneficial, or to confirm the purchase to his customer if it is not. No other trustee which I know of is allowed these days to occupy such a position." Concluding statements from GEORGE LOVET FRASER's investigation of the 1937 Hedley Amalgamated mine-salting scandal.

As the Depression took hold in the West, the VSE chose to deal with the bucketing scandals and the Crash of 1929 by pretending they had never happened. In the committee minutes for the months following October's Black Thursday and Black Tuesday, there is not a hint of anything wrong. No mention of the incredible drop in trading from a frenzied peak of 25 million shares and an average share price of $1 for the month of March 1929, to 10 million shares and an average share price of 30 cents for all of 1930. No mention of the number of listings, which had dropped from 155 (83 mines, 63 oils and 5 industrials) to a paltry 55 during the same time period. The VSE was so dedicated to the pretence of business as usual that president S. W. Miller ordered Bert Sprange to slip down to the exchange after hours and quietly remove two wings from the listings board. These wings, now conspicuously empty, had been erected in

1928 to accommodate the listings, which had jumped from sixty-two to ninety-three in less than a year. The vse management committee discussions centred around such topics as fines levied, where to hold the annual picnic and a debate about the creation of a clearing-house to alleviate the pressure on brokers who were doing their own clearing. The latter was hardly a pressing matter since trading was so light most brokers spent more time relieving themselves than they did buying and selling stock.

Brokers generally believed that once the worst market losses were shoved out of the headlines, confidence—and spending—would reassert themselves. But as the months limped by and the Depression took a firm grip on North America, it became increasingly clear to vse members that they had to do something or face ruin. They voted to hire a public relations firm in 1930 to place ads in all the daily and weekly papers to "educate the public about the purpose and function of a stock exchange." The full-page ads depicted the four services of an exchange: "To Give the Facts, To Deliver Promptly, To Trade Efficiently and To Inform the World." The calm, matter-of-fact descriptions of trading included delicate references to the Crash as "recent unsettled conditions" and to the 1928–29 pandemonium as "largely illusory." Illusory or not, the public wasn't buying the message, and a few months later the campaign was abandoned.

The PR strategy wouldn't have worked anyway, but any effectiveness was blunted by yet another scandal, this one involving I. W. C. "Ike" Solloway, one of the country's most famous and respected brokers. Ike Solloway, who appeared frequently on the social pages during the 1920s, was a prominent western financier, a broker and an entrepreneur. Rakish and handsome with a Chaplin-style moustache, he was a bit of a legend in the West. Born in Oxford, England, he came to Canada in 1900 at the age of twelve with a head full of frontier dreams and a boyhood passion for wide open spaces. He distinguished himself in the First World War, rising to the rank of captain.

Solloway was a visionary, and after his wartime experience he became convinced that the future of transportation and communication lay in the air. In the early 1920s he established Commercial Airways of Canada, based in Edmonton. His bush planes did everything from delivering mail and medicine to ferrying ministers into isolated communities for wedding ceremonies. The Commercial Airways pilots were a sterling lot and included the legendary Wop May, Roy Brown (the man reputed to have shot down Baron von Richthofen) and

Grant McConachie (the founder of Canadian Pacific Airlines). Part of Solloway's brilliance lay in his restless energy and curiosity, but those qualities led also to his downfall. At the same time that he was establishing the airline, he began to form what would become the largest mining brokerage house in the country. By 1929 he had thirty-eight offices across Canada, as well as branches in the United States, and had seats on the Montreal, Toronto, Standard, Calgary and Vancouver stock exchanges.

Solloway simply overextended himself, and VSE records show that he and his partner, Harvey Mills, were constantly being charged with trading infractions. No one knows how much Solloway lost in the Crash, but it must have been significant because he turned to crime almost immediately. The activities of the two men soon caused a scandal but not until January 1939 were Solloway and Mills charged with four counts of fraud for issuing false prospectuses in Calgary and Toronto. After a long, messy legal battle, Solloway was fined $150,000 and sentenced to four months in prison, Mills $25,000 and one month. Both served extra time because their firm, Solloway Mills and Company, was in ruins, and they could not raise the total amount of their fines.

Not until the two partners were actually hauled off to jail did the VSE suspend their membership. This had less to do with justice than with the fact that the exchange simply refused to admit that one of its members was a crook, especially after so many years of pointing out to the public that the people bilking them did not hold seats on the VSE. The only bright spot in the scandal was that it centred in Toronto and Calgary, a raw and restless city that bobbed, like a corked bottle, on the ebb and flow of a fledgling oil industry. The Solloway Mills case was the first time a VSE member had been suspended for something other than being in arrears and was the first time any member had been convicted of a criminal offence.*

The scandal was followed by yet another outpouring of indignation, but this time it was the press that fell upon each other like rabid dogs. The *Financial Post* became the champion of the blue-chip brokers and senior exchanges, while the *Canadian Mining Reporter* called the *Post* editorials

---

*D. S. Patterson, the first Toronto broker to buy a VSE seat, had been arrested and charged with fraud in 1932 but was never convicted.

a dastardly attack on one body of brokers to protect another and worse body of brokers from the punishment of their sins which is long overdue. If millions have been lost in the mining market, billions have been lost in the industrial market. It is the Cockshutt plows that have got the stenographers' dollars and the Massey Harrises that have swiped the office clerks' savings, while it is also the big brokerage houses that have cleaned out the public on International Nickel and Noranda.

The *Reporter*'s three-column-long article went on to castigate the banks for coming to the aid of the large eastern brokerage firms by announcing, late in 1929, their willingness to lend brokers up to 85 per cent on stocks selling for $30 and up. It exposed the fact that many of the eastern houses had been offering to their clients margins as low as 15 per cent, whereas mining brokers had stuck to 33⅓ or 50 per cent. It obliquely accused the *Financial Post* staff of playing the market and establishing "intimate" relationships with listed companies and not so obliquely attacked the perniciousness of wash sales, bucketing and other malpractices in the big eastern brokerage houses.

Solloway Mills and the verbiage of the eastern press was bad enough but worse was to come for the VSE. The ticker-tape service, as integral to a stock market as horses to horse racing, had to be cancelled when the exchange fell behind with the monthly fee. The ticker was a vital link to the trading world, but the VSE simply couldn't afford it. Although New York, Toronto and Montreal stocks were not traded on the VSE, the exchange provided information about daily trading on the major exchanges to its members and the local papers. The ticker gave the VSE a place in the network of international markets and allowed it to transmit its daily statistics to other exchanges. Without a ticker tape, the exchange had to rely on the mail to deliver the market quotes, a week or more after the trades had happened. Of the thirty seat holders only C. M. Oliver had its own ticker service, and in 1931 that too was cancelled. The VSE, far from informing the world, became totally isolated from the daily affairs of its cousins in the East.

Business became so bad that during the first two years of the Depression, the annual general meetings touched painfully on the possibility of closing down the exchange. The niceties of the gentleman's game were gradually dispensed with. Committee meetings became terser, and fewer members bothered to attend. In 1929 the management committee had met 197 times, but in the first three years of the Depression they met less than a hundred times. Until 1930 the exchange had been a considerate employer: the management committee once debated for hours about whether or not to fire G. T. Webster, a clerk, after he was caught drunk during office hours, and had voted to give him a second chance. But the decimation of trading made civility and compassion too expensive. Those hired during the recent boom years were fired with few apologies, and the salaries of even faithful employees like Bert Sprange were dropped and dropped again. His salary was so eroded that he was forced to take a part-time job, and special arrangements had to be made to open the exchange on the mornings he was absent.

The outlook was bleak, but the exchange didn't give up entirely. The newspapers were now publishing only sporadic market reports and the VSE couldn't afford advertising, so VSE president Charles Pennock dispatched Sprange to persuade the editors to let him write a regular column on stock markets in hopes of generating investor interest. In one column, Sprange pointed to the solidity of West Coast brokerages by citing the fact that only one VSE member had gone bankrupt in the years following the Crash and that demise was largely due to losses in the East, not on the VSE. Sprange didn't mention that more than 50 per cent of the VSE members were technically insolvent. A separate subsidiary of the exchange, Howe Investments Ltd., had been created to absorb and hold seats on a nontrading basis until members could afford to pay their fees and assessments.

The public, fixated on the growing food lines, dust bowl horror stories and unemployment, paid little attention. Inside the VSE, competition became fiercer for the dwindling trading. Scarcely a week went by without a broker being fined for offences ranging from calling a fellow member a "conniving sod" to failure to deliver stock or trading off the floor. Much of the infighting centred on the trading floor, and the presiding officer had his hands full containing squabbles over who bid or offered first. At times, the sessions resembled a barnyard where ill-fed, dispirited hens jostled each other for a meagre amount of grain. Brokers were continually undermining each other's bids by making private deals on or off the floor. When the officially recognized seller or buyer went to deliver or request the stock certificates to complete the transactions, his counterpart would innocently claim a clerical error and then take the deal to someone else for a better price. In some cases, the brokers simply received a larger commission for the fiddled transaction; in others, they actually pocketed the extra money, telling clients that a stock had been bought at 8 cents when in fact they had managed to get it for 7½.

The VSE's internal bickering became so intense that, for the first time in its history, the management committee called in outsiders to handle the problems. Checking on the validity of all the complaints was almost impossible since the VSE was badly understaffed and the brokerage houses so disorganized and behind in their paperwork that tracing a single trade had become a monumental task. The troops the VSE brought in to help were Butters & Chiene, the firm that was supposed to be doing surprise audits* of the brokerage houses. The auditing system never had worked properly because brokers were so resistant, but in 1931 the practice was resurrected with a vengeance. Butters & Chiene pursued their new mandate, but their determination was thwarted by constant abuse from companies who treated them like a social disease. One firm was tipped off about their impending arrival when a junior clerk spotted the auditors getting off a nearby tram. The firm's president hastily sent everyone home and tacked a "Gone to Funeral" notice on the door.

Audits that should have consumed a few weeks often took six months or more to finish. Finally, Butters & Chiene asked permission to notify their prospective victims in advance, reducing the element of surprise but speeding up the process significantly. By 1933 the VSE had invested considerable powers in Butters & Chiene, making the firm its informal policing arm. The two company principals were regular attendees of committee meetings, giving evidence about trading disagreements and many other complaints.

The VSE also began turning to the police for help. Only two letters of complaint from investors had been turned over to the police by the VSE in its first twenty-five years of existence, but between 1932 and 1934 nearly thirty were turned over.

In 1932 unemployment in Vancouver topped 30 per cent, and the city was virtually bankrupt. Three of the four adjacent municipalities were so indebted that provincially appointed commissioners were sent in to run them. Fortunately for the VSE, the speculative market frequently laughs in the face of adversity. In the years when the Depres-

*In 1928 the VSE had passed a bylaw calling for surprise audits of every broker. The eastern exchanges didn't bring in similar regulations until 1929, something that kept the VSE puffed up for years after.

sion was at its worst, VSE volume actually began to improve. Just under 10 million shares worth $3.2 million traded in 1930, but a year later volume increased by more than 50 per cent to 16 million shares valued at $2.8 million. Compared to the 1929 volume of 143 million shares, it was a pathetic showing, but nonetheless there was improvement. Average share prices, 16 cents for 1931 and 15 cents for 1932, were the lowest ever recorded, but the volume of trading indicated that many more people were willing to pare off a few precious dollars to gamble on the market. The market was probably also a fairly inexpensive diversion for many: as Sebastian de Grazia notes in *Of Time, Work and Leisure* (Anchor Books, 1964), participation in and spending on many forms of recreation actually increased at the height of the Depression. When things are at their most wretched, the promise of good luck is sometimes more bewitching than the offer of a square meal and a warm bed. In the West, that promise was gold.

The excitement began in 1933 with gold-mining companies such as Premier, Bridge River and Bralorne. (Bralorne Mines ran from 75 cents to $18 by 1934.) Trading on a single day in May 1933 of over 800,000 shares was greater than it had been for the entire month the previous year. By the end of May 1933, 2-million-share days were common, and the previously stagnating brokerages houses were faced with the happy problem of finding more staff. Some of the biggest firms, then employing fourteen or fifteen, increased the number of employees to sixty or seventy. Even so, brokers were working fifteen and sixteen hours a day, often eating all three meals at their desks and getting less than six hours sleep a night. It was as if the grime and pettiness of the previous three years had been magically sandblasted to be replaced with the hope of gold. Hoboes living on a dollar a week shuffled into the unfamiliar offices of VSE members, asking, "How much gold stock can I get for this? " and plunking down a handful of money. Housewives, who had reduced the family's butter ration to a tenth of what it had been four years earlier, scooped out hard-won savings and sent their husbands down with instructions to buy something. One elderly gentleman marched into the firms of Charles Pennock, the VSE's president since the Crash, and placed a sock full of coins on the nearest desk. "Gimme the best then pray fer it," he requested.

By the end of 1933 just over 88 million shares worth nearly $29 million had been traded. But not everyone had faith in the longevity of the market, and in 1934 a vicious circle of short sellers invaded the exchange. When share prices continued to rise, they used the deadly effective rumour mill to manipulate the market to their advantage. At this time, there were no restrictions on short trading, and it was not uncommon for a broker to sell a client the same stock he was personally shorting or planning to short. Since penny markets thrive on gossip, a few well-placed, disparaging words—particularly when a number of brokers were working together—could send a shiver of panic among shareholders, causing them to unload their stock. Once the price had been driven down, the shorters could buy back the stock and pocket the profit. Few companies of the time could survive a concerted short selling attack. Cariboo Gold Quartz Mining Company Ltd., one of the most active issues in 1933 and 1934, and one of the few with a legitimate mine, was almost destroyed by short selling but fought back. They attacked a slur campaign by placing a large advertisement in all the Vancouver papers, castigating those involved:

Cariboo Gold Quartz Mining Co. Ltd., has been financed on a mine basis and not for market play. The mine should produce the market—markets never produce mines. Unless the scurrilous methods of certain Vancouver brokers in circulating false and damaging reports concerning our operations at the mine cease, they will demonstrate, beyond dispute, the necessity of going outside of the province to develop even our most promising mining prospects. Some people wonder why only 15 per cent of our stock is held in British Columbia. What has been going on here during the last few days is the answer.

The VSE quickly countered with a press release stating:

Stock brokers in Vancouver are not interested in the dissemination of false information about properties, the shares of which are traded on the exchange. The members of the exchange have amply demonstrated that they are not only sympathetic to the legitimate developments of B.C. mines but play an important part in the financing.

As quickly as the gold market had begun, it was over, killed not by mere rumour but by the Wayside scandal. Wayside became the first VSE-listed company to be investigated by an authority outside the exchange. This time, public outcry was so vehement that the attorney general's department could not claim, as it had in 1929, that Vancouver was not on its beat.

Wayside rose in the froth and foam of the gold market. Between 1933 and 1934 it wobbled from a low of 6½ cents to a high of 70 cents and back down again. Accompanying the rise and fall were a group of brokers buying and selling amongst themselves, using companies they controlled as the buyer and seller of record. Wayside had no intrinsic value, and the buying and selling by brokers was designed to give the public the impression of strong market activity. The brokers were so sure of themselves that when they created a battery of companies to do the buying and selling, they didn't trouble to keep their names off the list of directors. The loudest cries of foul came from Toronto, where promoters hired by Vancouver brokers had sold bales of the stock at its height. Toronto newspaper editorials issued hysterical warnings against the folly of investing in the VSE. Vancouver papers, for once on the side of the VSE, retaliated: "This protest has been used as a subterfuge to keep Eastern money in Eastern mines." The VSE squirmed in the centre of the storm, unable to point out, this time, that the scandal had started elsewhere.

Investor reaction was immediate. Trading, which had reached 92 million shares in 1934, fell to 47 million the next year. Apart from the local investor exodus, Wayside appeared to be a disaster in other senses for the VSE: government involvement in regulating the exchange became a worry, and the lucrative eastern interest began to wither as the VSE was widely fingered as the speculative market where anything goes, including crime. The always willing Bert Sprange was dispatched once again to produce a series of articles emphasizing the exchange's vigilance in upholding ethics and the importance of the VSE in the general economic scheme. He also took this theme on the lecture circuit and during one talk shared the podium with Lobo, a three-year-old German Shepherd dog that "did a number of tricks and showed a remarkable fine degree of training." Lobo got a better review.

Sprange's efforts on behalf of the VSE did little to ease the public hostility. One "Constant Reader" in a letter to the Vancouver *Sun* wrote:

The brokers and the stock exchange have done B.C. an infinity of harm, and stand today as Public Enemy No. 1. The stock exchange committee, who are assumed to have disciplinary control of their members have been lax, and have allowed scandalous operations to take place with full knowledge and connivance. The results are obvious.

The public have absolutely lost confidence, and rumors and suspicions are rampant. The consequence is no one will put up a dollar for the many promising prospects.

Fortunately for the vse, the public's resolve is as fleeting as a hooker's passion. Investors disappear after every scandal and just as unfailingly return, aroused by another boom. This time it was oil that brought the speculators back. Late in the summer of 1936 a major pool of crude oil was discovered in Turner Valley in Alberta. The find unleashed a flurry of drilling and a corresponding increase in new vse listings. Nearly 100 million shares worth over $26 million traded that year. The next was even more hectic, and brokers were cheerfully likening it to 1929—but this time, they claimed, it was a real boom "with real substance and real mines." On January 23rd the exchange had to extend the afternoon session because so many brokers were left with unfilled orders. Just at the moment that the Turner Valley market was gathering its greatest momentum, the Hedley Amalgamated mine-salting scandal brought the vse once again to its knees.

Hedley Amalgamated had been listed since 1932 on the Curb Exchange,* trading between 8 and 15 cents. As the market, spurred by Turner Valley, picked up in early 1937, favourable assays on Hedley's property were published and the stock shot to well over $1. Shortly thereafter it crashed, as those involved quickly sold out their positions. Rumours circulated that the drill cores had been tampered with, and as reporter B. A. McKelvie solemnly noted in a front-page story in the Victoria *Colonist*, "Seldom has public indignation been so aroused." The government, even after the bucketing probes of the 1920s and Wayside in 1934, was still reluctant to get involved in the vse's affairs, but the legislature was like a battleground with accusations and demands being flung between members, occasionally even those from the same party. The management committee met so hurriedly on the evening Hedley broke that two members went without supper and stayed at the exchange until 2 A.M. to draft a telegram to the government and the local papers.

George Lovet Fraser was commissioned by the Department of Mines

---

*The Vancouver Curb Exchange was a separate entity run by the vse, designed to list stocks that for one reason or another could not meet regular listing requirements. In the 1930s this usually meant the company wouldn't pay the listing fee. There were also unlisted stocks that traded but had not applied for a listing. In 1932, vse records show listed, unlisted and curb stocks; in 1933, only listed and unlisted; then in 1934, only listed and curb stocks.

to investigate the Hedley Amalgamated affair. The report he produced a month later confirmed the rumours of mine salting and inflamed the situation still further. Pathetically evident was the fact that almost no one in the government really understood how the VSE worked, what rules existed, who was in charge of enforcing them and even what the mechanics of trading were. Fraser charged that both the mining engineer and mine manager were incompetent, and he also lashed brokers for being unethical and self-serving: "A broker who is trading both for himself and a customer is in a position to accept a purchase for himself if it is beneficial, or to confirm the purchase to his customer if it is not. No other trustee which I know of is allowed in these days to occupy such a position." This blatant conflict of interest between the broker and his client, clear to Lovet Fraser way back in 1937, is still present today.

Options had become very popular in the gold market of 1933 and 1934. An option is the right to buy or sell a certain amount of stock at a specified price. While options were not officially traded on the VSE, giving away options as sweeteners with the purchase of equities had become common in the 1920s. Fraser called options "evil," saying that a broker could help run up the price of a stock not only to sell his own shares but also to sell options, which would then be snapped up as bargains. The exchange was attacked for allowing options and escrowed shares to be sold without any concrete proof that development in the mine was progressing and for not cancelling all sales when evidence of crooked dealing was uncovered.

The VSE reacted as it had when the odour of scandal first fouled the air in the 1920s. The members portrayed themselves as helpless victims unable to fend off the corruption of people outside its control, and the VSE claimed it had no power to cancel sales, when it had already done so many times in disputes over transactions. It correctly noted that Mr. Garrett, the superintendent of brokers, was the only one who could give permission to release escrowed shares and that he alone approved options. However, Garrett was a busy man and the VSE was a small part of his responsibilities. Invariably he consulted with the exchange and deferred to its judgement over most matters. The VSE also rebutted the press's criticism of the exchange for not investigating thoroughly and immediately by saying that "all former attorneys-general have always requested the Exchange, not to complete their own investigations until the government's investigation had been carried out." But no detailed government enquiry had ever been carried out before. Besides, the vse vigorously maintained its right to police itself.

The vse's part in the Hedley scam was almost dwarfed by the free-for-all incited within the government. Garrett, the Department of Mines, the attorney general's department and the registrar of joint-stock companies were all busy vilifying each other. Vancouver's *Financial News* called Fraser's report "a damning indictment" of the government, and the paper also leaked news that an earlier report on the Hedley Amalgamated property, made by A. M. Richmond, a government engineer, had been suppressed. It was, as president of the B.C. Chamber of Mines W. B. Burnett called it, a "rotten mess." The press, excited by government bickering, police investigations and increasingly less veiled threats of Ottawa's possible intercession in the "carnival" of western markets, gleefully played up Hedley well into 1938. Trading showed the inevitable result, and volume for 1938 amounted to only 29.6 million shares compared to 120 million the year before.

The vse seemed to exist in a isolated world of its own, but sometimes global events did intrude. In August 1939 Germany overran Poland, and a vile tremor rocked markets worldwide. Once war was declared, it was almost with relief that brokers began to wind up their affairs. The 1930s had been cataclysmic, exhausting and often uncomfortably illuminating. Any breather was welcome, but no one envisaged a six-year hiatus.

By 1941, the exodus from the vse was massive. Of the fifty members in 1938, thirty-four remained, and of those, only eighteen were active. Johnny Jukes, vse president in 1939, was one of the few brokers to continue to man his firm full time. The vse staff was back to five employees, including Bert Sprange. On one day in 1940 only 5400 shares traded, the fewest since the infamous blizzard of 1935 had taken down phone lines all over the city and left thousands stranded in their homes. There was a single board marker who spent most of his time leaning back in his chair reading comics. Some traders dozed against the wall, others played cards. Jokes echoed across the hall with no competition from cries to buy and sell.

The indomitable Sprange continued to spread the gospel of the exchange at every opportunity. In a 1940 speech he called the exchange "the recruiting office of the country's capital," playing up the war theme. (Bert Sprange, certainly the vse's most loyal and longest-serving employee, left in 1942 to run the wartime Prices and Trades

Board. He was succeeded by V. A. Simmons.) Most of the VSE members turned their efforts to the two Victory Bond campaigns. "Canvassing was very thorough," recalls Cecil Stone, who was an assistant organizer of Victory loan districts. "Toward the end of the war we would have men going around door to door in uniform [whether they'd ever seen service or not], so it was pretty hard for the public to refuse. I met my partner on the war loan. He would go around in his naval uniform; he was a terrific salesman but the uniform helped a lot too."

About the only excitement to tickle the market came in early 1943, with the drafting of the Canadian-American securities agreement. The federal government accepted all aspects of the proposal without consulting the stock exchanges. The agreement would subject Canadian brokers to the terms of the American Securities Exchange Commission (now called the Securities and Exchange Commission), regulations that had been adopted after the Crash and were viewed as the toughest, some said punitive, in the world. The same agreement would make it an extraditable offence for a Canadian broker to buy from or sell to an American any security not registered by the commission. The VSE, unsurprisingly, was appalled at the prospect. In a rare display of solidarity, it banded together with four other stock exchanges (Montreal, Winnipeg, Toronto and the Canadian in Montreal) to fight successfully against adoption of the draft.

One of the oddest outcomes of the six-year wartime trading lull was that the VSE acquired a new image. Not that it had done any housecleaning, but the inactivity was such a contrast to the prewar scandals that others took it to be a sign of reform. Dr. Joseph Crumb, a professor of economics at the University of British Columbia, praised the VSE members for their self-discipline, not that they had much choice in the matter. He told them that they should forget "the gold old daze" of the gold and oil boom years because those times were over forever and brokers would have to make their livelihood from then on with "intelligent stock analysis."

At the end of the war, VSE trading crept back up to levels once regarded as dull. The volume topped 11 million shares in 1944 and reached 27.6 million by the end of 1945. But it wasn't until 1950 that trading again passed 30 million, and it would be another twelve years before the Depression gold market volume of 100 million was reached.

CHAPTER 5

John McGraw, the King

"This is a tough game. There are friends and ethics, but no one should ever go into it if they can't take the knocks —and I don't just mean the losses." JOHN MCGRAW'S philosophy about the speculative stock market, as told to his son Robert.

The years between the end of the Second World War in 1945 and the great mining booms in the early 1960s are conspicuous for their relative tranquillity. Few scandals erupted, few mines were found and the exchange, on many days, resembled a racetrack in the off-season. There was time to play cards and to pitch pennies on quiet Saturday mornings. The most exciting articles written about the VSE in those two decades were features on the life and times of the board girls—the six attractive young women who inhabited the platform above the floor and recorded quotations. The volume of annual trading varied between 16 and 89 million shares, with an average share value of between 35 cents and $1.90 a share. After the cataclysmic booms, busts and scandals of the late 1920s and all of the 1930s, it was as if a calm power had stepped in and taken control. These placid times made few national headlines, but out of them emerged one of the wealthiest and most powerful men ever associated with the VSE. His name was John McGraw.

To friends he was Johnny, and to anyone else he was "sir" or "Mr. McGraw." Young traders quaked when he strode by, and even his peers had a healthy respect for his influence. From the mid-1930s until his early and sudden death in December 1970 at the age of sixty-two, John McGraw ran the vse as if it were his own personal fiefdom. He controlled every aspect of the exchange's business through his complete domination of the board of governors (on which he sat from 1931 until 1970), his close personal ties with the regulators of the time and his considerable skill at floor trading. He was president of the vse three times, in 1938, 1954 and 1955, but even when McGraw wasn't in the chair, the exchange community still treated him as if he were. Another source of McGraw's authority was his ability to get at inside information, assess its strategic importance and then, ruthlessly, capitalize on it—all without anyone realizing what he was up to.

To this day, McGraw is something of a mystery even to those who knew him best. Unlike Alvo von Alvensleben who preceded him and Peter Brown who was to follow, McGraw preferred to blend into the background, at least as far as the public was concerned. His only concession to flamboyance were his convertibles, and even they weren't very flashy. Although his wife drove a white rag-top Cadillac, he preferred a considerably more ordinary Mercury. Over the four decades of McGraw's ascendancy, only a handful of newspaper stories even mentioned his name and none was a detailed profile. Whenever he was quoted, all he offered were terse one-line comments on trading or excerpts from turgid state-of-the-union speeches presented at annual general meetings. McGraw had very clear ideas about whose business his business was. While he was not exactly secretive about his work, his children were given no information they didn't ask for. "In my entire lifetime I only went to the exchange once, and I was only allowed to look in the door," recalls his second-oldest son, Robert, now a prominent Vancouver orthopaedic surgeon. "The only reason I knew when there was something going on was because the bloody phone would be ringing with calls from all over the continent. I would have to ask him if he was involved in whatever stock was causing the excitement."

John McGraw was born in Hamilton, Scotland, in 1908, the son of a fruit importer. His family emigrated to Canada while he was still a child, settling in Penticton, British Columbia, where his father took a job with the CPR. Young McGraw joined Pemberton and Sons Ltd. in 1926 as an office boy at the age of eighteen. Pemberton was a large firm with active real estate, insurance and bond sale divisions. Contemporaries remember McGraw as able, hard working, a little abrasive and always an enigma. "He was a very cute customer even then," remembers Stan Booth, an accountant who roomed with McGraw in 1926 and 1927, "affable but evasive. When you talked to him, it was as if he was holding back things."

McGraw was only a raw clerk when he ingratiated himself with Stanley Burke, the majority owner of Pemberton. The older man was impressed by McGraw's youthful competence, his almost arrogant confidence and his willingness to seize the initiative. Although they came to be close friends, McGraw never called him anything but Mr. Burke. Early on McGraw endeared himself to Burke by saving him considerable embarrassment with an important partner. In 1927, Burke signed a partnership deal with a leading New York bond firm but, caught up in several other business ventures, he forgot to set aside office space for their representatives. McGraw stepped in and completely reorganized Pemberton's office, creating a separate space for the newcomers, and managed to do it without upsetting anyone. From that point on, McGraw became Burke's protegé, and in 1928, when Burke formed Continental Securities Corporation Ltd. to take over stock market transactions, he put McGraw in charge.

Until then, Pemberton did not have a seat on the exchange. It had been funnelling its small amount of VSE trading through C. M. Oliver. But in 1928 new listings were flooding into the exchange at the rate of one a day, and Burke, like everyone else, wanted to get in on the action. He bought a seat in John McGraw's name for $35,000 just weeks before the price jumped to $50,000. That made McGraw, at twenty, the youngest member in the history of the VSE.* McGraw, who wasn't yet schooled in the jargon of the market, was suddenly faced with running a new company himself and hiring ten additional people to help him. Even with the extra bodies, trading was so hectic that the firm couldn't keep up with the paperwork.

Disaster for everyone else often turned out to be money in McGraw's pocket. The Crash of 1929 was no different. Brokerage houses that went bankrupt during and after that grim year were often dragged down by clients who couldn't pay off their accounts. The stock held by the firms as security against margins was almost worth-less. Miller-Court, a vse member, was saddled with $1 million in bad debts. In contrast, Pemberton, with only $75,000 in bad debts, was relatively well off. Burke could have hung on for a few years, but when trading got worse in 1931, he decided to sell Continental. At the time, a stock brokerage firm was the last thing any thinking business-man wanted, but McGraw knew that Continental was a viable enter-prise. Although carrying $75,000 in debts, it had $125,000 in capital, cash and bank loans, leaving a healthy surplus of $50,000 and making it one of the most stable in the West. McGraw borrowed $2,000 from his father and relieved Burke of Continental. Because the firm was still in good financial shape, he didn't have to sell out all his clients' accounts to pay their debts to him. Years later, when the market im-proved, some of them went on to become very wealthy men and con-tinued to do business with him.

Just as McGraw was completing the Continental deal, he got in-volved in a feud that almost tore apart the exchange. The vse had been building up a steady surplus since 1925. After the Crash, several members suggested that the accumulated $80,000 be distributed among the beleaguered seat holders. A. N. Wolverton, by then a senior member of the exchange establishment, was vehemently op-posed and managed to stonewall any efforts to take the idea further. In mid-1931 the suggestion was put forward again, and for six months the debate divided the seat holders into two bitter factions, one headed by the gruff and irascible Wolverton and the other by the young upstart John McGraw. Wolverton argued long and eloquently in favour of banking the money, pointing out that the vse had problems of its own, namely the Hamilton Street property purchased inadvisably in 1910 at the height of the real estate fever for an inflated $41,000. Wolverton claimed the property had cost the exchange over $150,000 in lost interest, decline in value and maintenance. He dolefully at-tributed the relatively low value of vse seats, compared to Montreal and Toronto, to years of such bungling management. He also argued that since many of the members were doomed, with or without the money, giving it to them would be like throwing it away.

McGraw realized he had neither the experience nor the clout to counter Wolverton's arguments directly, so he attacked more subtly. He began a campaign of back-room politicking, dropping hints here and there about what would happen to the price of seats and investor confidence if too many members went under. Gradually, McGraw put the fear of total failure into the minds of a majority of members. When the question was put to a vote late in 1931, the McGraw faction won. Each member's share was about $2,500 and was indeed sufficient to keep some of them solvent until the gold market of 1933 and 1934 once again brought prosperity to the VSE. McGraw's victory was astonishing, but it wasn't just fleeting good luck. At the same meeting he was elected to the board for the first time.

During his first couple of years, McGraw was a cautious trader, following the lead of more senior members while he learned the business, but from the first day he demonstrated a natural trading acumen. He could feel when a stock was beginning to slide or poised to shoot up. He seemed to understand the motivation of other traders just by watching them. If shorting was going to be successful, he would be the first one in, even though other traders would laugh and say, "Johnny, what are you doing? This one's a winner; you're going to lose it all." McGraw would just smile and keep on shorting. By the 1933–34 gold boom, he was the acknowledged master of the floor.

When McGraw died in 1970, he had served thirty-nine consecutive years as a board member. It was an extraordinary accomplishment because board positions, especially the presidency, were treated as a distasteful but necessary duty. Since there was only a handful of employees, board positions were very time consuming. The board ran everything from listings and membership to public relations and compliance. The board also communicated with the securities commission and the government, and when that was done the executive sat down and answered letters from irate investors. It was a huge mandate even on a sleepy little exchange. Most years between the Depression and 1960, the board committees met three or four times a week, and some of the more industrious members served on several committees at once. Many members did the bare minimum, but McGraw knew that the information he gleaned through his committee work would be repaid manyfold. McGraw was not altruistic but the VSE was his life, and being part of the executive was a natural extension of his outlook. His office was the trading floor and the exchange itself, not some suite of rooms removed from the action. He presided over the heart of the market; he didn't observe it passively through his employees.

When war broke out in 1939, Stanley Burke re-entered McGraw's life. He had foreseen the strife back in 1937 and sold out his share of Pemberton. Burke had a long fascination with aircraft so few were surprised when C. D. Howe, Liberal Munitions and Supply minister during the Second World War, asked him to be president of Vancouver's Boeing Canada plant. Burke was stubborn, arrogant and very persistent, and he didn't see the point of trying to build airplanes without the proper facilities. His constant lobbying paid off, and he persuaded the government to provide funds for a new and bigger manufacturing plant on Sea Island (where the Vancouver International Airport now is). The plant was built, and Burke set about establishing a wartime empire.

One of the first people Burke hired was John McGraw. Burke didn't ask him to leave the exchange so much as he ordered McGraw to pack up and follow him. Burke was one of the few people in the world who could have spoken to McGraw that way. McGraw became Burke's detail man, solving problems from transportation to personnel. The latter was a huge headache. "At the time I didn't appreciate his [McGraw's] capabilities," recalls Bill Kaseburg,* superintendent of the main Sea Island plant between 1941 and 1943. "Most of the employees came in as beginners; some of them had hardly even seen an airplane before, and within a few months they were our senior people. I don't know how he kept the whole thing going." At the peak of its production the Boeing plant employed over 6,500 people and was churning out one PBY reconnaissance craft every day.

After the war, C. D. Howe tried to hang onto McGraw by offering him the presidency of Canadair, the federal government's aircraft manufacturing plant in Montreal. Although McGraw had been enormously effective working for Burke he had been essentially on his own and had little desire to step into a large bureaucracy, particularly one owned by the government. He also disliked the thought of moving his family away from the West. In his later years, McGraw gained the reputation of being faster after a buck than any trader on the exchange, but there were other things that mattered more to him—and being a westerner was one of them.

McGraw quickly resurrected Continental Securities Corporation Ltd., and as the prewar brokers straggled back and new ones reapplied, the exchange moved slowly back into action again. Before the war, Continental's business had been largely with retail clients, but afterwards McGraw decided to deal mainly in wholesale trading for other

---

*After the war, Kaseburg, an aeronautical engineer, went on to become a key man in American space research. He was manufacturing manager for the building of the Lunar Orbiter and the Lunar Rover, which ferried Neil Armstrong and Edwin "Buzz" Aldrin across the moon's surface.

brokerage houses that didn't have VSE seats. It meant he would handle fewer numbers of people and have access to much bigger deals. "What he enjoyed most of all was playing with the big guys who never cried over a loss," says Robert McGraw. "He had no patience with the kindly, retired, spinster schoolteachers who always wanted to hit a big one and were never prepared to take a loss."

During John McGraw's long reign, the trading floor was the soul of the exchange. Today the VSE's soul exists in the penthouse offices of promoters and in the art-strewn halls of the brokers who do most of the underwriting. But then, the physical act of trading separated the best from the rest. McGraw's mind was quick, he was willing to take risks and as he grew more powerful he knew which rules were flexible. He was also an intimidating figure, not terribly tall, about 5′ 9″, but with a presence that was much larger. When his burly, not quite fat but hardly lean, neatly dressed figure strode onto the floor, the atmosphere changed. It was as though the traders said collectively and sotto voce: "The Boss is here." The mystique of McGraw was exemplified by his clothing: hand-stitched, hand-starched shirts, immaculate suits, trim hats, burnished shoes—nothing frayed, nothing tarnished. It was a quiet trademark that was at once impressive and menacing. Whatever else went on in his mind, on the outside he was never in disarray. Although McGraw was known to be a gentleman, polite to women and nice to small children, he let very little get in his way. "He was tough," remembers Harry Laidlaw, who was a young phone boy in the 1950s when he met McGraw. "He had a deep, tough voice. You didn't fart around with John McGraw. On the floor, if you said that's my trade and John said it was his, you'd say, 'Yes sir, Mr. McGraw, that's yours.' "

McGraw could never brook stupidity or slothfulness and consequently rode herd on his small staff like a general. Many looked at his second-in-command, Gus MacPhail (who owns Continental today) and wondered how he could work for such an uncompromising employer. Once, for example, one of Continental's four phone boys had been making a hash of some paperwork during a trading session and at some point inadvertently stepped on McGraw's foot. McGraw turned to MacPhail and boomed: "Whoever he is, fire him!" Gus gave the kid his walking papers that day.

Another source of McGraw's power was the fact that Continental Securities was one of the few sole proprietorships on the VSE. McGraw had no one to answer to, and because he did most of his own trading had complete control of every transaction. In other firms, a trader might lose valuable time when a stock began a fast climb because of having to consult with a principal. Not so McGraw. If there was action to be taken, he did it on the spot. He loved the risky excitement of the floor, and he never bothered with games of chance like cards or the ponies. "Hell!" he'd say, "I do that for a living."

McGraw employed only two salespeople in the 1950s, though Continental's trading accounted for 25 per cent of the VSE's volume. McGraw was also the largest underwriter on the VSE from the war until the late 1960s. But in those days, a 200,000-share financing at 15 cents was a big deal, and million-share-days were a just a faint memory. "One day," remembers Gus MacPhail, "I crossed* 20,000 shares of Canam Copper at 16½ cents and got so excited that I phoned John McGraw at the Vancouver Club and I said to him, 'I just doubled the volume of the exchange.' "

Underwriting was, in many cases, a personal thing, more like grubstaking than impersonal financing. "John McGraw and George Tapp would grubstake these prospectors," remembers Ian Falconer, now a vice-president of Midland Doherty. "The amounts of money we are talking about were big in those days, infinitesimal today. If a guy put up $5,000 as an individual to grubstake a prospector, you know that was big money." Sometimes the grubstaking was just that, a loan, with little expectation of return. Sometimes it was something more structured, like an underwriting, either to get the company listed on the VSE or to raise additional capital for one already there so the prospector could go back into the bush and bang together a few more rocks. McGraw's agreements, whether done with a backwoods miner or a major brokerage house, were always clinched with a handshake. And the bigger the deal and the more money involved, the more pleasure he took out of sealing it with his gentleman's word.

McGraw's personal power was substantial, but another source of his influence was his close friendship with J. Stewart Smith, superintendent of brokers from the end of the war until 1962. It is indicative of the times that Smith, who was supposed to be the impartial regulator of the securities industry, treated mining and prospecting like hobbies. "He was a man who believed in mining and was willing to take a chance on grubstaking somebody," says Bill Irwin, who worked for

---

*When shares are crossed, it means that a firm has matched a buyer and seller, bypassing the floor trader.

Smith and succeeded him as superintendent of brokers. "So any prospector who came into his office and needed $100 or $200, he would
grubstake them. He really loved mining and he loved British Columbia. He thought that if this fellow gets into the field with the $200 he
gets from me and $200 he gets from someone else and he hits some-
thing, that's great. It's going to do something for B.C. and I will probably get something out of it."

Until 1962, Smith ran the Securities Commission with a
paternalistic hand that had less to do with the letter of the law than
with whom he knew and liked. His downfall came from the deals he
cut with prospectors and promoters who were only to happy to give
him a few shares in exchange for badly needed cash. Eventually, word
leaked to the press about his relationship with the people he was supposed to be regulating, and conflict-of-interest accusations screamed
across the headlines. "Stu left under a cloud," says Irwin. "I really
don't think, knowing the man and knowing the temperament of the
press at that time, that he got very fair treatment. You can't win getting into a pissing match with the newspapers."

But that was later. While Smith still ruled securities from Victoria,
he and McGraw developed a friendly oligarchy. The two of them
quietly sorted out problems over drinks in the Georgia Hotel or on the
patio of McGraw's Shaughnessy mansion—problems that today would
hit the papers, inflame politicians, excite another orgy of rule making
and result in police investigations. Doubtful promotions, companies
that rose a little too quickly, prospectuses in which the shareholder list
seemed more fanciful than real—he and McGraw discussed them all.
In reality it was a kangaroo court, but the two men kept the VSE running smoothly without public scandal for twenty years. McGraw and
Smith viewed themselves as colleagues, not adversaries. Of course,
having the superintendent of brokers as a good friend didn't hurt when
McGraw wanted to hurry a prospectus through the approval process.
And when a market began to pick up, as it did during the uranium excitement of 1954–55, McGraw could actually get verbal approval for
an underwriting of a VSE-listed company and the consequent issue of
new shares, though it was irregular, even then, for a new company to
appear on the board before the paperwork was completed. "If you have
a good drinking buddy, who knows, that doesn't necessarily mean
you're doing anything wrong simply because they give you a little bit
of preferential treatment," observes Ian Falconer of the relationship
between McGraw and Smith.

McGraw's domination of the VSE was also buttressed by his alliance with the enormously popular and long-term board member George Tapp, senior partner of Doherty Roadhouse & McCuaig Bros. Tapp, like McGraw, considered the VSE to be an avocation, and he served a total of seventeen years on the board, including three in a row as chairman (1968–1971). Tapp was a friendly, extroverted Albertan of Irish descent with an engaging sense of humour. He had a strong character, but unlike McGraw he wasn't aloof; even the cleaning staff privately thought of him as George.

Handsome, lean and friendly looking, even in official photos, Tapp was also a self-effacing man. In the late 1960s, he lived with his second wife Pat in West Vancouver's posh British Properties and drove a white Cadillac to work every morning, but it wasn't until the big white boat was three years old that he stopped apologizing for it. Personality aside, what really counted in the alliance between McGraw and Tapp was that both of them believed the VSE should take care of its own affairs and problems. A speech Tapp gave in 1968 exemplifies his attitude:

It is important that the Vancouver Stock Exchange present a united front to the public. And in this regard we have been quite upset at some of the glaring examples of bad taste shown last year by some members in their statements to the press. It is a selfish way to get publicity and I would suggest that if any member has a grievance or a problem he should, in all decency and respect for fellow members, present it in writing to the exchange, and not look for the nearest outlet to let off steam. This type of action reflects poorly on the exchange and your fellow members.

Tapp served another purpose for McGraw: he was vocal, visible and had a good relationship with the press, especially people like Jack Wasserman, the influential Vancouver *Sun* columnist who mingled regularly with the Howe Street crowd. McGraw in contrast was a very private man, and the media barely knew him.

McGraw kept his coups to himself, but some of the risks he took are immortalized in stories still passed between traders who admire such things. One such incident in the 1950s is remembered by a few. Westcoast Transmission of B.C. and Pacific Northwest Pipeline Company were both in the running to win a lucrative gas sales contract to supply the Pacific Northwest region. McGraw was reading the Dow

Jones tape when the message came across that Westcoast had lost the contract. He ripped the message off the ticker, stuffed it in his pocket, then systematically shorted Westcoast and all the related gas and oil companies on the board at the VSE. Nobody else knew what was going on and, of course, the stocks inevitably collapsed when the news filtered through. The next day, he bought them all back at the deflated prices.

McGraw could be a devastating short seller, a technique he had perfected during the mercurial markets of the 1930s. In the 1950s and early 1960s mine companies, particularly those with eager promoters and not much good news to report, would invite brokers and the press to tour their properties, hoping to encourage them to fire up some action in the stocks. Such trips were often called "the kiss of death" and were considered to be the mortal rattle of a hopeless prospect. Whenever McGraw heard of a mine tour underway or proposed, and he heard of them all, he was the first on the floor to start shorting the stock. Usually he was right, and the company was destined to be history and a little more profit in McGraw's pocket.

The day of John Kennedy's assassination is also part of the McGraw legend. Virtually every person in the western world was stunned by the news, and stock exchanges throughout North America closed their doors immediately. New York was the first to close at 2:10 EST, followed by Toronto thirteen minutes later. But McGraw kept the VSE open until 11:55 A.M. (2:55 EST), and panic selling ensued. McGraw and another trader, Cecil Stone, bought heavily. "John McGraw and Cecil Stone were standing there and they were just buying everything they could of the quality stocks," remembers Gus MacPhail. "B.C. Telephone had been selling at $25 or $30 and it dropped to $12 or $15." The wires were buzzing with rumours that a black man had killed Kennedy, and there was talk of a revolution in the States; some predicted that North American exchanges would stay closed for an entire week. McGraw knew, however, that even the death of a president doesn't disrupt the flow of money for long. He kept buying privately over the weekend. On Monday morning, markets opened again on schedule, and it wasn't too long before the battered stocks were back in their former positions. McGraw netted $1 million for his three days of work.

After the frenzy of the Pyramid market in 1965, John McGraw, only fifty-seven, began to slow down. He took the summers off and handed over more work to MacPhail who, by 1968, was doing virtually all Continental's trading. He spent more and more time on the patio of his Shaughnessy home and at his summer place in Penticton. But if there were big plays to be made, McGraw ensured that Continental was in there making them. During the 1968 oil and gas bull market, the firm's trading equalled that of the top three retail houses put together. He also kept tabs on what was happening by encouraging the VSE to install cameras on the floor so he could monitor trading from his office. Figures weren't good enough; he had to see the people.

Most say that McGraw eased out of the market because he had been in it for forty years and was tired. The real reason, however, was that he foresaw change. He realized that what was happening to the VSE in the aftermath of Windfall and Pyramid was irreversible. The men who were streaking to the West Coast with pockets full of companies and big, promising smiles were not the men with whom he was used to doing business. Not that they were any better or worse, but he didn't know them. He also knew he couldn't hope to hang onto his control of the street when it was increasingly peopled with strangers. "He did tell me that it wasn't as much fun anymore," says his son Robert. "Deals that used to be made over lunch and a handshake had to have forty lawyers and miles of documentation. The freewheeling was gone." Within the VSE itself, things were also changing rapidly. By the late 1960s there were rumblings of discontent from the national houses about the direction of the VSE and talk about moving the exchange into more respectable securities. McGraw didn't want any part of it. He was a speculator, a risk taker, not just a guy who serviced orders—any clerk could do that.

Not only were the street and the VSE changing but so was the very nature of his company. McGraw traded for himself and other brokers. He didn't want the complications of a retail business. The action from 1965 on convinced many of the Toronto-based brokerage houses to buy their own seats on the exchange. Eight of the eleven new members of the exchange between 1963 and 1965 were national houses. McGraw could see that, soon enough, he would have no choice but to sell to the general public.

What convinced him to spend more time on his sundeck and less time trading all came to pass in a few short years, though he didn't live to see it. In 1970, McGraw died suddenly of a heart attack. The next year his era ended for good with the first palace coup and the assumption of power by the national houses. Had he been alive, McGraw might have allowed himself a small smile—after all, he had been right, as usual.

PART II

The Coming of Age

The events of the 1960s and early 1970s are critical to an understanding of the story of the VSE and junior stocks in Canada. The VSE was transformed, mostly by external events such as Toronto's Windfall Mines scandal and discoveries like Dynasty and Pyramid, into the centre of speculative trading. Unprepared for the promoters, the money and the sheer volume of activity that arrived overnight, the VSE was almost destroyed. Undreamed of profitability, coupled with limp regulatory and management supervision, ate away at the foundation of the exchange. During this period of chaos, two groups, the one bent on changing the VSE into a sedate and respectable mini-TSE and the other determined to capitalize on its speculative roots, waged a bitter power struggle. Not only did this struggle confirm, probably forever, the VSE's status as a speculative exchange, but it produced another formidable leader to succeed John McGraw: Peter Brown, the principal of Canarim Investment Corporation Ltd.

CHAPTER 6

The Transformation: Windfall, Pyramid and Dynasty

"That bull [the Pyramid and Dynasty market] was the horniest son of a bitch you ever saw. There wasn't anyone that was going to get in the way of that market —certainly not a bunch of fairy-assed regulators, that's for sure." A LONG-TIME VSE SEAT HOLDER.

During its first fifty years, the Vancouver Stock Exchange alternately envied the status of the Toronto Stock Exchange and blamed it for its problems. Toronto, and to a lesser degree Montreal, were the Canadian centres of junior mining until the mid-1960s. Toronto's Bay Street, now dominated by the austere high-rises of respectable financial firms, once was alive with scores of brokers hustling junior mining stocks. These people made such effective and unscrupulous use of boiler rooms, phony tout sheets and high-pressure salesmen that they inflamed the U.S. Securities and Exchange Commission, which in 1951 accused Toronto brokers of swindling Americans out of $52 million annually.

The love/hate relationship between the VSE and the TSE still endures and makes it especially ironic that the VSE owes much of its present prosperity to the TSE's decision, usually demarcated by the 1964 Windfall scandal, to rid itself of undesirables: i.e., junior mining brokers and promoters. That decision, coupled with a phenomenal string of mine discoveries spearheaded by Pyramid and Dynasty in late 1965, were crucial steps in the VSE's coming of age.

Aside from events in Ontario, the burgeoning prosperity of the 1960s had an impact on the dozing western exchange. That decade was the beginning of unprecedented prosperity in North America. Disposable incomes were growing, and people were using their extra money to buy a plethora of consumer goods and, increasingly, securities. The Dow Jones average, which had been at 404 in 1954, more than doubled to nearly 900 ten years later. In Vancouver the VSE benefited from the general optimism as trading volume leapt from 21 million shares in 1960 to 104 million in 1962. But it wasn't until Windfall that all the factors coalesced to thrust the VSE into the early stages of its modern era.

The 1964 Windfall Mines manipulation, sometimes called the Core Hoax, is often pinpointed as the sole reason the Toronto Stock Exchange moved so vigorously to restrict its junior mining promoters, but in fact the TSE had been informally blackballing undesirables since the late 1950s. What Windfall did was to provide inescapable public proof about something TSE insiders already knew—that junior mining brokers and promoters were running wild. The public and the media couldn't help but ask: if the perpetrator of Windfall, the highly respected president of the Prospectors and Developers Association, Viola MacMillan, was a stock manipulator, what were the real lowlifes doing? Windfall also uncovered an unhealthy intimacy among promoters, the TSE and government officials. Major corporations listed on the TSE, like INCO, Imperial Oil and Noranda, were aghast at the mining broker antics and privately threatened to move to the New York Stock Exchange if the mess wasn't cleaned up. In truth, Viola MacMillan was just one of dozens of stock promoters dancing a wild jig to greed. Unfortunately for her, she had no chair to sit in when the music stopped.

Viola Rita MacMillan, née Huggard, an extroverted hustler barely five feet tall, was commonly known as "the Queen Bee of Mining." MacMillan had been president of the Prospectors and Developers Association (PDA) for twenty-one years in 1964, and when anyone talked about the tireless spirit of prospectors and junior mine promoters, she was the sterling example. MacMillan was the thirteenth of fifteen children born to the Huggards in the Muskoka district of Ontario. Her parents were market gardeners, but the whole family turned their hand to anything that brought in a few extra dollars, from operating a sand and gravel pit to offering a summer boat service to vacationers. In 1923, Viola married George A. MacMillan, a quiet, unassuming man. George had been nurtured on the myths and legends of mining and prospecting by two uncles, Black Jack and Alex MacMillan, who had been involved in the Cobalt Lake silver rush at the turn of the century in Ontario.

Together, George and Viola MacMillan embarked on one of the most unusual careers in the history of Canadian mining. They began it as a favour, staking claims in northern Ontario for Black Jack. But rock breaking grew as a kind of fever in them, and by the mid-1930s they were prospecting full time. Every possible moment was spent in the bush, and they only emerged to keep their small real estate development firm going and to whip together investor syndicates to grubstake their latest activity. Over the years Viola and George prospected in virtually every Canadian province, often being out in the field for eight months or longer. They were involved in a number of finds including the Canadian Arrow Gold Mine in the Kirkland Lake District; ViolaMac Mines Ltd., a lead-silver-zinc mine in British Columbia, and Lake Cinch Mines Ltd., a uranium property in Saskatchewan. They became members of the PDA in 1935. George was president from 1941 to 1944, but his contribution has been all but forgotten in the shadow of Viola, who took over the reins and ruled the association from then until her disgrace in 1964.

In addition to being a tireless saleswoman and promoter, Viola MacMillan was also a mentor to other prospectors who approached her for legal advice, even going so far as to represent some of them in court. Not only was she a pillar of the junior mining establishment but she was a respected prospector too. "I'm a miner," she proudly told interviewer Christina McCall in 1957. "I love this business, and I want to stay in it until I die." One of the sad truths about the seductive but backbreaking world of prospecting is that the payoffs, which can be extraordinary, are rare nuggets in a stack of fool's gold. Viola and George were making a decent enough living from what they did, but the essence of prospecting is the big strike. As time passed and their dreams of bonanza never quite arrived, they increasingly chose the faster track of stock promotion to achieve their wealth. It was in this role as stock promoter that Viola MacMillan met her ruin.

The Windfall stock promotion began innocently enough. During

1963–64, the MacMillans staked twelve claims, which they sold to their TSE-listed company Windfall Oil and Mines Ltd. The property was adjacent to Texas Gulf Sulphur Company's huge lead-zinc find in Timmins, Ontario, one of the biggest ore bodies of its type in the world. The MacMillans were only two of a horde of proximity hounds crowding in, hoping the Gulf Sulphur glitter would rub off and send the price of their stock rocketing.* Their promotion was a masterful performance, with the MacMillans subtly feeding the rumour mill by what they didn't say. Early in July 1964, the first hole was drilled on the property. The samples were assayed in great secrecy. When the MacMillans were informed verbally that the assays were worthless, they ordered the rig to continue the drilling program, usually a positive sign, and then used every stratagem possible to delay receiving the written assay results. Then word somehow filtered out that the evidence of sulphide mineralization in the cores was so rich it was visible to the naked eye. While all this deception was going on, Viola, a veteran trader, had been painstakingly grooming the market. She created a sense of activity through purchases by other companies under her control. The price moved up and down between 40 and 80 cents until mid-July, when the rumours began circulating and the price shot up to $5.50. Trading in Windfall stock was heavy, totalling over $36 million during the three months of the manipulation. Viola MacMillan was said to have been personally involved in 40 per cent of all trading.

Viola probably would have gotten away with the manipulation, but she became too greedy. She let the stock get too high, and the volume was too great to ignore. When the negative assays finally surfaced at the end of July, the stock crashed and trading dried up. MacMillan netted $2 million from the three-month scam, far more than she and George had made during thirty years of legitimate prospecting. The resulting scandal, royal commission and trial cost MacMillan her good name and eight weeks in prison when she was found guilty of fraudulent manipulation. The post-Windfall hearings also hinted at the influence junior mining companies exerted: one of the directors of Windfall had convinced the provincial government to intercede on Windfall's behalf when TSE president Howard Graham threatened to halt trading if he didn't receive more information about the company's activities.

---

*In fact, the geologist who originally staked the property for Texas Gulf was part of a secret group that made a fortune selling worthless claims adjacent to the strike zone.

The furor over the Windfall affair lasted for years, and not until Black Friday hit the VSE in October 1984 was there another national stock market scandal to equal it.*

The Toronto Stock Exchange, reeling from the public, media and corporate backlash created by Windfall, threw itself into a frenzy of regulation destined to drive the penny stock market out of Ontario for twenty years. Vancouver's reaction was condescending. "It can't happen here," was B.C. Attorney-General Robert Bonner's pronouncement. He explained that "daily" communication between the stock market and the provincial securities commission monitored stock prices to catch any erratic or unexplained activity. Bonner emphasized that Viola's trading spree would have been halted long before the crash if it had happened on the VSE.

For a brief period in 1965 the Ontario Securities Commission actually looked to Vancouver as it studied how to clean up the effluent left behind by the Windfall scandal. Fraser Robertson, associate editor and business columnist with the Toronto *Globe and Mail,* also went to Vancouver that year to study the West Coast way.

> Conscience-stricken Toronto, mulling over the Windfall scandal and other unhappy operations, has been doing some housecleaning recently. For example, it recently hired a full-time stock-writer, part of whose duties will be to prevent the market from being rigged by sharp operators. Vancouver has had one for a long time. . . . The B.C. securities laws are almost word for word like those of Ontario, but there is this difference: the exchange and the commission work in harmony here.

No one in Vancouver enlightened Robertson as to the real reason for the observed harmony. The OSC's workload was heavily devoted to listed companies. In contrast B.C.'s superintendent of brokers had very little to do with the exchange; less than 5 per cent of its work concerned VSE listings. Later, when contact increased between the VSE and the superintendent of brokers, the harmony disappeared abruptly.

*In *The Discoverers,* the 1982 official history of the PDA, a three-page biography of Viola makes no mention whatsoever of the Windfall scandal. In 1983 John Woods, publisher of the Vancouver-based *Stockwatch,* commissioned a painting of the TSE floor in action. He had already commissioned one of the VSE. He tried to talk Viola MacMillan into posing, like a wraith, in the visitors' gallery overlooking the trading floor. She refused because she didn't think it was proper.

PYRAMID AND DYNASTY

"Pyramid started out like any other dog," wrote Frank Keane, a Vancouver stock market columnist, in 1981. But, during the brief eighteen months it took to get its pedigree, Pyramid altered the character of the Vancouver Stock Exchange forever. Pyramid Mining Company was originally formed by prospector John Tancowny to finance exploration and drilling in Aspen Grove near Merritt, B.C. One of the people who held a significant stock position in the company was his accountant, Alec Lenec, a stocky, stogie-smoking man who had given up his comfortable government job to become an accountant specializing in mining. The property turned out to be just another chunk of moose pasture, and the time spent discovering that fact swallowed up all the money that had been raised privately. Tancowny, desolate over the failure of what he fervently believed was a sure thing, resigned from the presidency of Pyramid and asked Lenec to try to resurrect something from the shambles before they all went bankrupt.

In November 1964, Lenec approached Alfred E. "Ted" Turton, a local broker-dealer, to help them raise money. Pyramid had only $7 and some odd cents left in the treasury. The company needed a new property before anything could be done to rekindle their investment, so Lenec talked to mining engineer Henry Hill in the summer of 1965 to see if he had any ideas. Hill was interested in two areas, the Stikine copper district in B.C. and Pine Point in the Northwest Territories. Pine Point Mines, owned 78.2 per cent by Cominco, had already made major lead-silver-zinc discoveries in the region but had abandoned a large number of claims on the periphery of the main ore body. Hill staked and optioned a total of 434 claims for Pyramid. Lenec, though eager, wasn't a promoter, so Turton did the legwork in drumming up investors for the necessary exploration capital. He conducted two underwritings, one of 175,000 shares at 35 cents and another of 175,000 shares at 50 cents, as well as a private placement of 200,000 shares at 75 cents, grossing the company $298,500. "I had trouble even giving the stock away at 35 cents," remembers Turton.

Turton sold to anyone he could collar. Friends, many of whom bought a handful of stock as a favour, began to avoid him lest they be pressured into adding to their portfolios. Lenec was just as single-minded. "If you walked into Tiny's [the local bar and grill hangout for promoters, brokers and prospectors] and you saw Alec there, you just turned around as fast as you could and got the hell out of there. If you didn't, you'd end up with more of that damned Pyramid stuff," chuckles one thirty-year veteran of the street who now, thanks to that "damned stuff," spends most of his year in St. Kitts. As a result of Turton and Lenec's efforts, Pyramid had one of the widest distributions in the history of Canadian penny stocks.

Hill commenced surveying the property in the fall of 1965, utilizing the relatively new Induced Polarization Technique (IPT), whereby electrical currents are sent into the ground and the resulting "playback" gives the engineer an inkling of the mineralization. The results were so good that Hill decided to drill, even though the temperature was hovering around -45° to -50° and the crew's skin froze the minute they set foot outside the camp tents. He was excited about the IPT results, but the real reason for the haste was the group's suspicion that Cominco employees were shorting the Pyramid stock. Shorting stock often drives the price down and inhibits trading. Since the principals of a company depend on selling shares from the treasury or conducting a new offering to finance operations, a depressed stock price could destroy their ability to raise money.

Lenec and Hill had to use radiotelephone to communicate. As a security measure to foil eavesdroppers, they created an elaborate code, with the hours of the day corresponding to various drilling results. If Lenec asked Hill what time it was, and Hill replied "three A.M.," that might mean a strike had been made. On Friday, October 28, 1965, Henry Hill called. He had been into the sauce a little bit so he had some trouble organizing his thoughts. While he was trying to tell the group huddled around a radiophone in Vancouver what he had found, they kept overriding him to ask what time it was. Finally, in exasperation, Hill said, "I don't give a fuck what time it is, we're all fucking millionaires." And they were. Turton and Lenec each owned 100,000 shares, giving them a paper worth of $1.5 million within a week. Hill's 50,000 shares made him worth $750,000.

By the time the official assay results arrived, the exchange was closed. Pyramid was not yet a VSE-listed stock, but when exchange president John A. Van Luven saw that the first hole indicated commercial grade ore of 5.37 per cent lead and 14.16 per cent zinc, he knew the market would go wild. Brokers and VSE officials got an avalanche of calls about Pyramid all weekend, and Van Luven hastily called a board meeting. Pyramid, which was only part way through the listing process, was suddenly on the board by 7 A.M. Monday morning. He explained this unprecedented move as an effort to maintain an orderly market, but the real reason was to enable the VSE to receive its percentage of the trading commissions and a share of the prestige of bringing in a winner. It was a wise decision. An incredible $1 million in stock was traded in the first hour that Pyramid was listed. When the market closed at the end of Pyramid's first day, 4.2 million shares had changed hands, establishing a new VSE record. In comparison, trading during the whole of that October was only 20 million shares. Even the revelation that a second drill core had negative results didn't diminish trading.

The frenzy was intoxicating. By 6:00 A.M. on Tuesday crowds were milling around outside brokers' offices, and by 9 A.M. cars were heedlessly double- and triple-parked along Howe Street. Taxi companies frantically put as many cabs as possible into the downtown area. From one end of the brokerage community to another, phones rang without pause. "I had clients you couldn't even talk to because we were so busy," recalls Brian Graves, now a vice-president of Brink Hudson and Lefever Ltd. in Vancouver. "We'd just go like mad, take all these orders and relay the fills back. . . . I'd go back to the office when the exchange was closed, and my father and I would try to balance the previous day's business. I'd get back to the office at one or one-thirty in the afternoon, and he'd been at it since nine in the morning. I would have a few moments to phone my clients, then I'd sit down at a typewriter and type out contracts for that day's business. You'd struggle home to bed at nine or ten o'clock and collapse until six the next morning."

Pyramid was front-page news all week. On Monday, the Vancouver *Sun* printed a detailed map of the Pine Point area, showing the claim locations of all the mining companies. On Tuesday, an enthusiastic customer stormed into one of the brokerage houses and demanded: "Buy me a bunch of that Great Slave Lake. I've seen a map in the *Sun*, and it's in the Pine Point area." Later in the week another client rushed into C. M. Oliver, shouting, "A band is playing out there! They've found more ore in Pine Point!" The band was from the Salvation Army and it was playing for Remembrance Day contributions. "You just couldn't talk fast enough to put your orders on the floor," marvelled George Wright, then assistant manager at James Richardson and Sons.

On Tuesday, November 2nd, the pace was gruelling. Between 7:00 and 10:00 A.M. that day, 3.5 million shares traded. "People seemed to have lost their heads," commented one local broker. "Many are phon-

ing up and asking only, 'What's going up?' Then, 'Buy some for me.' "
Trading was so backlogged that if an order to buy was put through at
$7, the price was $10 by the time it was filled.

On Wednesday, when positive results from the third hole were
released, the previous two days seemed like holidays. Over 6.5 million
shares traded. Floor traders, hoarse with shouting, were haggard and
sweat-stained. They were also very, very happy. Jimmy McKissock,
president of the local West Coast Securities, enthused, "Toronto's
had it for twenty-five years. It's B.C.'s turn now." Pyramid's stock
went from $4.40 at opening to a high of $16.50, and closed at $14.40
during the week of November 1, 1965. It was all based on three drill
holes. A total of 16 million shares (most of them cashing in on the
Pyramid find) valued at $17 million changed hands that week.
Pyramid, joined by a host of hangers-on, dragged up every stock that
had the remotest connection with the Pine Point area. Some of the
companies had extensive claims (many staked after the Pyramid results became public), some only announced they intended to purchase
claims and still others, like Ace Mining Company Ltd., went spiral-
ling up simply because Alec Lenec was on the board or Henry Hill was
listed as company engineer.*

Lenec, Turton, Hill and Tancowny had what every prospector and
promoter lusts for in his heart—a big, fat mine. For a while they enter-
tained thoughts of developing it themselves, but Cominco, which had
walked away from those same claims a few years before, was determined to buy control. Eventually they gave in, realizing the futility of
trying to fight off the giant. The deal they made was for $33 million in
stock and another $5 million in cash. Pyramid stock, which Lenec had
been called a fool for buying on the open market at $15, promptly
went to $20. For Lenec, it was a dizzying turnaround. Just a year before
he had been earning barely $50 a week. Lenec could have retired and
smoked the best havanas on some endless beach. But mining is rarely a
short-term disease; he gathered up his booty, joined forces with Hill
and went looking for more. He never did find another Pyramid, but
few could boast of that much.

Pyramid was to remain an exciting stock, even through the pre-

---

*Other companies that traded heavily included Madrona Explorations Ltd., Croydon Mines
Ltd., New Cronin Babine Mines Ltd., Chataway Mining Company Ltd., Trojan Consolidated
Mines Ltd. and Buttle Lake Mining Company Ltd. None had even begun exploration work, and
none of the more than thirty companies with location bets ever found anything.

development depression that generally follows a discovery and causes prices to slump until the ore is actually produced. In a normal market the weeks following Pyramid would have seen a gradual tapering off of interest as all the companies with locations bets burned out. But those times were not normal. Just as the Pyramid hysteria abated, Dynasty rolled in and swept the exchange back into a trading blitz.

Dynasty was the offspring of Dr. Aaro E. Aho, a geological engineer, and a small group including Alan Kulan, a prospector, R. E. Gordon Davis, also a geological engineer, and Ronald V. Markham, a financial expert. Aho was a scientific prospector. Complex instruments were his divining rod, and he used them with extraordinary success. The original claims in Vangorda Creek, Yukon, were staked by Alan Kulan, who had explored the area on his own and in conjunction with other companies before joining Dynasty Explorations Ltd., a syndicate formed by Aho in 1964. Aho, a native of Ladysmith on Vancouver Island, was convinced that a major mine existed in the Yukon. The initial surveys were promising, and he was able to talk the Yukon government into the expensive job of plowing a 137-mile road in the middle of winter to allow more intense exploration including 30,000 feet of rotary drilling, diamond drilling and more detailed geophysical surveys.

Markham conducted two private placements, raising $200,000 in 1964 by selling 700,000 shares at 40 cents and early in 1965 another $200,000 worth with a share price of $1. But money was getting progressively harder to raise. Markham and Aho approached a number of major mining companies for a partnership deal but barely got past the receptionist with most of them. Finally, the treasury naked, Aho took a chance and went to California. After weeks of turndowns in Canada, they hit pay dirt with their first appointment. Impressed with Aho and with Dynasty's results, Cyprus Mines Corporation handed over a cheque for $50,000 one day after their first meeting and agreed to fund the remainder of the exploration. During the spring of 1965 a further $250,000 was spent on exploration and claim staking, but they found nothing. More than twenty drill holes had been sunk. Then, in June, the camp moved, and Aho pitched his tent at dawn over what was to become the Faro No. 1 orebody. Ironically, they had started drilling in the only place in the whole area where there wasn't significant mineralization. Dynasty and Cyprus kept their find under wraps while they consolidated the surrounding property. In all, they staked 2,400 claims covering 130,000 acres in the area.

Dynasty, which had been trading over the counter in the $1 range, was listed on November 9th and opened at $15 on the strength of rumours and a promising, but ambiguous, announcement by Aho. "Initial results on one of two zones now being drilled on the Faro property have indicated massive sulphides with good tonnage possibilities, but further drilling will be necessary before the average grade and indicated tonnage can be established." Like Pyramid, only a handful of holes had been drilled. In contrast, Cominco had drilled 1,500 holes to fully establish their Pine Point property. But Aho's news was sufficient to propel trading to a near-record level of 4,388,275 shares the first day. As Dynasty took off, it sparked a staking rush even bigger than Pyramid's. Newspaper accounts called it the most extensive since the Klondike gold rush. In the weeks following the public listing, another 2,000 claims were staked, and dozens of vse companies touted property in the area to sell their stock. As with Pyramid, none of the companies with location bets found anything. A sad irony of Dynasty's success is the fact that the two men most involved in its discovery, Aho and Kulan (who became multimillionaires), died tragically early. Aho was killed in 1977 when a tractor rolled over him on his Ladysmith farm, and Kulan was shot to death in Ross River, Yukon, in 1976.

On the day that Pyramid was listed, Vancouver out-traded Toronto by one million shares. It was the first time ever and it set the Toronto brokerage community back on their heels. When Dynasty joined in to add to the Pyramid excitement, more attention was being paid in Toronto to the Vancouver tickers, as crowds wanting a piece of the action gathered around them, than to tse-listed companies. The eastern brokerage houses acted quickly to capitalize on the boom. James Richardson and Sons, then the only national house that operated an active seat on the vse, flew in seven extra traders and floor clerks from Winnipeg and Toronto. William Thompson, a senior trader for the firm, was sent west via the night plane with only six hours' notice. Cameron Jones, Gairdner & Company Ltd.'s number one trader had similarly short advance warning for his western trek. Doherty, Roadhouse and McCuaig Bros. announced that they would bring in traders from the East to begin trading their seat. Until then, they had been relying on jitney brokers like John McGraw of Continental Securities. There was an unseemly rush as brokers and senior executives fell over each other in their hurry to get to Vancouver. When the news of Dynasty hit the wires, two Toronto-based brokerage houses with vse seats notified the exchange that they wanted second seats, and several others indicated that they were considering purchasing seats. Seat prices tripled between 1963 and 1967, jumping from $12,000 to $35,000.*

Dynasty and Pyramid are heralded as VSE winners, but they were both already successes before becoming listed. The Cyprus deal with Dynasty and the Cominco deal with Pyramid and all the early financing had nothing to do with the VSE. The mines would have gone into production whether they were ever listed or not. The main reason they went on the board was to give shareholders a ready market to sell their stock.

Aside from the brokerage community, the Pyramid-Dynasty action on the VSE galvanized another Toronto group: promoters. Although the Ontario Securities Act, strangling the junior mine industry in the East, would not come into effect until 1967, anyone associated with mine promotion knew that the game was lost. Between 1964 and 1967 the backbone of the Toronto penny stock market, the sharp-eyed, quick-tongued promoters, masters of hyperbole, slid into Vancouver en masse. Where the promoters led, the junior mining brokers were quick to follow. Their timing was exquisite. Pyramid and Dynasty led a surge of real mineral finds, all discovered over just seven years: Lornex, Highmont, Valley Copper, Stampede, Bethlehem and Afton became lucrative producing properties. Hundreds of claims were staked in the vicinity of these mines, piggybacking on their success. Almost all amounted to nothing, but they fed the long bull market that lasted almost unabated until 1970. In 1968 the value of trading was almost double that of 1967. In early 1969 the VSE rang up several 5-million-share days. In late January the tape ran twenty-three minutes late as 3 million shares traded in two hours. Then, on January 28, 1969, the Pyramid record was broken as 7 million shares were sold.

Not even the brokers themselves understood what was happening. One hoarse and weary trader, asked for an explanation in 1969, croaked, "How the hell do I know? The thing starts for no reason that

---

*In 1965 trading totalled 300,502,360 shares worth $302,201,821—a 37 per cent increase in value from 1964. Most of the increase was attributed to Pyramid and Dynasty during the final two months of the year. The 1965 breakdown of the VSE's over $300 million trading was mines 76 per cent, industrials 17 per cent, oils 6 per cent and the rest banks. It was estimated that the unlisted market traded 78 million shares at a value of $68 million—more than 20 per cent of the VSE's volume.

I can see, spreads faster than a flu bug and before you know it we've all caught it."

The VSE, the police and the superintendent of brokers (SOB) were totally unprepared for both the flood of trading and the sudden bloating of the once minute promoter community. In 1964, the SOB's office was still headquartered in Victoria with a staff of just two investigators. Only a small percentage of their work was devoted to VSE-listed companies, and days would go by without a glance at market activity. The VSE was even more poorly prepared: it had no compliance department to ensure proper filing of financial reports, little in the way of systematic records and no means of investigating either perceived or known problems with listed companies. Although there was one man, Bob Mullock of the RCMP, who was frequently assigned to commercial crime cases, he had no market experience, little time and no mandate to concentrate solely on the exchange.

The VSE stoutly maintained it could deal with the influx of promoters. "There's always some fellow who comes along with a new twist to try and beat the public," Van Luven, then the exchange's executive vice-president, told the press. "But our listing committee and board of directors have a good many years experience among them and they're on the alert." Van Luven's much touted listing committee was formed in 1962, when the Securities Act gave the VSE more responsibility for policing listed B.C. stocks. The committee was made up of four members of the board of governors and Van Luven. The identity of the other four members was kept secret to decrease lobbying by promoters who had listing applications pending, but the committee was hardly formed before their identities ran up and down Howe Street like a flame in a paper tunnel. That was bad enough, but at least the public didn't know, so the committee still had the illusion of secrecy—for a while. But shortly after Windfall broke, the VSE mistakenly published an uncaptioned but very clear picture of the listing committee in action. No more was said about that particular safeguard.

In fact, almost no one was paying any attention to the picayune problems of regulation. Pyramid, Dynasty and their successors dwarfed everything. By 1966 there were thirty-one broker-dealer firms in the city, almost as many as the forty-two brokerage houses, and they were, for all intents and purposes, unregulated. Despite rules to the contrary, many of the brokerage houses were working with broker-dealers, and a large proportion of the eastern promoters were using them to operate their phone campaigns. "You never knew what those guys were up to," confesses one former securities official. "You just shut your eyes and prayed they didn't create too much of a stink while they were doing it, or burn the mayor or something."

In 1969, four years after the series of mine bonanzas had broken the cosy community of the VSE wide open, the industry was still denying that the junior stock market had been altered one whit by eastern promoters. Superintendent of Brokers Bill Irwin only tacitly admitted in a Vancouver *Sun* interview that during the previous four years his office had been desperately trying to clean up the problem that didn't exist: "There aren't the fast buck boys here [from Toronto] that came in the Pyramid Mines days. We are finding out who they are and they are being dealt with accordingly."

Windfall, Pyramid and Dynasty did much more than set the stage for, and then fuel, the longest bull market in the history of the Vancouver Stock Exchange. Those three events metamorphosed the soul of the VSE and altered forever the character of stock speculation in Canada. From a higgledy-piggledy group of brokers, prospectors and promoters scattered across the country's exchanges, the heart of the junior stock business coalesced into a well-organized knot of smart, educated, cunning and aggressive individuals, located in Vancouver, who attacked the penny punch board world with precision and determination.

CHAPTER 7

The Struggle for Power:
Two Palace Coups

The VSE had become highly visible during the trading binge of the 1960s, and even that venerable British publication *The Economist* called it "one of the leading venture capital markets in the world." Unseen by everyone outside the exchange, however, was the disintegration within. From the trading floor to the board of governors, the exchange was like the wreck of a house the morning after a motorcycle gang party. First, the VSE had no leader. Its last strong man, John McGraw, began to ease himself out of the business in 1966. The bureaucracy was frayed at the edges from the many years of prosperity that had diverted attention away from the business of running the VSE. The exchange's seat-of-the-pants administration, which had worked well enough when trading volumes were low and when John McGraw was in control, disintegrated during the long onslaught of the bull market.

When there is a power vacuum, inevitably some force will move in to fill it. Between 1965 and 1970, eight of the eleven new VSE members were from Toronto. Ironically, the brokerage houses that flocked to Vancouver were the same ones that had carefully kept their distance in the past. If the VSE had been strong and well organized, the growing eastern membership would have had little effect. But, just as penniless prospectors who strike it rich in the back of beyond become a target for big mining companies, so the weak VSE became an attractive honey pot for national brokerage houses. Their presence led to the two coups that ultimately turned the VSE into the money machine it is today.

John (Jack to his friends) A. Van Luven, president of the VSE since 1965, tried to step into John McGraw's boots. Van Luven had been an accountant in the provincial sales tax department before joining the VSE as manager in 1957. He immediately improved the VSE's casual and antiquated book- and record-keeping system, which had changed little from the 1930s. Articulate and vocal, he also became the VSE's badly needed spokesperson, as John McGraw didn't have a good relationship with the press and rarely allowed himself to be interviewed.

Van Luven and McGraw held similar philosophies about the conduct of life and business. They were both gentlemen who believed fervently that transgressions and disagreements should be dealt with behind closed doors, and who deplored any washing of the VSE's linen, no matter how soiled, in public. Van Luven was convinced that the quiet word and the tacit agreement were far more powerful than the documented regulation. It was a flexible approach, and promoters, who were all on a first-name basis with the VSE staff, knew that as long as they were bringing trading volume to the exchange and not creating a public disgrace, they would have no problems. Van Luven also forcefully opposed any intrusion by outsiders into the exchange's domain. He even regarded the B.C. Securities Commission as a meddler and successfully resisted repeated suggestions by the government and press that there be public representation on the VSE's board of governors.*

This gentlemanly approach was effective during the 1950s and the early 1960s when growth was unspectacular and the promoter community was limited and well known. But in the mid-1960s it all changed abruptly with Windfall and then Pyramid. The VSE was deluged by promoters from Toronto, many of whom had never met a gentleman, much less knew how to act like one. Van Luven's little world mushroomed from 200 listed companies, $1 million in underwriting and $40.5 million worth of trading in 1960, to 650 listed companies, $46 million in underwriting and $1.2 billion worth of trading in 1969. He assured everyone that the VSE was in control, and the board, oblivious

*The first VSE public governors, lawyer David Huberman and accountant Peter Stanley, were appointed to the exchange board in 1972 during Thomas Dohm's brief presidency.

to administrative duties during the orgy of money making, asked no penetrating questions.

By 1971, however, Van Luven's civil servant bookkeeping and back-room diplomacy was coming apart at the seams. There were no compliance files, listing records were scanty and sometimes nonexistent, and most information existed only in the heads of the exchange staff. The employees were underqualified and poorly paid, and most had been demoralized by the preceding years in which their peers in the brokerage community had made $100,000 a year. It was hopeless to try to hire people acquainted with the market when the exchange could offer only a fraction of what they were already making. Also, by 1971, Van Luven was publicly feuding with some members of the media and Superintendent of Brokers Bill Irwin.

The Palace Coup of 1976 is often mistakenly called the first in the history of the exchange. Neophyte brokers today are told it was the first time the incumbent board's recommended slate for the next year's election was ever contested.* They are told the coup alone was responsible for guiding the VSE out of the drunken melee of the 1960s and into its modern era. Brokers, however, have a poor sense of history. That coup, though pivotal, was actually a reaction to the real first Palace Coup, which took place in 1971. That was the year when the national brokerage houses, and those that aspired to be like them, joined forces to take over and do things the right way—the Toronto way.

The first Palace Coup in 1971 was more an evolution than a revolution. Aside from the internal disarray, the character of the VSE had been changing for years. Many of the high-volume traders, like McGraw's Continental Securities, had lost a great deal of their jitney business when the national firms bought VSE seats and no longer needed middlemen like McGraw to do their trading. And, as the emphasis shifted to retail sales, the physical act of trading itself became progressively less important. Just a decade before, the principals of the most influential VSE firms had often done their own trading, but by 1969 the only proprietor who spent any time on the floor was John McGraw. As the national houses moved in, traders became mere employees. (Once the centre of VSE power, the position of traders has

---

*In fact, the slate of governors for VSE elections had frequently been contested in the early years. But once John McGraw became president in 1938, the board's recommended slate was usually unchallenged.

been emasculated to the point where, now, the board of governors are planning on replacing them with computers.)

Mike Ryan, who was elected to the VSE board in 1970 at the age of forty, is seen by most as the ringleader of the group who instigated the 1971 coup that quietly replaced McGraw's cohorts with like-minded national and local brokers. Ryan graduated with a B.A. in commerce from the University of British Columbia in 1953. He was well connected in Vancouver, being a lifelong friend of Art Phillips, the popular two-term mayor who also headed his own investment firm, Phillips, Hagar & North Ltd. From 1961 to 1964 Ryan was a partner in the securities firm of Stevenson and Ryan Ltd., and in October 1964 he struck out on his own with Ryan Investments Ltd. One of Ryan's favourite stories concerns the $131 he spent to buy three shares of Bell Telephone in grade eleven, and how he later made a nice profit by switching the investment to Brazilian Traction, Light and Power Company Ltd. (which became Brascan in 1969). The story illustrates why Ryan would become the lightning rod for the animosity that led to the second Palace Coup in 1976: he was biased towards blue-chip stocks and established markets. Although he defended the VSE at every turn, he was among the faction who believed that the exchange had run amok during the late 1960s and that if it was to progress away from the turbulence of periodic mining booms it had to emulate Toronto.

Ryan is an intelligent, personable and attractive man who was an effective spokesman. When he was elected chairman of the VSE in 1973, he was one of the most communicative ever to hold the position. He was quoted more often inside a month than many of his predecessors had been during their entire year in office, but he made the mistake of speaking publicly about the exchange's weaknesses.

In 1973, while addressing a group of Vancouver executives, Ryan admitted that the stock exchange's image was of a self-protecting institution fighting against "them"—the public and the government. "When the press has criticized us editorially, we have usually deserved it," he said. Ryan then committed the ultimate heresy by saying that some of the governors forgot that they were there to protect the public's interest as well as the interests of VSE members.

After the 1971 coup, Ryan talked of building up the "investment grade" listings on the exchange and spoke hopefully of the day when a national stock exchange would be formed. Unspoken was the fact that Toronto would be the headquarters and Vancouver a subsidiary.

Ryan's pro-Toronto comments were guaranteed to stick in a westerner's craw, but they were not the only thing that goaded conspirators into instigating a second coup to toss out Ryan and his group.

The VSE should have been building on the bull market of 1965 to
1970. Instead, it was directionless and unprofitable. Between 1971
and 1976, the exchange ran through four presidents: Van Luven,
Dohm, White and Scott. One of the first acts the national houses did
on taking over in 1971 was to fire Jack Van Luven. The rift between
Van Luven and the board had been growing for years, but as well, the
VSE staff was close to mutiny. Two exchange personnel, administrative assistant Michael Petch and lawyer Angus Ree (later a provincial
MLA), had previously gone over Van Luven's head to tell the board
that there was a communication breakdown between Van Luven and
the staff, and chaos in the organization itself. "It finally got to the
point where we were so dissatisfied that other than walking out there
really wasn't anything we could do," Petch told the Vancouver *Sun*.
Van Luven fired the ringleaders, and Petch's public statements gave
the new board yet another reason to get rid of Van Luven. Being fired
was a bitter moment for Van Luven, who had come to view the VSE as
his own domain and to see himself as fireproof. The memory of his dis-
missal is so painful that his widow still will not tolerate mention of his
career at the exchange.

The man hired in December 1971 to replace Van Luven was a high-
profile Vancouver lawyer and judge, Thomas A. Dohm. Dohm's handling of hearings into the city's 1971 Gastown riot and allegations of
police overreaction had earned him great community respect for dealing with "a ticklish situation impartially and concisely." He was a
popular choice and even the Vancouver *Sun*'s often critical business
writer, Bill Fletcher, cheered the appointment. A careful reading of
Fletcher's comments gives an indication of how badly things had
deteriorated at the VSE:

> There couldn't have been a happier bunch of people in town that [sic]
> the Vancouver Stock Exchange members who gathered in the Hotel
> Vancouver Thursday night for their annual dinner and to meet their
> new president Mr. Justice Thomas Dohm. Directors fairly bubbled with
> enthusiasm over the "new image" they foresee for the exchange starting
> next Tuesday. I hope they do get the new image they envisage. But
> they must take some share of the blame for the "old image"; they were
> around while it was being fostered so it cannot all be laid at the door of

the former president John Van Luven. "Things won't be so free-
wheeling," said one broker. "You won't see promoters walking all over
everybody. It's a whole new lease on life for the exchange." Suppose
Tom Dohm does crack down on the wheeling and dealing that took
place in the past and earned the exchange the sobriquet in some
quarters of a "penny punch board". When the members go along with
his decisions it will mean that they have recognized their past errors
and are now about to make amends.

The selection of Dohm was one of the last universally popular
moves made by Ryan and the new leadership. Dohm worked hard to
mend bridges, making new contacts with the regulatory authorities,
the Montreal and Toronto exchanges and the media. He sent a clear
message to listed companies that the VSE's filing and other paperwork
requirements were serious business by delisting ninety-two stocks—
only twenty had been delisted in 1971. The delistings were because
the companies had failed to file financial statements, had a substantial
deficit in working capital, had become dormant or owed money to the
VSE. The measures had some effect in smartening up the paperflow
but barely dented the real problem: promoters and brokers who were
flouting regulations. Some VSE members were using broker-dealers to
run boiler-room operations for them and were, in effect, actually
promoting companies. It wasn't uncommon for brokers to take positions on the boards of listed companies,* using promoters to massage
the market so they could sell off their founder's shares, purchased at 10
cents, for an enormous profit. The conflict of interest made a joke of
the VSE's oft-repeated description of itself as "a free marketplace for
the trading of shares."

Dohm was well intentioned but distressed his employers by speaking
out against practices that were the heart and soul of speculative trading. Ryan and his supporters wanted reform, but they weren't about to
go bankrupt for the cause. Once, during his tenure, Dohm, provoked
by a report that accused short sellers of undermining even the
worthiest VSE stocks like Afton, wondered publicly why short selling
was permitted at all. The VSE members were horrified. Short selling
could be fabulously profitable, and they saw no reason why, if you

*Today regulations prohibit brokers from taking positions in listed companies, though the princi-
pals of brokerage firms can still be on as many boards as they wish.

could bet on a stock rising, you shouldn't also be allowed to bet on it falling out of bed.

Dohm was gone within just ten months of assuming the job. The official explanation was that he resigned over a disagreement with the board of governors over his acceptance of a directorship with the Bank of B.C.

The vse found another high-profile head in Cyril White, a highly intelligent but harshly abrasive and arrogant man who had been head of the B.C. Workmen's Compensation Board for many years. He took over on February 1, 1973, little more than a year after Dohm's much-heralded arrival. White hired key staff from the compensation board, thus alienating the already dispirited exchange employees, and managed, through his manner, to re-establish the divisions among the vse, the press and the regulatory authorities. "About the only good thing you could say about Cyril was that he wasn't a crook," says George Cross,* publisher of *The George Cross Newsletter*. "He specialized in not working and spending vast amounts of money. The vse had always prided itself on having a surplus† to tide itself over the bad times. White got rid of that during a moderately good market." White wasn't knowledgeable about the securities industry, and he saw no difference between the exchange and any other corporation when it came to whipping it into shape. He cared little about the idiosyncrasies of the penny stock industry, which bear no relationship to any other organization on the face of the earth.

White wasn't any more successful at straightening out the exchange than Van Luven or Dohm. They were all attacking the symptoms rather than the cause. Promoters, who had settled on the exchange

*George Cross is one of the great characters around the vse. His father, a cofounder of the *Financial News* in 1929, started the newsletter in 1948. It has been an authoritative source of information ever since. George's first personal experience with the vse was in 1949 or '50. "I bellied up to the bar at Richardsons [Securities] and put my $100 down. The broker told me to fuck off kid, it's mine now. Three trades later it was." At the time Cross was making $20 a month from his paper route. He hit his first bonanza while at university. "Grand Duke Mines was nearing the end of the season and was selling at $9. I sold it short and bought Pyramid short, using the credit gained by selling Grand Duke short. It was called pyramiding short and was legal then. I made a fortune that summer, five years' wages." Cross was making $200 a month at the time. "I thought I was unbeatable, and for the next year I tried to destroy myself with drink."
†The surplus was accumulated largely from trading during 1972, which exceeded 900 million shares, an exchange record. One of the biggest stocks of the year was Afton. The following year was the fourth busiest ever at 592 million shares, but the dollar value was well below the $1.1 billion set in 1969.

like maggots on a corpse, had the upper hand, and they didn't have the slightest compunction about using their advantages. The promoters were better financed, at least as well organized, in many cases smarter, and in all cases more richly rewarded than the men who were supposed to control them. Van Luven, Dohm and White learned that the promoters, with their hands firmly clasped around the VSE's tender parts, could turn any regulation on its ear and destroy its original intent.

In 1973, for instance, in an effort to weed out marginal companies and to encourage brokers to underwrite larger deals, the VSE increased the minimum underwriting price of a stock from 10 to 15 cents per share. Rather than forming new companies with real value, promoters immediately subverted the intent by using a classic stock gambit. They embarked upon an orgy of reverse stock splits, or consolidations. One share was exchanged for two, three, sometimes even fifteen shares, neatly multiplying the price overnight, yet complying with the rules. There was an added bonus to promoters in this type of manoeuvre, for it invariably gave them greater control of the company, by isolating many small blocks of stock.

Valnicla, a marginal mining company, underwent two consolidations in thirty-four months between 1970 and 1973. The net result was that stockholders who had owned 1,000 shares suddenly found that their holdings had shrunk to 67. (Another company, Gem Explorations, was rolled back one-share-for-four in 1968, and the promoter, obviously someone with a sense of irony, changed the company's name to Consolidated Gem Explorations. Then, in 1973, Gem was rolled back again, one-for-five, and the name changed to Brendon Resources. A 1,000-share board lot of Gem was then equal to 50 of Brendon.) Selling such odd lots was almost impossible, so many people just shelved the stock and forgot it. With so much stock voluntarily out of action, it was far easier and less expensive for the promoters to get and maintain control. Exchange officials were aghast at the result of their rule change and announced that they were preparing new rules to counter the rollbacks. The promoters spread the word that if the VSE disallowed rollbacks, they would simply walk away from their shells, and the stockholders, who were unhappy with 67 shares, would, in effect, have none. The VSE was left with no choice but to endorse the reverse splits. "The consolidations give the investor another kick at the cat," rationalized Mike Ryan.

The history of the VSE follows a pattern of boom, bust, scandal and cleanup. There were no major scandals in the early 1970s to encourage a cleanup, but there was a growing wave of public discontent with the conduct of the securities industry generally and the VSE in particular. Broker-dealers, the odd fellows in the modern exchange-oriented securities world, came under increasing fire from everyone. Their boiler rooms and covert relationships with VSE members prompted many suggestions that they should be forced to join the exchange or close down. (Broker-dealers were forced out in 1973, and a handful of them did eventually join the exchange; many others became promoters.) Superintendent of Brokers Bill Irwin was badly outmanned and, being in Victoria, removed from the action. Even in the brokerage community itself there was a feeling that corruption had become endemic to the exchange.

Bob Scott, who later became president of the VSE, had first-hand knowledge to confirm the vague feelings of unease. In 1973, when he was vice-president of compliance at the exchange, he was involved in negotiations over a stock that had been suspended. "The lawyer [of the listed company] asked me if I would come downtown and discuss this. I walked into his office and sat down in the chair and looked down, and there was this hundred-dollar bill lying on the floor. It would have been the easiest thing in the world for me to drop a handkerchief or something and bend down and pick it up. He said it must have been a previous client who dropped it out of his wallet. Whether that was the case or whether it was to see if I was on the take, I don't know." Scott never had the chance to find out since he gave the money back. But during his time at the VSE he heard plenty of rumours of those who didn't give the money back. "I used to hear stories all the time about [another vice-president] being pieced off," he says. Scott eventually got tangible evidence of the corruption when Chris Caulton, vice-president in charge of listings in the early 1970s, was charged in 1980 with ninety-four counts of bribe taking and conspiracy during the period from 1970 to 1976. A web of promoters, including Dennis Johnstone, who wasn't charged and convicted until 1986, had been using his services to ensure that their listings were approved quickly with a minimum of scrutiny. Caulton fled Canada for England in 1977, shortly after the RCMP investigation began, so he has never been tried on the charges.

The VSE probably could have weathered the legion of vilifying headlines in the early 1970, but for the election of the provincial New Democratic Party. The one good thing about that event, as far as the exchange was concerned, was that the NDP gave the VSE members something tangible to take the blame for their problems. The stock market was extremely suspicious of the socialist NDP horde that threatened to take over the provincial telephone system, to tax business punitively and to slap a mineral royalty tax on the mining industry. In the two months following the NDP's assumption of office, there was a 12.84 per cent drop in the market value of the common shares of British Columbia's fifty largest listed companies. In comparison, during that period, the TSE's industrial index and the Dow Jones were only marginally lower, 3.89 and 3 per cent respectively.

The worst news of all was the 1973 publication of an RCMP report on commercial crime in the province of British Columbia. The report covered all aspects of commercial crime, including loan sharking, tax fraud, bankruptcy fraud, credit card fraud, and trafficking in stolen and counterfeit securities. It also focussed on stock fraud "because it appears to be a major problem in British Columbia."

> Several stock frauds are committed in this province every year. Promoters, salesmen, known criminals and a myriad of others are continually conspiring to defraud investors in the market. The law enforcement agencies have estimated that approximately 20 to 30 per cent of the mines and local, junior industrial stocks listed on the Vancouver Stock Exchange are manipulated. Many of them have been created solely for this purpose. In other words, the directors and promoters of such companies are not interested in developing a viable business or mine, merely in using it as a vehicle for defrauding the public. The authorities are aware of the key individuals suspected of perpetrating many of the stock frauds. The suspects are a few promoters and a number of dubious individuals with long criminal records who may be financing the criminal ventures. . . . The key individuals do not act alone, however; there is usually a group co-ordinated by a promoter. Some promoters have a number of salesmen in Vancouver, eastern Canada and the United States who buy and sell stock on instructions. Associates of organized crime syndicates from the East have attempted to engage in activity in the Vancouver market. In addition a number of known local criminals, including drug figures and gambling promoters, are, or have been, involved in the market. It has been estimated that there are about 25 to 50 people with criminal records involved in some way or another. The Securities Commission knows of people with long criminal records who associate with major criminally-oriented

promoters, but in the final analysis the true extent of criminal involvement in the market is unknown to anybody.

The report concluded with the disquieting statement that because of
lack of manpower, the RCMP and the local police were helpless to control the VSE.

The VSE board, led by Ryan, decried the report as scandal-monger-
ing without a shred of evidence to back it up. Nonetheless, investor
confidence dipped again. By the end of 1973 the VSE was $58,000 in
the red, the first time it had posted a deficit since 1931. Ironically, it
was also the first time in the VSE's history that the exchange had
released a financial statement. The board had voted to do so earlier in
the year in an attempt to counteract criticisms that the exchange operated like a private and secretive club. Had the governors known how
badly the year would end, they likely would have shelved that resolu-
tion. The VSE lost money again the next year, and in September 1975
Cyril White shocked everyone by announcing that the exchange
might have to close for lack of business.

The four-year regime of the 1971 Palace Coup clique was dogged by
bad luck, poor timing and blundering. Not surprisingly, the leadership
became increasingly unpopular. Discontent was erupting from every
pore, and talk about the need for radical changes soured the working
life of the exchange from the trading floor to the president's office.
Nothing could happen, however, without a leader, and the exchange
had been without one since John McGraw. Ryan had proven he had
plenty of charisma and organizing ability, but he didn't have the
toughness in the clinches to keep the obstreperous VSE in line. As
well, Ryan's vision of the future ran counter to the trend of events.
There were plenty of conspirators in the wings, but no one stepped
forward. It took a small, seemingly insignificant incident to galvanize
them into action.

Warring Clarke, president of McDermid Miller, had been on the
VSE board for years and in 1974–75 had served as honorary secre-
tary/treasurer. In 1975 a lawsuit was pending against Clarke's company, and he and his partners felt his presence on the board might be
an embarrassment to the industry. He agreed to serve out his term and
re-evaluate his position at election time. But a few months before the
1976 elections, he learned that the board, without consulting him,
had left his name off the slate. This event, supposedly an example of
the heavy-handedness of the incumbent board, became the rallying

cry for the group that sparked the second Palace Coup.

Mike Ryan's board might have dropped Clarke in any case because they were determined to get more representatives of the Toronto viewpoint on the board and because they certainly didn't want Clarke, who was known to be be unhappy with their growing presence, to become chairman in 1978. "Even today there is a pecking order," says Brian Graves, now president of Brink, Hudson & Lefever Ltd. and then one of the "establishment candidates" who was acceptable to the coup group. "You start out as honorary secretary/treasurer and you go to vice-chairman and then chairman. Warring Clarke was the number three guy on the totem pole. He was one of the people who the establishment felt should step aside and let one of the national people on." It was a minor slight to Clarke, but the incident was used to win over the brokerage community to the dissident camp.

The 1976 Palace Coup was one of those pivotal events that, years later, become romanticized by revisionism and muddied by the fact that everyone remembers being part of it, whether they were or not. The generals were Peter Brown, president of Canarim Investment Corporation, and Ian Falconer, vice-president of Midland Doherty. The foot soldiers were Clarke, Dick Thompson of Pemberton Securities and Bob Atkinson of Loewen, Ondaatje, McCutcheon & Company Ltd. Their action ranks as one of the greatest business coups ever, turning out to be worth over $125 million in profit over the next ten years to Brown and his Canarim partners alone.

These days, when the story of the 1976 Palace Coup is told, the prominent role is held by Peter Brown. In fact, Ian Falconer was the brains behind the whole thing. Falconer is a slender, fast-talking, gregarious man. He is widely respected, both for his senior position with a major national brokerage house and his willingness to use his knees and elbows when the occasion necessitates. Falconer had been privately bitching about the board for years, even though he'd been a member of it as recently as 1973–74. He'd been approached before about taking action, but the timing was never quite right. When Clarke complained to him about the board's actions, he knew he had the perfect issue.

Falconer, a subtle man who believes in spreading his risks, suggested that Clarke talk to Peter Brown, whose personal contempt for Mike Ryan was well known. "[Ryan] gathered around him a coterie of guys who really believed that the guys who were doing the volume were either dishonest or crooked. They became, as a group, very heavy-handed with the local members. Guys like myself," Brown says. Brown seized on the idea of the coup with the fervour of one who sees the main chance and persuaded the supposedly reluctant Falconer to enlist in the fledgling conspiracy.

"Finally, I said, I like Warring," remembers Falconer. "I'm mad as hell that they did that to him. I'll do it under one condition; that we only put up four people to run on our slate. We don't want it to appear to the industry that we're trying to control the VSE. If we get elected, the present people on the board will certainly get the message that, look, the members out there want change. We don't have to have a revolution."

Other than his own presence on the board, Brown's only demand was the exclusion of rival Gus MacPhail. "When we got on the board, Peter was absolutely adamant that MacPhail not be allowed on the board," says Falconer. "What was I going to do? I said I don't give a damn. I'm not going to fight someone else's fight."

Falconer's strategy was superb. By not challenging the senior board positions, the dissidents reassured nervous seat holders that they weren't going to turn the exchange upside-down. At the same time, Falconer hedged his bets; he knew that Brown would attract most of the animosity and criticism if the coup didn't work. "You've got to remember that Peter had absolutely no credibility," Falconer says. "Not an ounce, none at all. I had a hell of a job running around talking to those dealers about him. . . . Peter had to keep himself pretty invisible in those days, or otherwise we would probably have lost the election."

Falconer and Brown worked hard making phone calls, visiting brokers and amassing proxies. Brown devoted himself utterly to the cause. "For the weeks that preceded that VSE annual meeting, Peter did nothing else but solicit proxies," says Brown's partner, Brian Harwood. By the night of the annual general meeting they had a clear majority of the votes. The atmosphere was formal and tense as the board presented their twelve-man slate and the conspirators presented their four alternatives: Clarke for secretary/treasurer, with Brown, Falconer and Atkinson for the board at large. Out of the 56 potential votes, Falconer got 44, Warring Clarke around 40 and Brown got 35. (The ballot was supposed to be confidential, but after the vote, two VSE employees, eager to ingratiate themselves with the dissidents, trotted over to give them the final tally.) Two of the existing board, realizing which way the wind was blowing, voted for the opposing slate. No one expected such a decisive victory, and there was considerable fear of what new directions the vse would be taken in. "The claim was they'd given over the keys of the bank to the burglars," snorts Brown.

The last thing that Brown and the other brokers wanted was more rules or even better ones. "People say it [the vse] is unregulated," he said ten years after the coup. "But it is because of the volatility of the trading and that's because of the types of issues you have. The fact is that I think it has got to the point where it's overregulated. If you've got 2 per cent breaking the rules, new rules won't stop them." What Brown and the others wanted was a president who would balance the vse's books and create a better public image for the exchange. In essence, they were looking for another front; one who would look good to the public and who would keep the exchange running efficiency and quietly. They knew that the exchange couldn't afford to hire another public figure who knew nothing about the stock market. When they chose a regulator for the job, the brokerage community was astonished. Robert Scott, former vse vice-president of compliance, former investigator for the superintendent of brokers and, at that time, head of the Alberta Securities Commission, was a man so squeaky clean and so appropriate that critics of "the burglars" were immediately silenced. Scott had ideas of his own about what the job was all about. "Their perception was that the vse had to get back in the black," recalls Scott. "I remember a couple of them [board members] would ask me out to lunch and they would bend my ear about the financial problems for an hour or so and ruin my digestion. But I saw my job was to improve the relationship with the police, the commercial crime people, with Bill Irwin's office, with the public, with the media, and tighten things up."

Bob Scott is a short, almost delicate-looking man who has retained a boyishness well into his fifties, yet he is one of the toughest men to ever work any side of the vse. Scott combined his toughness and stubbornness with an elemental and visceral understanding of the functioning of speculative markets. It was the kind of understanding shared by John McGraw and Peter Brown. Scott took a radically different approach to the job than his predecessors. Instead of issuing new rules and regulations, he sent promoters and brokers an unmistakable message with his handling of the crash of Avalanche Industries in 1976. Avalanche was a typical vse stock. It had a brief soaring ascent until it was magically transformed from a bird into a bag of cement, when the promoters stopped supporting the market. Scott, in defiance of all modern vse tradition, suspended the stock before it hit bottom. The year before, Mike Ryan had justified the exchange's more typical move of delisting only after a crash by saying: "It's a tough area. We tend to halt trading far more on the way down, yet there was probably an indication of something wrong on the way up. Can you imagine the outcry of some person who has held a dog for years, and we halt it on the way up?"

Scott's action wasn't unprecedented. Early trading halts were not uncommon before the Second World War, though the reasons were often curious. Sometimes it was because the directors had abandoned the company or changed its name without informing the vse. One coal-mining company in 1933 decided gold was more to their liking, so they simply issued more shares and tacked the word gold onto the company name. The vse halted the stock and politely requested some clarification. In 1937 another listed company changed its name and began trading on the board; the same company was trading under two different names for several weeks before anyone caught on. But the classic vse halt is the four-day cease trade of Boulder Mountain Minerals in 1919 when it was suspended shortly after declaring both revenue and profit for the year. The declaration was such a rarity that the exchange was immediately suspicious.

Suspending a stock before it crashes, or preferably on the way up, is an extremely effective way to control market manipulation. Another is to increase the margin on a stock to 100 per cent. If a suspicious stock is suspended early, the regulatory authorities are in a strong position because, more than likely, the promoter hasn't taken his trading profits out and there is still some money left in the company treasury. If the company is legitimate, with real trading, experience has shown that a brief halt doesn't harm subsequent trading. But if the vse waits, as is still the common practice, to suspend and investigate a stock after it has crashed or on the way down, it has very little, if any, leverage. The promoter and insiders have their profits, and the treasury is usually empty.

Scott discovered that less than half of the primary distribution in Avalanche had actually been sold to the public. The promoter, Ronald Mcdonald (no relation to the hamburgers), couldn't unload the rest. Mcdonald took the remaining stock, put it in several nominee accounts that he controlled at Davidson and Company, bought the stock himself and then reimbursed himself from the company treasury. The net result was that the public was left with the impression that the initial distribution had been snapped up, which generated further buying. "Strictly speaking, it's probably theft from Avalanche," says Scott. "Plus it was a false statement of material facts. It wasn't an underwriting at all. He induced people to buy stock by telling them that they would get a portion of his escrowed shares. He had all this stuff in writing, and we had copies of all these documents."

Scott put the brokers and promoters on notice with his handling of Avalanche. In turn, the brokers, promoters and shareholders tried to intimidate Scott. He was besieged the minute he suspended Avalanche. And not all the pressure came from the VSE's slimy underbelly. A powerful B.C. mayor who later became an influential provincial cabinet minister was part of the lobby group harassing Scott. "I was working in my office one day and I was told a Mr. X was there to see me. He didn't have an appointment and I was busy, so I said I would see him when I can. So he waited about half an hour and he became very irate and demanded to see me because he was the mayor of Y. Well, that pisses me off. I said that's very good, where's Y?" When Avalanche appealed Scott's decision, he rolled up his sleeves and personally defended the VSE in court. He did it because "the exchange was broke" and as another message to investors, promoters and brokers that he wasn't just a figurehead.

Scott knew that he couldn't directly control each and every promoter, so his tactic was to focus on a few and let the implicit warning get out along the highly efficient market grapevine. Murray Pezim was one of those with a permanent place under Scott's microscope. Scott had a gut feeling that there was something not entirely kosher about one of Pezim's companies, Cutlass Exploration, which was trading furiously and moving up to the $5 range. "I phoned Murray one day and I said, 'Where's all the buying coming from?' " remembers Scott. "He said, 'You don't have to worry, Bob, it's all good solid buying.' I said, 'That's fine Murray, but where's it coming from?' He said, 'Toronto, New York, Montreal, all good solid buying, no problems at all. It's all good solid trading.' " Scott checked around and, as he suspected, Murray was generating the majority of the trading himself. Rather than halt the stock, he ordered a 100 per cent margin, meaning that everyone, Pezim included, would have to pay cash for Cutlass or put up stock of equal value as security. If the buying was broadly based, as Pezim claimed, the order would cause only minor inconvenience as people scrambled to make good the margin. But if, as

Scott believed, Pezim's buying in Cutlass was an elaborate web with the purchase of one block of margined shares providing the security for another, selling out his Avalanche account would precipitate a hasty collapse of the company's artificially inflated price. (If Pezim couldn't meet the margin, the brokerage would have been forced to sell Pezim's shares until the account balanced.)

Scott's order went out at 4:00 P.M. That evening he was working in the deserted executive offices when he heard a mighty crash as the gate dividing the reception area from his office was kicked open. "Does anybody in here know what the fuck they're doing?" bellowed Gus MacPhail in the booming voice that he used to dominate the trading floor. MacPhail was furious at Scott's edict because Pezim was his best customer—a favourite Howe Street observation is that Mac-Phail's Rolls was paid for by Murray Pezim—and MacPhail would have to take the loss if Pezim couldn't come up with the cash. "Gus had got into the sauce a little bit and when he found out about this 100 per cent margin he lost his cool," Scott chuckles, "so we got into a bit of a slanging match. He was quite irate."

Bob Scott's determination to involve himself in every aspect of the exchange eventually cost him his job and his health. Not only was he the VSE's public relations spokesman and lawyer for many years but he also sat on every conceivable committee, frequently met personally with brokers and promoters who had grievances, and visited the floor two or three times a week to find out if "a stock should be running and whether there was a promotion going on." He even began vetting company announcements. "We would test the credibility factor," he says. "If they said we've found six ounces per ton, we'd say, 'Over what distance?' If it was half an inch, we'd make them say that." Few could have enveloped an organization as Scott did, and in the end it broke him. By 1981 Scott had lost control. His hands-on approach, personal integrity and energy brought a new credibility and profitability to the VSE. But he was never an administrator ("I told them that when they hired me") and when the exchange ballooned again, dwarfing even the Pyramid days, Scott's once-effective leadership was overwhelmed. In 1976 there were 65 VSE employees. By the time he left in 1981, there were 225. Daily trading had grown from an average of 1.5 million shares at 65 cents in 1976 to 9 million shares with an average value of nearly $2 in 1981.

The man who was called "The Sheriff of the Wildest Exchange in the West" was close to a nervous breakdown in 1981. "I couldn't stay

awake more than half a day. I was asked to resign, and I resigned."
While many in the stock market community criticized Scott for being
pigheaded, narrow-minded and uncompromising, there was probably
no one else who could have coaxed, bullied and cajoled the VSE
through the toughest few years of its existence.

The Palace Coups of 1971 and 1976 were necessary steps in the
evolution of the VSE into the money machine that it has become. The
eastern-dominated 1971 coup swept out John McGraw's old order.
That four-year reign in turn became the reason for the 1976 coup,
which laid the foundation for the VSE's modern era. But most importantly, the 1976 coup heralded the emergence of the long-awaited
new strong man, Peter Brown.

CHAPTER 8

Peter Brown, the Successor: From Wastrel to Workaholic

"Look back to your own school days. Remember the schoolyard bully. Very insecure. Spends his time beating up and belittling others. Brown's just like that. Most of his actions are rooted in contempt for the other guy." A BROWN FAMILY FRIEND trying to describe what motivates Peter Brown.

Peter Brown is betrayed by his eyes. Although pouched and reddened by years of hard living, they demand attention like a slap in the face. When you look into them, the camouflage of urbanity—the relaxed soft voice, the monogrammed silk shirt, the signet ring, the even, milky suntan, the manicured fingernails—drop away. The eyes are glacial, with a deep, very deep, molten core. In the space of an instant, they have sized you up, calculated your net worth, evaluated your political leanings and gauged your nuisance potential.

They are the eyes of a man who has driven himself first as a wastrel and then as the fastest, smartest and toughest in the sea of sharks that surrounds the Vancouver Stock Exchange. In fourteen years he has transformed an insolvent bucket shop, now called Canarim Invest-

ment Corporation Ltd.,* into the most profitable brokerage firm in
the country. Starting from nothing, he has amassed a net worth of at
least $55 million. His income from commissions on retail sales alone is
as much as $180,000 a month, even in bad times. Along the way,
Brown has become one of the most powerful and influential non-
elected people in the province; he's also one of the most envied and
hated. Such is Peter Brown's power that few will allow their names to
be attached to any criticism of him.

Peter Brown doesn't own the VSE—it just seems as if he does. What
he does own is the dominant brokerage house on the exchange, Canarim. He exercises his control of the exchange through the sheer force
of his will, his proxies on the board, his singular political connections
with the ruling B.C. Social Credit party and because of the simple fact
that he is willing to work with a ferocity others find hard to compre-
hend. "Work is a habit and lack of work is a habit," states Brown
bluntly. "So I got onto the work habit and I couldn't get off. I work all
the time, seven days a week, twenty hours a day. I work like a dog."
Panting after Brown are a bevy of aspirants to his lifestyle, his wealth
and his influence. They are his 125, mostly young and mostly male,
salesmen. "The trouble with working for Peter Brown is that they are
all crazy about him and they are all trying keep up," laments the wife
of a Canarim broker who leaves home at 5:30 A.M. and rarely comes
back before 6 P.M., even though the trading floor closes at 1:30.
"They feel like they have to work the same hours or else they're out of
favour. They hang around him like hungry puppies, hoping for tidbits
like a piece of the next deal or a referral to a big client."

Brown was born in 1941 with a silver spoon in his mouth, but he
chewed it up and spat it out long before it could do him much good.
He was born into a well-off, well-connected West Coast establishment
family. His grandfather and father were provincial managers of Crown
Life Insurance Company, and were influential, back-room, Liberal
money men. Young Peter trod the private school road and ran with an
upper-class crowd, and he still retains the indelible private school
stamp. It's easy to imagine him scampering around in matching shorts,
tam, tie and blazer. If Brown had been born in Toronto it would have
been Upper Canada College, but in Vancouver it was St. George's

*Hemsworth Turton & Company became Canarim in 1973. Intercan Holdings Ltd., created in
1981, now owns 100 per cent of Canarim. Intercan is owned by Peter Brown (40 per cent), Ted
Turton (40 per cent), Brian Harwood (15 per cent) and Channing Buckland (5 per cent).

and Shawnigan Lake, and today he retains all the learned polish and niceties that such education buys. He also demonstrates genuine consideration for employees and friends, a characteristic that has earned him enduring loyalty inside and outside Canarim. On the other hand there is a deep streak of rudeness toward and contempt for lesser beings that shows up when he feels someone isn't worth his time.

Friends and acquaintances remember the school-age Peter Brown as moving a little faster and always going a little bit farther than everyone else. He was a superb rugby player and a devastating tackler. "He never got involved in anything that he wasn't the fastest, the toughest, the best. He was a very good card player. He was a great bluffer; it's in his eyes," says Robin Lecky, former publisher of the *Vancouver Courier* and a friend since private school days. "He always had a car around. He liked to drive fast. There was never a party that Peter ever missed or wasn't the first to arrive or the last to leave."

Brown graduated from St. George's with straight As and enrolled in the University of British Columbia (UBC) at the age of fifteen. Despite his high marks, his intelligence was unfocussed; his energy, however, was not. As a member of the exclusive Zeta Beta Tau, the wildest and most social of UBC fraternities, Brown easily became its hardest-drinking and hardest-partying member. Many of his escapades are part of UBC fraternity legend. Then as now, Brown provoked as much dislike as admiration, and one member of another fraternity who rubbed shoulders with him remembers Brown as "an arrogant young man who came from too much money and was just coasting through life."

Brown left university without a degree in 1963, having failed the frosh term three times in five years. "I was a fuck-up as a student," he says in a now rare admission about his early life. "I spent five years at university and did three. Most of the time, in those days, I wanted to be good at playing around." He was hired by Greenshields Inc., which sent him to Montreal and later Toronto to be trained as a registered representative. For three years, he worked under Brad Firstbrook in a three-man corporate finance department. "Firstbrook really turned my life around," Brown is fond of saying. "He changed me from a wastrel to a workaholic."

In 1968 Brown moved back to Vancouver but only stayed with Greenshields a year. Then he was hired as sales manager of Hemsworth, Turton and Company. His new employer was distinguished only by its unsavoury past. The firm had been incorporated in 1950 as Pacific Securities Ltd. and was later bought by stock

promoter Harold Hemsworth, who renamed it H. H. Hemsworth &
Company. When Murray Pezim got interested in Vancouver, he
bought his way into the VSE by purchasing a 49 per cent piece of
Hemsworth in 1966 for "a couple of hundred thousand." Pezim
brought little but hard times to the firm, which nearly went under
supporting Bata Resources, a company he was promoting. Pezim,
according to his own account, was being "shorted to death," and
Hemsworth was eating up its capital trying to make good his margin.
By the time Ted Turton came along in 1967, Hemsworth was scrambling for any no account deals it could get. It was, in Brown's words,
little more than "a bucket shop."

Turton bought Murray Pezim's share of the decimated Hemsworth
for $23,000. "It was one thing to buy it," he remembers, "it was
another thing to put the capital in. It was very easy to buy. They
desperately needed the money." The first thing Turton did was sign a
bank loan for $100,000 just to keep the company, renamed Hems-
worth Turton, afloat. His injection of cash did keep it going, but
Turton wasn't the man to stem the chaos within the company itself.
"I'm a salesman, not an administrator," he admits.

The bull market of 1968 and 1969 was a wild period for the VSE, but
nowhere did things get as extreme as at Hemsworth Turton, which
was more a nonstop melee than a stock brokerage firm. Forty or fifty
clients would pack into the small office space, cheering or hissing as
quotes were marked up on the board. Salesmen were besieged by
phone calls and shouted orders. Sometimes clients couldn't get close
to a broker's desk so they simply wadded up their money and threw it
over the crowd. Nobody was in charge, and Bill Irwin, then superintendent of brokers, was worried about the solvency of the company.
"Each salesman seemed to be running his own deal. Rather than the
firm sitting over the salesmen, saying, 'Yes, this is a good deal, your
client should be in it,' or 'No, it's not a good deal, don't put your
clients in it.' "

Today, Brown likes to tell the Hemsworth Turton story as if he had
immediately begun to turn the company around. In fact, he fit into
the freewheeling atmosphere a lot better than he likes to admit.

For most western securities firms, the speculative market has been
an endless cycle of riches and rags. When volume is high, profits are
high, and the money goes to life's indulgences. John McGraw often
criticized this behaviour, saying he could always tell when a firm was
on the upside of the cycle because three new cars appeared in the

driveway of every broker. When times were bad, companies like Hemsworth had little left to tide them over until things improved. The period between 1965 and 1969 was a time of unprecedented and almost unbroken prosperity for the vse, but not even the pinnacle of this cycle could entirely rescue Hemsworth Turton from its excesses in previous years.

Thanks to Pezim and an exceptionally loose idea about administration, the firm was teetering on the brink of collapse when the market soured in 1970. Brian Harwood, a banker by training, inclination and outlook, saved the company. When Brown offered him a job, Harwood was senior assistant manager at the Bank of Montreal's busy Tenth Avenue and Granville Street branch, one of the largest in the province. The branch handled the Brown family account, and Peter Brown also maintained his personal account there. Harwood had few illusions about Brown. He viewed him as "an orangutan, [a] wild man, . . . a roustabout, a man about town." But he also saw his potential. Harwood moved into Hemsworth Turton in 1970 to clean up the credit mess. That job was crucial, but even more important was the role he came to play as Brown's foil, his straight man, his counter-balance.

Brian Harwood is immaculately groomed and genuinely friendly. The openness of his manner only serves to emphasize his steel hide and the confidence of a man who is able to say no and make it stick. "Brian's the ghoul here," Brown says. "Every man should have a devil's advocate. It works really well. Brian was my banker, and he was such a tough little cunt that I hired him." It is a mark of Harwood's pivotal role that others in the industry use him as a benchmark. If a firm is doing poorly, it's because "They don't have a Brian Harwood."

Back in 1970, Harwood was appalled by what he found at Hemsworth. He took a fiscal machete to unpaid accounts, credit granted to clients with no ability to pay and little intention of doing so, and salesmen whose honesty was doubtful. He personally vetted all trades and purchases and eliminated margin accounts. His actions riled many salesmen, who saw their paper commissions fizzle overnight. Harwood's strong medicine took about a year to cure Hemsworth Turton's most obvious ailments. The firm was still shaky, but at least it was under control.

Reining in Peter Brown was another matter. Harwood's victory in the Great Backgammon Battle was the pivotal engagement in that war. During the dog years of 1970 and 1971, Hemsworth Turton more closely resembled a gambling den than a brokerage house. Dice clicked and chittered all day and sometimes far into the night as salesmen rolled and wagered feverishly over their backgammon boards. At the centre of it was Peter Brown, hollow-eyed, shirt open at the throat and sweat crowning his brow as he passed the dice time after time until there was no one left to oppose him. "It was one of those obsessive periods he had and backgammon became everything," recalls Harwood. "He was a very good player. Times when I thought should be devoted to business, they were all playing backgammon. But it was hard to control the salesmen when Peter was doing it himself."

Unable to dilute Brown's obsession, Harwood surreptitiously began confiscating any board he could get his hands on. When he accumulated a pile he quietly sold them all at a garage sale. On the most expensive boards, he stole some of the pieces or the dice so the set was incomplete. "Then I started in on Peter," says Harwood. "He would bet me that it wouldn't happen again, and I was cleaning up. I would catch him a day after the bet. I was getting all these excess $20s, $50s at a crack. He would say, 'It's worth the $50, here's the $50. I'm going to play.' Eventually we stopped it."

The metamorphosis of Peter Brown is a matter of considerable conjecture among his friends, associates and enemies. Some say the change happened during the 1976 Palace Coup; others believe it wasn't until the boom of 1978. Some claim he hasn't changed at all. And Brown himself, when asked about it today, either looks at you as if you were vermin or maintains that the real change happened back in Montreal in the 1960s. There's a bit of truth in all points of view, even Brown's. One thing is certain, personal animosity was a powerful goad in fashioning the new Peter Brown. In 1972, Hemsworth Turton proposed Brown's name to the vse board of governors as the firm's new president. Vetting such appointments is required under the rules but has always been a formality. This time was different, and the board turned down the proposal. Today Brown blames one person for the ignominious rejection: "Mike Ryan had tremendous influence in the exchange, and Mike turned it down, for no other reason than he thought I was a bad guy. But he did me a great favour. When the smoke cleared, I asked myself how could I have got myself into a position where I could allow a guy like that to interfere with my career in that way? It made me goal-oriented. I said, 'I must have an awful lack of credibility.' It made me think out the whole Hemsworth Turton—

Canarim thing. And I knew then that we had to upgrade considerably."

Another incident involving Mike Ryan in 1974 reinforced Brown's resolve. Canarim owned three seats by that time, and Brown wanted a fourth. The price of seats, which had hit $65,000 in 1969, had by then plummeted to $4,000. Brown bid $3,000 for one that had become available, ostensibly because no other bids were on the table and a vacant seat "didn't look good." The reaction of the board was startling. "I got hit so fast, it would make your head spin," Brown snorts. "These guys called an emergency board meeting and came to the conclusion that Peter Brown was trying to buy up the whole exchange." Part of Ryan's attempt to block Brown was probably because of his own chagrin at buying a seat at the peak. Letting Brown scoop up one for less than a tenth of the price would have been galling to say the least.

The VSE passed an amendment to the bylaws prohibiting any member from owning more than three seats. Brown took the matter to his lawyer and forced the board to back down until a shareholders meeting could be called. "Every time they turned around, they did something stupid. I told them in '73 that by '75 we would run and throw them all out, and they just laughed." At the time of his threat, he was twenty-seven years old. Brown's contempt for Ryan is still clearly palpable. He criticizes and belittles him at every opportunity. "Mike's diplomacy stunk, I hope you quote that." For his part, Ryan refuses to retaliate. When asked about Brown, he invariably responds with the same compliment: "Peter Brown knows more about the underwriting of speculative stocks than anyone else in Canada. He's two or three times as smart as anyone else in Canada on that, and always has been."

Brown waited until 1976 to get his revenge, spending the years in between grooming Canarim to dominate the VSE. From 1973 until 1976 everyone from miners to brokers was moaning about poor world mineral markets and the NDP government's tax on mineral royalties. Brown ignored the carpers and doubled the size of Canarim's Vancouver sales force, hiring top producers away from the other firms. At one point he began raiding Ian Falconer's staff at Midland Doherty. Falconer was furious and told Brown "to keep out of my goddamn way." Brown said he would and shortly after began raiding the salesmen again. He also opened new offices in Prince George, Whitehorse,

Winnipeg and Regina. "Upgrading is not an easy thing," observes Brown of his struggle. "It sounds easy, but if you're little Hemsworth Turton, good people don't want to work with you." Brown wasn't just after image, however. Under Harwood's prodding, he set about building and hanging on to Canarim's capital, meagre though it was initially, and put all the profits between 1972 and 1978 back into the firm. The philosophy of Brown and Harwood was to develop a large enough capital base so that when the big deals came along, Canarim could handle them itself, without having to bring in partners. And with a good capital base, a risky deal going bad or a downturn in the market wouldn't ruin the firm. They were years ahead of themselves. In the 1980s investment house mergers littered the financial pages as eastern firms chased after each other in their efforts to increase their capital. Brown foresaw that the little deals that once propped up many of the VSE firms would give way to much larger ones. He also suspected the competition from banks and foreign brokers wasn't far off.

Despite Brown's fledgling resolve to drive Canarim forward, he never knew one month whether he would still be in business the next. "His firm had very little capital," says Falconer, "maybe $100,000 or $200,000 which was really skinny-assed to work with, really nothing. I remember him [Brown] telling me that if the market didn't pick up, he didn't think he could carry on for many more months [and] he would finally have to close it down." It was only the sheer force of Brown's salesmanship that kept Canarim alive. "We joke about it now," Harwood says of those years, "but I would often go to Peter and I would say, 'Here are the numbers. We're going to lose some money this month. We aren't going to make it.' We had a very low overhead, but there just wasn't the business being generated, and Peter thrives best under those sort of circumstances. By the end of the month we always broke even or made a small profit. He would go out and drive in the business and get on the phone and talk to companies about underwritings. He never ever let up."

Today, selling is still Brown's greatest skill. He personally participates in at least 50 per cent of Canarim's underwritings, either by instigating them himself or because salesmen bring their deals to him. The latter isn't just for show or an attempt to ingratiate themselves, it's simply because they know that Brown can sell any deal. Early in 1986, for example, Canarim's much vaunted Multiple Opportunities Fund (an unusual mutual fund investing only in VSE juniors) was languishing, only halfway to its goal of $8 million in subscriptions.

Brown was preoccupied with his position as vice-chairman of Vancouver's Expo 86, and his salesmen were listless and uninspired. When Harwood told Brown that he thought the slow placement was damaging Canarim's prestige, Brown got on the phone and within a week raised $5 million. The turnaround was dramatic as his salesmen followed his lead, and shortly the fund was oversubscribed.

The coup of 1976 was only the beginning of change. Although Brown was only a junior board member, he took control of the new board almost immediately. His first and probably most critical move was to hire Bob Scott as the new VSE president. He did it because it was precisely the last thing the others would have expected. "When we hired a regulator, they were surprised," says Brown savouring the memory. Scott was a well-known stickler, sympathetic to and blessed with a rare understanding of the industry, but not a man anyone could push around. He created new regulations and saw to it that the old ones were enforced.

Once the events of the Palace Coup were completed, Brown went about showing the VSE how to make real money. Since its inception in 1907, the basis of the exchange's business had been the trading floor, the place where everything important was conducted and where key individuals spent all their time. Principals of firms stayed so close to it that when something important came up, miniboard meetings were held right on the floor. Underwriting was part of the business, but it was the gravy, not the meat. Brown recognized the diminishing importance of the trading floor. He believed the key to making serious profits was underwriting and retail sales. His philosophy was simple: churn out the issues like sausages and take a position, through founder's shares, options, etc. in each. The potential profit was far higher than could be gleaned from trading commissions and far more reliable.

A typical Canarim underwriting from that period would go as follows: Acme Gold comes to Canarim wanting an underwriting, either through a private placement or a public issue offered through the VSE. Acme Gold owns a piece of property that it wants to explore. The property was previously owned by one or more of the company's principals who traded it for a chunk of escrowed shares—shares they can't sell until some exploration work has been done. Canarim agrees to underwrite 500,000 shares at 50 cents a share in exchange for 100,000 shares at 10 cents. These are the so-called founder's, cheap or seed capital shares—their cost to Canarim is $10,000. In a good market, with a decent promoter who has to get rid of his stock too, the shares can be counted on to reach at least $2. If the majority of them are sold, then the profit for the Canarim is $190,000, not counting the minimum 20 per cent commission (amounting to $50,000 in this case) on the underwriting itself. If only half of the underwritings make this kind of money—and in a bull market, half is extremely conservative— the resulting profit is enormous, legal and relatively risk free. The above example is a fairly conservative one. Brokerage companies could and would take larger positions. The stock could be blown off at far higher prices. And the pot could be sweetened still further by options, warrants and unwritten deals whereby the company owner is forced to sell back shares at a nominal price at a later date to the brokerage firm.

The faith Brown has in this system is indicated by the positions he takes in the companies that Canarim underwrites. By 1980, he had major equity positions in more than 180 vsE-listed companies. Until 1980, there were no restrictions on the amount of founder's shares underwriters could retain. Then the figure was set at 20 per cent.

In 1976 Canarim made $5 million, its first real profit since 1969. Three years later it had clearly established itself as the force. Canarim's $90 million of underwriting was half of the vsE total. Brown didn't ignore the trading end of things either. Canarim's volume amounted to 20 per cent of the vsE's total, thus rivalling Continental, which had been the number one trading house for decades. Canarim's top dozen salesmen, of a total staff of around 120 in Vancouver, earned an estimated $250,000 each in commissions, and their least successful salesman was taking home $60,000 to $70,000.

By 1981 Canarim had eliminated all contenders for the dominant position. That year it underwrote $200 million, nearly the entire vsE financing, and also accounted for 20 per cent of all trading. Canarim was the most profitable brokerage house in the country, netting over $30 million—not counting revenue from extensive real estate holdings and other investments. In comparison, two large national firms, Dominion Securities with 223 employees and Richardson Greenshields with 212 employees netted $24 and $21 million respectively. The top-grossing salesman at Canarim made $2.2 million in 1981, and it wasn't unusual for others to make $700,000 annually. Brown bragged that twenty Canarim salesman in the previous eight years had become after-tax millionaires from commissions and investments.

The figures document a relentless march toward utter control of the western speculative market, but they tell only half the story. The success of Canarim in those years had as much to do with Brown's leadership as it had to do with dry business goals. As a leader, he's made of the same stuff that made Bear Bryant, the Crimson Tide football coach, the most successful in the history of the sport. Apart from his achievements, employees and colleagues admire and like Brown for the raucous, arrogant young man who still lurks within. The brokerage community is a bit like a military platoon or a football squad: hard-living team players with a spit-in-your-eye self-assurance are much respected. Brown is also appreciated for a host of unpublicized small kindnesses. If someone is sick, he's the first one to visit them in the hospital. A dozen perfect roses might show up on the desk of a woman who is celebrating an anniversary. When promoter Morris Black was jailed for wash trading in 1976, Brown immediately sent off a sympathetic letter to him. "It was a very nice letter," says Black's youngest son, Jeffrey. "It meant a lot to him at the time."

Brown expects as much from his staff as he does from himself, but if one of his reps is in financial trouble, Brown makes it his problem. Canarim, like all the Vancouver houses, has a horde of young brokers who started during the incredible boom years of 1978–81. It was easy for a beginning rep, just a few years out of university, to make $100,000. The money was irresistible to most, and they spent it on weekend-long parties at Whistler, expensive vacations, trendy condos purchased at the height of the market and sleek, low, foreign cars. When the bear market took over, a few forgot to stop spending. In order to support their indebtedness and standard of living, some started churning client's accounts, buying and selling without permission just to generate commissions. Brown preferred to deal with problems like these in-house, rather than firing the broker and ruining his career. His philosophy wasn't altogether altruistic. He ensured that reparations were made, and Canarim kept a chastened employee with a loyalty bordering on love.

Brown may have a good memory for his friends, but when it comes to paying off his enemies, his memory is elephantine. Gus MacPhail, principal of John McGraw's old firm, Continental Securities, and Brown have been at odds since the late 1960s. There is considerable conjecture about the source of their enmity, but it boils down to the fact that, at the time, Continental had the bulk of the VSE's business and Brown wanted it. MacPhail is from the old school and, like

McGraw before him, worked the floor long after it was fashionable or appropriate. He also disdained Brown's hard-nosed collection tactics, preferring to offer credit to the high rollers. By 1980, Brown's Canarim Investment had pushed Continental firmly into the background. A 1984 incident shows the bitterness of their rivalry. It was during one of Murray Pezim's periodic bouts of insolvency. He owed about $1.5 million each to Continental, Canarim and Midland Doherty. Each brokerage firm had shares covering the amounted owed, but Midland Doherty was in the best position with the most solid security. Both Continental and Canarim were "sucking wind" in the words of one insider. Brown, in a masterly move, bought Midland's security, and then quietly dumped the whole lot on the market. This had two results. By averaging the value of the shares held by Canarim and Midland, Brown managed to recoup most of the money Pezim owed him. And by selling the shares, Brown drove down the value of the shares Continental held as security. It was a neat trick: Brown made good his own losses and just about drove Continental out of business at the same time.

Brown's style, as much as his accomplishments, are what earned him a place in Peter C. Newman's 1981 book, *The Acquisitors*. In a city jaded by the gargantuan excesses of the J. Bob Carters and the Nelson Skalbanias, Brown more than held his own. Nicknamed "the Rabbit," his office was adorned with bunny knickknacks, including a six-foot stuffed version. At one point he considered putting a rabbit on his business card. The press loved the stories about Brown, even if they couldn't penetrate the man himself. He bragged to journalists about his seventy pairs of Gucci loafers ("I have a very high arch and a wide foot and they're the only shoes I find comfortable") and the separate closet he built to accommodate them in his 8,000-square-foot Georgian mansion. He spent so much money, more than $2 million, remodelling a 4,000-square-foot cottage on Bowen Island, that he cornered the market in local tradespeople. "Shit, I can't even get somebody to fix my pool because all the good tradesmen are up at Bowen doing Brown's place," complained one friend at the time. He ordered 150 triple bullshots at once in a Las Vegas bar and impressed a Palm Springs waiter by calling for a case of Chateau Lafite Rothschild '61 (then $166 a bottle). "Give me a case of this Lafite shit," he told the man. His possessions seemed endless: his houses, his Mercedes, his Rolls Corniche, his four boats. Brown spent money like it was water.

It was as if he wanted to rub his success in the face of those who had once thwarted or doubted him.

During this period also Brown demonstrated a taste for practical jokes, many of which had a subtle or not so subtle undertone of maliciousness. One day in 1979, the vse staff sent Brown a live white rabbit bedecked with red ribbons. There was no response from Brown until a few hours later, when a waiter delivered to the vse a roasted rabbit wearing the same ribbons and reposing on a silver platter. The staff later learned that the cooked rabbit had been purchased from one of Umberto Menghi's restaurants and was not the pet bunny they had sent to him. Nonetheless, the incident left a sour taste in many mouths.

Today Brown, who no longer answers to Rabbit and has shorn his office of rabbity mementoes, would prefer to talk about his charitable contributions, his board seats* and his art collections than his past hijinks. Brown and Canarim are among the largest, if not the largest, corporate donors in Vancouver. "Our corporate goal has been to give a million and raise a million for charity every year," he says. He and Ted Turton donated $250,000 to keep the Emily Carr collection in Vancouver.

Brown's pastimes and generosity leave no doubt about his largesse and vitality, but as with all his passions, there is something sterile, almost calculated about them. He appears to capture and mount his hobbies like exquisite butterflies. When he took up tennis in his late thirties, he had to master it, taking lesson after lesson. He played with a ferocious intensity that left no room for idle recreation. "He hates to lose. He's not designed to lose. Accepting losing is difficult for him. He may try to hide it, but he wants to erase the loss right away," says his friend Robin Lecky.

Brown talks about his cherished Canadian duck decoy collection as if he had embarked upon it for public consumption, not personal joy. He doesn't speak of the intricate workmanship, the fine detailed beauty or the pleasure they bring him. He calls it the biggest, the best, the most expensive collection and, without prompting, throws around

*The boards Brown has been on recently include: Investment Dealers Association of Canada, the vse, the University of British Columbia board of governors, the Vancouver Art Gallery, the B.C. Lions football team, B.C. Place, B.C. Enterprise Corporation and the Big Brothers. He was vice-chairman of Expo 86, second in command only to Jim Pattison, and is a member of the Atlantic Institute for International Affairs, a think tank.

the latest prices for a single specimen. He talks with relish of the $319,000 paid by an American collector in 1986 for a pintail. His joy in the hobby is the joy of possession, of conquest. "You go into his house and there's all these gorgeous things, thousands of them, stacked cord upon cord like so much firewood," observed playwright and author John Gray in amazement after a visit to Brown's home. Brown's display of the birds in his games room is actually a meticulous history of duck decoys in Canada. They are all arranged according to region and the gun clubs that carved them. The entry of Brown into decoy collecting had an enormous effect on the price of the birds and the character of the market. In two and a half years he spent several million dollars buying 80 per cent of the top quality Canadian decoys available. "I've gotten rid of all my birds," observes one collector ruefully. "There's no fun in it anymore."

Brown admires Toni Onley, the West Coast painter who has achieved the seemingly impossible for an artist of becoming rich in his own time. Brown doesn't own a few Onleys or even a handful: he owns the Canarim Collection, which consists of 68 paintings. Seven from the collection are mounted in the main lounge area on Canarim's executive floor. The famous ghostly landscapes hang so close together and against such a mottled background that they resemble a bunch of drugstore posters. Brown also owns a gorgeous Emily Carr, which an expensive lighting system in his home manages to turn into a black velvet painting. "I've always had an interest in art. I've got some of the premium works in the country," says Brown. "I've got Casson's *Country Crisis*, which is clearly his number one painting, Lismer's *Spring in Sackville*, which is his biggest canvas. I've got other major, major artworks. Premium pieces."

Brown has turned to politics with the same kind of calculated zeal that he unleashed on tennis, ducks and art. His involvement with the Social Credit party in British Columbia started back in 1973, when he realized political influence could be a prop to his ambition. It was the year that Dave Barrett's New Democrats took power. Brown's intention was to counter the threat to mining, and therefore the VSE, that the NDP posed. His initial contribution was raising money from corporations. The man he worked for was Bill Bennett's chief bagman, Austin Taylor, now president of McLeod Young Weir Ltd., then in charge of the firm's Vancouver underwriting department (where he was responsible for attracting such clients as Westcoast Transmission Company Ltd., Finning Tractor and Woodward's Stores Ltd.). After the election, Taylor received most of the credit for the fund raising, and McLeod Young Weir was named as the province's fiscal agent for bonds issued by the government and for a plethora of Crown corporations, an appointment worth millions in commissions. Brown got something even more valuable: he and Premier Bill Bennett established a mutual admiration society.

There was an immediate affinity between the two men. It's been written that Brown "idolizes" Bennett, though it's hard to imagine Brown idolizing anyone short of John D. Rockefeller. What attracted them to each other was basically an emotional bond, surprising in two men from vastly different backgrounds. Bennett and Brown discovered they were both sensitive to criticism and intensely loyal to friends. What's more, they preferred the straightforward, no-nonsense conversations of the sort favoured by Richard Nixon. By the time Bennett announced his retirement in 1986, Peter Brown was one of the three people who had immediate access to the aloof premier.

In March 1982, Sandy Ross, well-known author of *The Traders*, asked Brown if he had ever considered politics. "Too many skeletons," Brown replied. "To be in politics today, it's almost like being a monk. A guy has to make up his mind what he wants to do at eighteen, and lead that life. I'm trying to keep my nose clean, but it's tough." Four years later, Peter Brown's name was the first to surface as a possible successor to Bill Bennett. Vancouver *Sun* columnist Denny Boyd handicapped the field and made Brown his favourite at 2-to-1 odds. "Bet this one and you'll wear diamond bracelets," he wrote on May 23, 1986: "Is probably the closest civilian to Bennett in the province, has acted as Socred bagman for several years and is regarded as heir apparent. Worships Bennett. May have been given verbal promise of future party leadership as reward for significant campaign fund raising." Brown thought seriously about joining the race, even though he had never been elected to public office, not even to the PTA. He may have been tempted, but the skeletons won out; after calling around to test the opinion of influential friends, he decided against running.

While he now works hard at portraying the new Peter Brown, his trademark sense of humour still seeps out. In May 1986 when the Socred leadership campaign was just beginning, the front runner was Bud Smith, a Kamloops lawyer who had been Bennett's principal secretary for two years. A reporter was interviewing Brown, who let it slip that Bud Smith was a few floors down secretly meeting with promoter Murray Pezim. The reporter, with film crew in tow, arrived to catch

Smith and Pezim as they left the meeting. On the CBC-TV news that evening, Smith was so astonished at the appearance of the media that he had the furtive look of someone caught red-handed. The incident was a devastating blow to Smith's leadership hopes, and his opponents used it to successfully brand him as a back-room operator. "It makes you want to gag," wrote the *Sun*'s lead political columnist Marjorie Nichols, "this stock market promoter meeting in a closed room with a couple of men who have never run for public office to discuss the ownership and presumably the financing of the highest office in B.C." Smith never recovered from Brown's prank. "It backfired," Brown now says lamely. "I didn't mean to hurt Bud, and I think it did."

Brown's maverick image has been tucked away with his rabbit mementoes, and he's even allowed himself to be co-opted by the establishment—providing he starts at the top. A case in point is his once well-publicized distaste for the Investment Dealers Association (IDA), the national self-governing organization of stock brokerage firms. "They're such a pack of assholes," he said of the IDA during an interview with Sandy Ross. "If I joined them, I'd have to wash my hands every half hour. They're hypocritical. . . . If I join them they can't speak for me. And in terms of venture capital, they not only don't speak for it, they've hurt it. They've been a great detriment to it. Ideologically they just can't see it. And the hypocrisy they practise, this holier than thou. And then you look at some of their transactions . . . Christ, if I operated the way some of those guys operate, in terms of insider trading and inside information, if we did the same things those guys pulled, we'd be put out of business. Two sets of rules. And I'm not going to subject myself to that—ever."

Thirteen months later, however, Canarim Investment Corporation joined the Investment Dealers Association, and Peter Brown was immediately made a director. "They represented Toronto and they represented national firms who didn't understand our business," says Harwood of the IDA. "Peter was the voice, and he went on the national executive, which was a big jump. You don't normally do that unless you've been in the IDA for a while. They wanted him on. They recognized that what he said was true."

Brown would like to shed his past like a skin. But it keeps coming back to haunt him. Once he was happy to be portrayed as a rich buffoon and a flamboyant boy wonder pushing people into swimming pools, boasting about his collection of Gucci shoes, rating how good a day he was having in terms of bottles of champagne—a one Dom day or a two Dom day—and correcting people who didn't make the stories extravagant enough. Now he wants to be taken seriously, to be given his rightful place as the man who turned the VSE around and to be respected for the tenacity and drive that put him where he is.

Whatever you think of Peter Brown, and it's impossible to be ambivalent, his actions are directly responsible for much of the VSE's current financial success and way it operates. The exchange would have limped out of the 1970s and into the bull market of 1978 without him, but Brown pushed it to do more. He taught the VSE what it really means to take control and make money.

PART III

Ripe for the Picking

Promoters have become critical to the success of the VSE. Where once they were a tolerated evil, a means of selling stock when all else failed, the stock promoter is increasingly the power and the brokerage community the follower. The profiles of a handful of promoters in this section illustrate the changes they have undergone and the impact they have made on the VSE.

Egil Lorntzsen personifies the old-time prospector who trudged through the bush for years before he found his mine. But Lorntzsen is something more. He is one of the rare prospectors who became his own promoter, cracked a good deal with a major mining company and then was canny enough to keep his fortune intact. The story of Norman Keevil, Sr., and Teck Corporation is surely one of the most amazing in the history of Canadian mining. In the space of thirty years, Keevil has gone from being a perfectly happy university professor to being the perfectly happy principal owner of Cominco, one of Canada's largest mining companies. Along the way, there's hardly a facet of Canadian mining that he hasn't mastered including his own unique style of promotion. Morris Black is one of the most singular characters in the history of Canadian business, let alone speculative securities. His career parallels the shift in focus of Canadian speculative securities from Toronto to Vancouver. Murray Pezim and Bruce McDonald are each the most powerful promoters of their time. McDonald, in particular, illustrates the changing face of stock promotion at the VSE.

CHAPTER 9

Promoters and Prosperity

"The real story of the Vancouver Stock Exchange is the promoter. If you tell their story, you've said it all." B.C. SUPERINTENDENT OF BROKERS RUPERT BULLOCK in 1985.

VSE PROMOTER JOKES:
Q: How do you know when a promoter is lying?
A: When he moves his lips.

Q: What's the difference between a bad and a good promoter?
A: One's in jail and the other isn't.

In this age of managers and administrators, stock promoters, admirable and otherwise, are still endowed with the free-wheeling, turn of the century, capitalist spirit. Unlike brokers, who are trained, licensed and beholden to an institutionalized code of conduct laid down by the Investment Dealers Association of Canada, stock promoters are not subject to licensing or ethical codes. And anyone can become a stock promoter. It is one of the few professions in Canada—and by far the most lucrative—to which people can belong by simply saying that that is what they are.

Without promoters, the VSE and many brokerage houses would

cease to function overnight. The triad that supports the exchange consists of the speculating public, the brokers who are the intermediaries and the promoters. The smart money recognizes this relationship and bets not on a company, its assets, its potential or even on the quality of its management, but on the promoter. "Let's face it, I'm in the business of making money for my clients, not making mines," says stock salesman Harry Laidlaw bluntly. "That's one in a thousand. . . . Even in our junk market, our crap game, you go with the people. If you've got good people, you've got it made. If they got a good record of taking a stock at 15 cents and manipulating it up to $2, then that's a good investment for my clients."

The VSE faces a difficult problem. It has a single product to sell*—the shares of nearly 2,000 companies. Generally, this product has little intrinsic worth; its value is promise—the promise that one day shares bought at 25 cents will be worth $1. Remove the stimulation of promoters, and the majority of these companies would have as much future as a bucket of dead fish. Of course the exchange, brokers and promoters will deluge you with impressive reasons why *your* company will become a producer. In the trade this is called "the story," and its effectiveness is often the determining factor in the success of a company. Privately, however, most of them will admit that the product and the promise are basically as described.

Another problem is that there is no particular reason for the average person to buy shares in a VSE-listed company. Few of the companies have revenue, even fewer ever provide dividends; and there is no guarantee that, once purchased, the shares can be sold again— even at a loss. Millions upon millions of gaudy stock certificates that may still be worth a few dollars now repose in shoeboxes around the world, because the promise is gone and consequently no one wants them—at any price. In any given week, 25 to 30 per cent of VSE-listed companies won't trade at all. Not one share.

The person who generates the promise and the reason to buy is the promoter. IBM, Canadian Pacific, the Royal Bank and Cominco don't need a persuader to encourage people to buy. Even the market illiterate has heard of these companies and believes that they have intrinsic value. If the corporate name isn't familiar, the public still feels

*Actually, the VSE now sells a few more products thanks to the bad times of the early 1970s and earns revenue with its clearing-house and other services, but the meat of its existence is still the shares of the companies it lists.

comfortable buying shares listed in the sombre edifices of the Toronto and New York stock exchanges because they believe that the company will be around the morning after. It's called investment. The act of buying shares of companies like IBM and CP is, to most of us, an act of saving and investment. Speculation, on the other hand, connotes neither saving nor investment, merely gain or loss—usually the latter. Speculation is not part of our school training; it is not what our parents had in mind when they walked us through our first bank account and it is not what our grandmothers intended when they gave us ten shares of Imperial Oil for our coming of age celebrations.

Although the Vancouver Stock Exchange is the world's largest stock market dealing primarily in speculative issues, someone still has to get out on the streets, into the back rooms and increasingly into the board rooms to convince people that the promise of gain (usually quick) lies in one stock or another. Someone has to promise investors that there will be a buyer for their stock when they want to sell. Someone has to get people talking about Urea High Mining and make sure information about its "fabulous" new property becomes affixed to the market grapevine. That someone is the promoter. Some floor traders, who are close enough to the action to know, maintain that as much as 70 per cent of all trading on the VSE is generated in one form or another by promoters.

The VSE has always recognized the importance of promoters, if only covertly. Despite the importance of promoters to the VSE's existence, there are only a handful of instances in its entire early history when the subject has been mentioned in board minutes. The first time that VSE officials publicly admitted the importance of promoters was in a 1940 article in the Vancouver *Province* when a reporter quoted exchange president Johnny Jukes:

> Mr. Jukes thought it was a great pity that the expression, company promoting, had come to be regarded by some people as synonymous with shady business. A little reflection should establish the fact that every joint stock enterprise has to be started [promoted] at some time and that company promotion is an integral part of the modern financial system.

In 1960, the VSE monthly bulletin broke with its long tradition of silence on the subject of promoters by printing an article on the value of this underrated and poorly appreciated group:

To be successful in B.C., a promoter needs to be of a type above the average in hardiness, vision, courage and determination. This being the case, it is certainly in the interest of the province that any honest, enterprising promoter should be regarded as a provincial asset and not just a costly parasite. The promoter takes nothing out of the world. He leaves it much the richer for his activity. If temporarily some prosper while many fail it is a small and fair price for society to pay for progress and prosperity in which all participate.

The reason the bulletin gave for British Columbia needing these visionaries had nothing to do with the speculative nature of the market but with the fact that B.C. suffers more keenly from geographic handicaps like mountains and rivers than do other provinces. The implication seemed to be that these physical difficulties translate themselves into the market, making it more difficult to sell stock in B.C. than elsewhere with more forgiving terrain.

In the recent past broker-dealers did most of the stock promotion around the VSE. They operated largely by purchasing controlling interest in a shell company,* then selling to it, at a premium, a piece of property or an idea. At this point the company name was usually changed and often some share rollback occurred. Vancouver had a circle of lawyers who specialized in these shells. The whole business was a roller-coaster ride. Most of the broker-dealer/promoters made a living and a few made fortunes, but generally it was a much-despised trade. Their methods of promotion included letters extolling the virtues of one stock or another and warning the recipient that time and fortune were about to pass them by if they didn't act quickly. One letter from the early 1960s pointed out a stock that was recommended at 10 cents and had reached a high of 70 cents, a 600 per cent profit, "to the astute investors who were guided by us, both on the time to buy and the time to sell." The letter also said the stock had traded over 10 million shares in 1961, giving the reader the impression of a very liquid market. The letter failed to mention that the company had gone

*Utilizing a shell company is an ever-popular promotional technique. A shell is a listed company, usually with no revenue, assets or share value. Its only value is the fact that it is listed. At any given time, between 250 and 300 shells are floating around the VSE. There are two main advantages in taking over a shell rather than forming a new company. The shell is already listed on the exchange, so taking it over will attract less rigorous scrutiny than starting a new company via a prospectus that requires quite wide-ranging information. Also, because the shell is already listed, it avoids the delay, as long as three or four months in some cases, that forming a new company entails.

through four name changes in six years and that the shares had been rolled back on the basis of one-share-for-five, making it seem as if the stock was rising in price. The 600 per cent profit was just so much hocus-pocus.

Archie Hanna, whose son Ken is one of the West's most respected securities lawyers, was a broker-dealer. "He was bankrupt a couple of times. He was very up and down," Ken Hanna recalls. "But he was also a very, very generous person. He gave away more money than he made. Even if he didn't have any money he'd give it away." Archie Hanna was typical of his time: he was everything, prospector, promoter and broker-dealer. He began drilling oil wells in Alberta and Saskatchewan in the late 1940s, and after the oil excitement died away, he moved on to mining in British Columbia. He was always on the move, always promoting, always hustling, always living dangerously close to the legal line, knowing that he and others like him were constantly being watched by the police, the vse and the Securities Commission. Although few broker-dealers were ever jailed for securities offences, they were considered dirty by definition, and if you were one of them you had to keep one eye looking backward all the time.

When a scandal erupted, it was most often the broker-dealer/promoters who raised the ire of the press and the public. In 1960, the Vancouver *Sun*'s business columnist, Bill Fletcher, wrote:

> What I can't abide are the promoters who lease, stake or pick up some two-bit property, run a bunch of misleading propaganda through a printing press and then take dead aim on the savings of widows, retired people and get-rich-quick innocents. If this type of promoter ever got a commercial oil well or mining property out of his deal, he would probably die of the shock. His primary intention is to run a market for his own benefit. And, when the project is milked dry, scurry around and find another scheme and start all over again.

Fletcher's column, referring specifically to broker-dealers, came at a time when the vse was on the verge of radical change. Before 1964–65, the Toronto Stock Exchange was a thriving haven to many of the same promoters who now grace the vse. As a result of their start in the East and their seasoning in the West, Canadian promoters are now the reigning monarchs of the profession—especially on the dark side of it.

The art of stock manipulation has a long and colourful history, but never before has it been polished to such perfection as with Canadian stocks. Canadian promoters are able to fleece Wall Street brokers as easily as they take the most unsophisticated speculators for a financial ride; only the approach is different. Greed is universal. . . . The vast majority of Canadian mining and oil stocks have little if any intrinsic value. Yet they do have a monetary value as long as buyers can be found, and it is perfectly logical to buy an intrinsically worthless stock providing you can be sure someone will be around to take it off your hands at a higher price in the future.

So wrote T. H. Mitchell, LL.B., Ph.D., LL.D., a noted Toronto economist, market advisor and international lecturer, in his book *Canadian Mining Speculation*. He was describing Toronto stock promoters before 1965. Since then, Vancouver promoters have refined their craft considerably.

After the Windfall scandal in 1964 and the Pyramid discovery in 1965, Vancouver became flooded with sharp-eyed eastern operators, many of whom were far more sophisticated than their western cousins. They were city slickers who had no intention of staking their own claims, let alone getting out and banging rocks together. Nor did they want to deal with actually selling stock as the broker-dealers did. The VSE and the B.C. Securities Commission, alarmed at the influx of these eastern promoters, which had begun in 1960, revamped both VSE rules and the Securities Act in 1962, significantly upgrading the requirements for listing a public company on the VSE. The toughened rules backfired by driving out the broker-dealers, small-time promoters and prospectors, making their more cunning colleagues virtually indispensable. It became more complicated for someone with a handful of claims to go public and get listed on the VSE. Gradually, prospectors began seeking out professional promoters who would buy their claims and then, at an opportune time, sell the property into a public company for cash and shares. Thus the prospector was eliminated from the promotion process. Today's VSE promoters differ from their earlier counterparts in that most of them aren't, and never have been, prospectors. Even when it comes to industrial ventures, promoters rarely come up with the ideas themselves.

The days of the broker-dealers were also numbered, not only as promoters but as stock salesmen. The VSE had always found them a convenient scapegoat in times of trouble but couldn't afford to get rid of them, since trading in unlisted stocks, the broker-dealers' liveli-hood, amounted to 30 per cent or more of daily trading volumes. The VSE received no percentage of the commission on these sales, but its member brokers did. And, since many of the unlisted stocks origi-nated with broker-dealers, VSE members didn't take kindly to frequent suggestions that their less desirable counterparts and the unlisted board be eliminated.

The broker-dealers hung on until 1973, and the unlisted stocks quickly followed them into oblivion. It wasn't the first time the un-listed board was banned, but it was the last. At least thirteen times in the VSE's history, the unlisted, curb or miscellaneous board has been banished from the exchange floor. Depending on how flush members were, the exile lasted anywhere from ten days to two years. If any scandal befell unlisted stocks, the VSE, which took no responsibility for them, simply shrugged and said, "We have no power to control what goes on there. The board is merely a convenience for our mem-bers." (Now unlisted stocks have now been incorporated into the VSE on the Development Board, where the listing requirements are less than for those of regularly listed companies.)

What eventually killed the broker-dealers was their inability to adapt to change. Full-time promoters were taking away much of their business, and the police were developing a keener interest in the semi-legal fringe of the securities industry. In 1967 the RCMP established a commercial crime squad. While most of its members were unschooled in the stock market, they at least had a mandate to look a little harder at anything to do with securities. One of the squad's first collars was Archie Hanna. "He, like a lot of people, simply didn't know what was expected of him," says his son Ken. "His particular problem was that he was just in way over his head. He was not able to adjust to the changing and more complicated legal requirements." Archie Hanna was charged with using money from one of his companies for his own purposes. It didn't matter to anyone that most of the money went to Hanna's pet charity, the Variety Club. He was just one more broker-dealer out of the way.*

Increased police scrutiny weeded out many of the less sophisticated

---

*Ken Hanna claims not to have been influenced by his father's experiences, but he has worked hard to improve the securities system and educate those in it. He instituted a director's course to teach the multitude of uninformed public company directors what their responsibilities are. He was also instrumental in creating the statement of material facts—a simplified prospectus, and he has been on the securities review committee for over ten years.

promoters. Bob Mullock, a former commercial crime squad member, chuckles at some of the gaffes that promoters made. "One of the first securities cases I ever did had to do with raising capital from about fifty or sixty shareholders. When we looked at the company we found the records showed the purchase of a bulldozer, building equipment, fencing . . . all the things you'd expect in mining." But when Mullock asked a few questions, he discovered that the man had really purchased a racehorse. The building equipment was for a barn, the fencing material was for a paddock and the fuel was hay for the horse.

Bob Scott, when he was in charge of compliance for the VSE, also stumbled across a few innocents. One of them was the promoter of a company that had been rising steadily on the VSE with a fair amount of trading activity. One day the price of the stock crashed, and there was no trading. "I called him [the promoter] in and asked him why. He said, 'I ran out of money.' I said, 'What do you mean you ran out of money?' He had bought the stock all the way up to a buck and a quarter, ostensibly maintaining an orderly market. And he kept on upping the bid all the time. Not only was he honest, but he was stupid." This poor schmo didn't realize that a promoter accumulates stock at the beginning of a promotion when it is cheap, sells it on the way up and buys it back on the way down.

There aren't too many of those kinds of promoters left today, mainly because they couldn't survive in the same game with the new breed who learned how to beat and rule the system. "They're confidence men, most of them, and they are the most charming rogues in the entire game," says Bob Scott. "Usually they are intelligent too. I'd rather deal with them than any dolt off the street as long as I know the ground rules. Some promoters are smart and honest, some are smart and dishonest. You rarely find them in the stupid category."

The game has become so impersonal that promoters often hire technicians who specialize in a single area of promotion. Specialists, for example, whose sole occupation is finding, taking control of and renovating for future use the three hundred or so shell companies kicking around the VSE at any given time. One such specialist was Harold Quin, who had a Ph.D. in English and assorted other degrees. "Harold's modus operandi was fairly simple if a little bent," wrote stockbroker Frank Keane in B.C. Business magazine:

Harold would sell off a bunch of cheap stock and do a primary* in a

*A primary is the original sale of any issue of a company's securities.

deal, putting some bread in the treasury. He would then live off the treasury until such time as a buyer showed up for the company. Once he had a deal, he would then repeat the process, taking money from the new company to replenish the treasury of the one he was selling. All his vehicles were clean and had a few bucks in the treasury and Harold was able to deliver just about all the escrow, cheap stock and the primary—that's why his deals were in such demand. Anybody who bought Harold's cheap stock had to be prepared to give it back, but always at a profit, when the call came.

The shady side of the promotion business has long been known, but it wasn't until James Colby Danielson testified in 1975 and 1976 about stock manipulation that most people got a glimpse of what was possible in the half-real world of penny stocks. Jim Danielson, a.k.a. Jim Daniels, a.k.a. A. J. McCandless, was a well-seasoned American stock manipulator who skipped his $35,000 bail in the U.S. and fled to Vancouver in the late 1960s. Described as a "real hotshot" by U.S. Securities and Exchange Commission officials, Danielson claims to have taken part in U.S. swindles involving 27 million shares of various American companies during the 1960s. But the vse was a much sharper game than even this veteran stock manipulator expected, as his wife, using the pen name Marlis Flemming, reported in her book, *Under Protective Surveillance*, published by McClelland & Stewart in 1976:

> The track is fast in the Vancouver financial community. My husband was soon to discover that you had to be extremely fleet-footed just to survive. The slow-witted are soon separated from their money and trampled underfoot. . . . From 6:30 in the morning, Monday through Friday, it [the vse] is thronged with the fastest guns in the Western world."

Danielson and his partner Steve Dineen* soon became chummy with several Vancouver promoters who explained the vse world to them. Flemming recalls them being told:

---

*Stephen James Dineen, alias Steve James, fled the U.S. in 1970 in the wake of a fraud conviction involving the Lord Bank and Trust Company of Nassau, one of the first of the exotic offshore banks. Dineen was president of the bank. He was also wanted in Florida for possession of $500,000 worth of stolen bonds.

All you have to do is lay a little cash on the line for your underwritings, cross the t's, dot the i's, and swear allegiance to the province and the Queen. Wait till you see a prospectus like they let slip through up here. It's all right down there in black and white how they're going to rip off the public. Only the public doesn't known how to read the cute English. They let promoters hide their stock in nominee accounts or in street certificates. They let the promoters control the companies through a big escrow stock position. It's rigged so the public can rarely get voting control.

Danielson found ready acceptance on the VSE. Other promoters and brokers hired him to act as a front or to spice up their trading. Danielson testified that he had a hundred people working for him at one point. They planted rumours with the media, the brokers and the public that a given company was on the verge of a significant mineral discovery. They also manned the phones, calling up thousands of investors, sometimes claiming to be licensed brokers or sometimes, simply, "a friend of the company." During his two years in Vancouver, Danielson admitted to having sold more than 3 million shares in this manner. His biggest problem was bribing brokers to recommend stocks to their clients. It was a problem, he claimed, because most were already spoken for: "All these other promoters operating in town at the time I was doing my deals here had their corralled salesmen who were being paid off, pieced off, bribed. . . . The salesmen were greedy, yes, because a secret commission, a 10 per cent bribe, was eight times the amount of their legitimate commission. Eight times that amount!"

The public was aghast at Danielson's revelations, but the VSE had fielded such accusations before and had always passed them off as a load of hot air. "Nobody on the VSE staff has been taking payoffs. I can't imagine anybody on the listing committee getting paid because no one member could swing it and it would cost too much to pay off the whole committee," retorted Jack Van Luven in 1967 when Toronto novelist Ivan Shaffer insinuated that the listing committee were in the promoters' pocket.

Good promoters are everything to the VSE. They provide the so-called orderly market, so necessary if the VSE is to maintain some semblance of normal trading. They provide bids when shareholders want to sell and offers when they want to buy. They also make the winners. Most people think of market winners as stocks like IBM or Xerox—real companies with big finds or inventions. But the VSE knows that companies like Pyramid, Placer, Endako, International Corona and Goliath are important for image only. The real winners have nothing to do with anything so mundane as finding a mine or developing the latest computer software. A real winner is a company that starts out at 15 cents, climbs up to $10 or $15 (though lately $50 and $60 is more like it) without attracting too much attention and then fades from sight in the same way. The brokers sell off their cheap shares, the promoters unload their positions and the insiders take their profits at or near the top. With a little bit of luck, a handful of investors who bought low will have had the courage to sell early and come away with money in their pockets.

Chopp Computers Corporation Inc. is a perfect example of one such winner. It also demonstrates what the real job of a promoter is. Chopp was listed on the VSE in April 1985 and, for a short while, traded for as little as 17 cents. Over the next eight months the shares were split twice (in all, six new shares for one old share) and by March 1986 were trading for $20. That meant the old shares were worth the equivalent of $120 each, making Chopp one of the most expensive stocks ever to grace the VSE board. The entire assets of the company consisted of the right to distribute a yet-to-be-developed supercomputer. That right could be exercised after the payment of $6 million to Sullivan Computer Corporation of La Jolla, California, the company supposedly developing the computer.

The people behind Chopp are the Huttons, Don and his wife Josephine. Also involved is Frank Mathews. Of Don Hutton, Bob Scott says, "I wouldn't touch him with a barge pole. I wouldn't let him near the exchange." The Huttons and Mathews have homes in Palm Desert, California, and Mathews is a resident of the state. They were all involved in the March Resources promotion of 1981 (Mathews was president), when the company shares shot up to a presplit price of $63.75 and down again to 50 cents after the much-vaunted U.S. oil wells turned out to be bone dry. The SEC (March Resources was listed over the counter in the States) investigated the company, which was suspended several times on the VSE. No charges were laid, and the company is still listed.

The Chopp (Columbia Homogeneous Parallel Processor) computer was touted as being able to "outperform the most powerful Cray computer machines by a factor of 100." Cray Research Corporation of Minneapolis dominated, and still does, the market for supercomputers —ultrafast, handbuilt machines capable of extraordinary feats. It was a Cray that simulated the minute detail of alien planet surfaces in the movie *The Last Starfighter*. Those machines cost as much as $7 million each.

At the same time that Chopp was climbing up to $120, the company began talking about a merger between it and Sullivan. Both the merger and the unveiling of the prototype passed deadline after deadline. Both were always unavoidably detained by legal details and testing problems. In December 1985 Chopp revitalized interest in the market by announcing that Randy Jackson, brother of rock star Michael Jackson, intended to buy $2 million worth of Chopp shares and warrants. By February that deal was mysteriously off.

In June 1986, the *Durant Livermore Cutten & Bliss Report*,* published in the West Indies, criticized the company, stating, "There is no viable supercomputer being developed." Chopp filed suit against the *Report*, which promptly countersued, alleging a massive conspiracy. The various suits are still before the American courts. From March 1986 to July 1986 Chopp shares yo-yoed up and down, finally ending at $7⅛ (equivalent to over $42 before the split), when the company requested trading be halted in its stock. Shortly after, Chopp's directors quietly delisted it, and the company left town. It was an auspicious time to bail out because the superintendent of brokers was starting to be concerned about all the missed deadlines. The Sullivan merger took place after Chopp was delisted from the VSE and was safely away from the probing eyes of the SOB, the RCMP and the exchange. The VSE heaved a massive sigh of relief when Chopp melted from sight. The company had rocketed to $120 a share, but there had been no spectacular crash or embarrassing scandal. At last word the company was preparing to list on NASDAQ,† the American over-the-counter market. There is still no sign of the supercomputer.

Whether or not there actually is a supercomputer in development, Chopp was a brilliantly conceived and elegantly run promotion in the classic VSE sense. The stock rose and fell in just over a year, coming down fairly gradually. There was always liquidity, always a buyer for a panicky seller. The company never dropped out of sight, though it was as low as $12 a share (presplit price), and when things started to get

---

*The *DLC & B* newsletter is a unique market service. For an annual subscription of $1,000 U.S., the report guarantees profits, through short selling opportunities, of at least 50 per cent yearly.

†NASDAQ stands for the National Association of Securities Dealers Automated Quotation System, an electronic exchange, now second only to the New York Stock Exchange in volume.

sticky, Chopp quietly had itself delisted and went elsewhere. The shareholders always had a chance, though many lost, no doubt, by buying at the top. The supercomputer claim is still relatively intact and ready to be revitalized. It is the kind of promotion that the street admires. "Regardless of what Chopp is proven to have or not to have, the Chopp market makers have been topnotch," commends John Woods, the respected editor of *Vancouver Stockwatch.** "The Choppers have run their market in one of the most professional manners I've ever seen a market run. Sure, no doubt Chopp was never worth $120. I'm not discussing the value of the company. I'm just discussing the method of the market making. And it was first class."

Outside Vancouver, however, the machinations of a company like Chopp rarely provoke admiration. In fact, so poorly is the promoting profession perceived by the public that many promoters have taken to calling themselves financiers, facilitators, corporate agents, entrepreneurs and the like. Ask someone around the TSE if he is a promoter, and the chill in the air could not descend swifter than if a truckload of dry ice were dumped on the plush Bay Street carpet. "We call them market makers here," snapped one TSE executive when asked about that exchange's control over promoters. There is none of this mincing shyness in Vancouver, where promoters are named as such and their role is even specifically defined in the Securities Act. "I'm a promoter, a money raiser, it's just that simple," states the VSE's current promoting genius, Bruce McDonald.

In Vancouver, promoters have gained such public acceptance that they have become important players in the political process. The 1986 B.C. Social Credit party leadership contest is a case in point. The leadership was a particularly juicy plum; the winner would immediately become premier of the province and would not have to call an-

*John Woods is one of the true gentlemen involved with the VSE and a student of speculative trading. He started out in the brokerage business in 1967 at age twenty-two, moved to the trading floor in 1968 and worked his way up from phone boy to assistant trader to floor trader. He was Canarim's floor trader from 1976 until 1982, when what had been a hobby turned into a brand-new career. In 1978 he began buying single shares in each of the companies listed on the VSE in order to receive their press releases, proxies and annual reports. "One of the overall pervading problems that the VSE has always had is that you, investors, cannot get information about listed companies in any coherent sort of format," he points out. He owns one share of almost every stock traded in Canada, approximately 3,200 in all, worth about $50,000. Woods fed the information into a personal computer, and by 1982 he had a formidable data base, which he used to assist Canarim's underwriting department. In 1984 Woods hit upon the idea of publishing a daily compendium of the information he received, and approached Peter Brown, who after a fifteen-minute meeting purchased 45 per cent of *Vancouver Stockwatch*.

other election for two years. John Reynolds, former Conservative member of parliament and a controversial figure, was the first to announce his candidacy. He would not have been challenged if he had described himself as a businessman with a wide range of interests, including an investment portfolio, but he repeatedly chose to call himself a stock promoter. Reynolds also made no bones about expecting the support of fellow promoter Murray Pezim, and Pezim felt comfortable coyly discussing with the media the merits and demerits of various contenders, saying he could raise "a few hundred thousand without much difficulty" for the candidate of his choice. During the campaign, several of those in the running, including Kamloops lawyer Bud Smith, then at the head of the pack, met with Pezim, presumably to solicit funds. But the winner of the leadership contest was Bill Vander Zalm, who had gone to great lengths to avoid back-room meetings with people like Pezim. Nonetheless, within two weeks of his victory, Vander Zalm paid a highly publicized visit to the VSE where he was seen cavorting with the floor traders. Reynolds ran near the bottom of a ten-candidate field, but he ended up as speaker of the legislature.

Promoters today are vastly more sophisticated than their predecessors were just a decade ago. And they are an increasingly faceless lot, having retreated into the camouflage of big offices, high-priced publicists, securities lawyers and other hired guns. There are still a few of their old-style counterparts around, hunkered down in modest offices decorated in early private eye and festooned with rocks. They're nice guys, for the most part, controlling one or two companies at a time, each with a bit of property that they fantasize will yield a producing mine or take off in the wake of a big find. Aside from the big score, their greatest hope is that their small companies will never be noticed or coveted by the sharks who've taken their place.

CHAPTER 10

Egil Lorntzsen,
a Raggedy-Ass
Prospector

"The rules of the VSE are set up by the members to stifle promoters and end up stifling the market. I said to hell with the whole goddamn thing." EGIL LORNTZSEN explaining why he avoided the brokerage community when he listed Lornex.

Egil Lorntzsen is one of the few remaining prospector-promoters. In many ways, his story follows the typical prospector path. He stumbled into prospecting with no formal training, and over a fifty-year period trudged across virtually every square inch of British Columbia as well as a considerable portion of the rain forests of South America, looking for mines. What distinguishes Lorntzsen from the rest is that he found one, the massive Lornex open-pit mine in the Highland Valley in B.C., profited hugely from it and has actually hung onto most of the money.

Success has broken far more prospectors than the failed search, but Lorntzsen, according to friends, is little changed since his big find. He happily holds court, surrounded by a feast of his memorabilia—rocks, plaques and photographs—in his roomy private office above Vancouver's Terminal City Club. He is still in the business, running a few companies with a handful of promising mining properties. What he does now is more hobby than anything else, the recreation of a man who loves his work.

Lorntzsen was born in Tromso, Norway, in 1908, and as a boy hunted seals on the remote islands located off Murmansk near the coast of Greenland. In 1930 he signed on as crew with a Norwegian merchant marine freighter and saw the world before jumping ship in the Caribbean in 1932. That year Lorntzsen emigrated to Canada, settling with relatives in Prince Rupert, B.C. He turned his hand to a variety of odd jobs including fishing, before signing on, in 1934, at the Minto gold mine in the Bridge River valley, about a hundred miles northeast of Vancouver. That summer, he explored the rugged Bridge River area. It was his first taste of prospecting, and he was hooked. Although Lorntzsen continued to work as a miner during the winter for several years, from then on he considered himself a prospector.

The trial and error tactics of other prospectors didn't suit Lorntzsen. He began reading every book, magazine article and scientific thesis he could find on mining and prospecting. So consuming was his quest for knowledge that he built up one of the largest and most comprehensive collections of mining books in the country. While he was building his library, Lorntzsen continued exploring the Bridge River area.

In the late 1930s Lorntzsen found his first mine, called the Tungsten King, a small but profitable tungsten mine, located near his favourite haunt of Bridge River. It was an extremely labour-intensive operation. "We [he and his Swedish partner, Gunnar] used to drill holes in the ore body with a steel and hammer. Then we'd blast it, put the ore in sacks and then haul the sacks down to the road by the cabin." Trucks from the nearby Bralorne Mine came by regularly to collect the sacks for refining at the Bralorne mill. It wasn't a bad life, but Lorntzsen wanted something more than a bachelor camp in the middle of nowhere, and he tried to talk his partner into selling out when Bralorne made an offer. "Gunnar—he had arms like Alley Oop —thumped his big fists up and down and said, 'I'm staying, I never change my mind.' He wanted to stay and mine that tungsten the rest of his life. I told him I was going to go to Vancouver and get married. Gunnar said, 'I didn't know you had a girl in Vancouver.' I said that I didn't, but Vancouver is full of girls; some of them must want to get married." In the end, Gunnar bought Lorntzsen's share.

Lorntzsen did move to Vancouver, and in December 1945 he married his wife, Iris. He set up an office with a mine developer named C. P. Riel. Riel died in 1945, and Lorntzsen soon realized he wasn't cut out to be a desk man. "When anyone came into the office, I was scared to death," he laughs. During this time Lorntzsen went looking for gold in South America where he bought two concessions, a hundred square miles in Dutch Guiana (now Surinam) and forty square miles in British Guiana (now Guyana). He found gold on both properties, but the Canadian government was supporting gold to keep the country's mines in operation and his New York backers pulled out. When the last of his Tungsten King money ran out in 1948, he donned a knapsack and headed back into the bush.

For the next six years, Lorntzsen supported his family by staking properties and selling his claims to mining companies. Typically, he was paid in cash and some shares in the company, most of which ended up being worthless. In between he prospected on his own at every opportunity. In the winter of 1954, the Highland Valley was alive with companies staking location bets hoping to cash in on Bethlehem Copper's massive find. That year and the next, Lorntzsen staked claims for a number of companies including fifty for Red Rock Mines and another hundred for what became the Highmont Mining Corporation. At the same time he staked over a hundred claims in his own name south and west of the Bethlehem discovery. The area just felt right even though it was covered with severe overburden, the detritus from glacial action. The land was virtually unexplored because the overburden made the surface hard to expose by traditional prospecting methods. It was a perfect area for scientific mine-finding techniques—or so Lorntzsen assumed. He optioned the property to different major mining companies for three consecutive years: first, in 1962, to ASARCO (American Smelting and Refining Company), the powerful mining arm of the Guggenheim family; then to Kennecott Copper, the huge American copper producer, and finally, to Noranda in 1964. Each found nothing. At one point during Kennecott's tenure, Lorntzsen, exasperated by the lack of progress, offered to help out. "Egil," the chief engineer said patronizingly, "we don't need a prospector, we are doing things scientifically."

Lorntzsen decided to try one last major. Knowing that Anaconda had optioned some property near his claims, he gathered up all the results and took them to the engineering chief, Dr. Glen Waterman. "I got a call one morning from Glen," remembers Lorntzsen. "He said, 'Meet me at the Georgia Hotel.' I turned to Iris and said, 'By God, I think I've got a deal!' " But Waterman simply returned the reports, telling Lorntzsen, "You've had three of the biggest and best exploration companies in the world looking at your property. It's been proven conclusively that there's nothing there."

Anaconda's refusal made Lorntzsen realize that nobody was going to explore his claims unless he did it himself. He decided to "get off my fat ass" and take a good look around. In the tradition of great prospectors, Lorntzsen operates viscerally as much as intellectually. The senses—smell, taste and feel—are important and uncannily accurate prospecting aids to such men. In 1948, for example, a prospector showed Lorntzsen a sample of cobalt uranium ore. The man didn't know where it came from, but Lorntzsen, after studying it for a few minutes, was able to pinpoint the origin within a few hundred yards. It was taken from Roxy Creek in the Bridge River area—a spot he'd prospected in thirteen years earlier. Lorntzsen and the other prospector went back to the area, confirmed his opinion and staked a number of claims.

On June 13, 1964, while tramping across his Highland Valley claims, Lorntzsen happened upon a moraine littered with broken granite. Every rock he cracked open contained copper mineralization. The big companies had missed the entire area. The next day his wife came out and stayed at the Highland Valley Lodge. Perched on a rock looking over the valley, she asked, "Egil, what are you so excited about?" Lorntzsen looked at her and replied, "Iris, I'm going to set up a company." His wife christened it Lornex.

Lorntzsen, together with David Ross, another prospector-promoter, set about raising money to explore the claims. They formed a private company, Lornex Mining Corporation Ltd., and began to approach well-known mine backers, all of whom turned them down—the Highland Valley was no longer the sexy prospect it had been a few years earlier. They raised a little money selling 10-cent stock to family and friends. Despite the difficulty, they never considered a VSE listing. "In those days we didn't need all that jazz," he says disdainfully. Finally, Lorntzsen called Superintendent of Brokers Bill Irwin. "He was down to his last nickel when he got me on the phone, I was in Victoria," recalls Irwin. "He said that he had 10,000 shares of Russian rubles or something. I said, 'What the hell are Russian rubles and what's it selling at?' " (Lorntzsen actually called it Bolshevik currency, the joke being that the stock was in escrow and therefore as useful to him as if it were uncashable currency.) Irwin agreed to release the escrowed stock, which Lorntzsen promptly sold for $6,000. He took the money, gave $1,000 to his wife and used the rest to rent a bulldozer. Back on his property, Lorntzsen had the operator open up a 750-foot-long trench, starting at the spot where he had found the granite. The entire trench showed strong visual evidence of copper mineralization, and further work revealed that it was spread over a considerable area.

After more trenching, engineering reports and a comprehensive drilling program using a new overburden drill developed in Sweden, Lorntzsen knew he had a mine. The question was where to get more financing to fully prove the discovery and bring the mine into production. His shareholders urged him to go and see a VSE broker who would do an underwriting. Lorntzsen was adamantly opposed. "I have no intention of going to a broker. For every $200,000 he'd raise, you'd have to give him sweeteners—some of my stock. If he raises a million dollars, there'll be damn all left in the treasury. And I'll probably end up with hardly any stock." He told the shareholders he was going directly after a major and was going to give them only 60 per cent of Lornex in return for developing it.* What's more, he was going to insist on being in control of how the first $500,000 was spent on the property. He didn't intend to let a major piddle away a few hundred thousand on the property, then get cold feet and pull out. The shareholders laughed. No one believed a big mining company would go for the kind of deal Lorntzsen proposed. Fortunately, Lorntzsen still owned more than two-thirds of the shares and his will prevailed.

Lorntzsen likes to characterize himself as "just a raggedy-ass prospector," but he got everything he wanted by skillfully playing off two majors, Rio Algom and Kennecott, against each other. He eventually made a deal in 1965 with Rio Algom, which bought 60 per cent, leaving Lorntzsen with 640,000 shares. The deal was structured, through the clever use of options, so that Rio Algom didn't assume full control for two years when the final options were exercised. In the meantime Lorntzsen served as president of Lornex and was in control of the exploration. It was only after the deal was cut that Lornex was listed on the VSE. The stock climbed up to $13 and eventually peaked at $85 a share. The raggedy-ass prospector, almost overnight, had a paper worth of over $8 million, and at the peak of the market his holdings were worth over $40 million. He indulged himself a little with a $1.2 million renovation of a house sitting on two very exclusive acres overlooking Vancouver's Spanish Banks.

*This would be an excellent deal. Seventy per cent of Endako's shares ended up in Placer's hands, and higher percentages for the majors were not uncommon.

Today Egil Lorntzsen is one of the most venerated members of the Terminal City Club in downtown Vancouver. Many of the old-timers who frequent the place recognize that he is something special. Not only did he make it big, but he made it on his own terms. He is a little stouter than he was when he spent his time breaking rocks, and the hair he once had has been replaced by a toupee. It has been nearly fifty years since Egil and Gunnar toiled over the Tungsten King, but in some respects, those days aren't far behind. He is still a prospector, just not quite as raggedy-assed as he likes to pretend.

CHAPTER 11

Norman Keevil:
From Junior to Major

"Opportunity can go by in a day." NORMAN KEEVIL, SR.'s credo.

D r. Norman Bell Keevil, Sr., has the relaxed, confident air of a
tenured professor; a man at the top of his profession who knows
that he cannot be touched. He even looks a little bit like a professor, the unconventional type with the unstylishly long hair and the
propensity to say and do the unexpected. Yet, as he slouches back in
his chair, long slim fingers hooked into his belt, enormous smile domi-
nating a lean, sharp-featured face, there are visible traces of a bush-
whacking prospector. His laugh, which has bounced off more than a
few gullies and moraines, isn't mannered or restrained. It's the laugh
of a man of huge accomplishments—first as a professor, then as a prospector and finally as chairman of Teck Corporation, the fastest growing major mining company in the country. It's the laugh of a man who
has lived life on his own terms.

It has taken Keevil barely thirty years to amass a quarter-billion-
dollar personal fortune. He has accomplished the rare feat of discovering a mine and using that discovery to fashion a mining company with
tentacles into significant prospects all across the country. Criticized as
a sharp takeover artist and an asset stripper in his early years, Keevil
has become a remarkable producer. In the past ten years, Teck Corporation has the incredible record of bringing in seven mines, under

budget and on time. Most of Canada's majors can boast of opening only a single mine during the same period.

Keevil was born in 1910 in Saskatchewan. His grandfather was a successful wholesale food entrepreneur in England, and he is one-eighth a Rothschild on his mother's side. The maverick that flourished in Keevil first showed itself in his father, heir-apparent to the family food company, who came to Canada to deliver a load of thoroughbreds and stayed—seduced by the tantalizing lure of the frontier. Keevil grew up on a Saskatchewan farm, getting his early education in a one-room schoolhouse. By the time he was a young man, Keevil was well on his way to becoming one of Canada's pre-eminent scientists. He earned his B.Sc. in 1930 and his M.Sc. in 1932 from the University of Saskatchewan, starting off with mathematics, then moving to chemistry and finally geology, qualifying for scholarships at every step. In 1937 Keevil took his Ph.D. at Harvard, and over the next three years shuttled between the twin pinnacles of North American scientific learning, Harvard and MIT, teaching and doing postgraduate research in geology. Then, in 1940, Keevil returned to Canada to become an assistant professor at the University of Toronto; it was the first Canadian professorship in the field of geophysics.

During the Second World War, Keevil's research led to the discovery that vitamin B2 decayed in sunlight. He also investigated the effects of bright light on human vision and advocated beer for the troops to improve their sight (after testing forty-eight different brands of suds). His most notable achievement of the time was his pioneering work in the relatively new areas of uranium and thorium: radioactivity, isotope tracers in explosive reactions, and the distribution of uranium and thorium in North American rocks. Keevil's research led to an invitation by Nobel Prize–winning scientist Professor H. C. Urey to join the Manhattan Project. But Keevil's FBI clearance for the ultrasecret project was slow in coming, and he missed out on the development of the atom bomb. Keevil may have been slowed up by the FBI, but he had considerable influence in Canada. One morning, his lab assistant F. J. Wank was called up by the Canadian army. Keevil made a few phone calls, and Wank was back at his workbench in the afternoon. During his scientific career, Keevil published forty-six papers, most of them containing original research.*

*Keevil still is interested in scientific research. Moli Energy Ltd., a VSE-listed company of which he is president, is putting the world's first rechargeable lithium battery into production. The Molicel, developed at the University of British Columbia, is to be manufactured near Vancouver starting in 1987.

After the war, science still held him in thrall. "I used to spend ninety-five hours a week doing nothing but pure research. I really intended to go back on the Harvard staff but never did get around to it. Too bad, it would have been a nice life," he says with a trace of wistfulness in his voice. But Keevil was the only geophysics professor in Canada, and it was natural that he be consulted by mining companies. He had never run a geophysical survey in the field until taking on his first such job early in 1946, so he had to borrow the equipment. He staked a few small claims on his first job, formed a company, Geo-Scientific Prospectors, and turned to consulting full time. "A few successes at the start, and word gets around," he says explaining his transition from academic to consultant. "In no time at all, I had fifteen parties out in the field. Keeping track of them was a job in itself. You couldn't worry about research or writing up a paper."

It was an abrupt career change for one so happily immersed in research. Keevil himself resists any analysis of the move, other than to state: "Opportunity can go by in a day." Norman Keevil, Jr.,* with the kind of insight an offspring can sometimes offer, says the leap from teaching to consulting, and then self-employment, was a combination of practicality and opportunity. "I suppose what shaped him more than anything was that he started out to build a fairly large family, larger than one supports on a professor's salary, even though he was one of the highest paid in his category at the U. of T., so he got out into the consulting business. And once you're there, it's a short step to trying to find your own mine instead of finding it for someone else."

Later in 1946, Keevil entered a partnership with Dominion Gulf Company, Gulf Oil's Canadian mining division, to conduct aerial surveys. During the war, Keevil had heard about the U.S. Navy's magnetic airborne detectors, used to find enemy submarines. He thought the device would be perfect for discovering mineral deposits from the air and bought the Canadian rights when it was declassified in July 1946. During the rest of 1946 and 1947, Keevil conducted what was, at the time, the most extensive aerial magnetic survey ever done in Canada. Geophysical mine finding, known as far back as the seventeenth century, uses magnetism to locate minerals. In 1906, Thomas

*Normal Keevil, Jr., worked at Teck and other mining companies during the summer while he was a student. He did his thesis at Placer Development's Craigmont Mine, where his boss was Bob Hallbauer, one of the most respected mine operators in the country, whom he later enticed into Teck's fold. Keevil Jr. almost became a university professor like his father. When he graduated from Berkeley, he was offered the opportunity to set up a department of geophysics at the University of Utah.

Alva Edison used a magnetometer to confirm the presence of copper-nickel-pyrrhotite deposits in Sudbury while searching for a source of materials for the storage battery he had invented. (He actually drilled a shaft but hit quicksand and gave up the search. Eighteen years later, another group in the same spot found the hundred-foot vein of nickel that became the Falconbridge nickel mine.) Airborne surveys were a great advance and, as the technological ability to differentiate minerals improved over the years, became increasingly important. But they didn't eliminate ground-level investigation.

Ironically, Keevil discovered the mine that was to be the basis of his fortune during an instrument test while ferrying the magnetic detector by plane to Canada from the States. "The very first flight line when I was just coming up from Pittsburgh, going up for tests, I plotted a course over what I thought was interesting geology, just here and there, up to Kirkland Lake. We ran across the biggest magnetic anomaly, not necessarily in intensity though it was very high, but the biggest in size—the largest that's ever been found anywhere." Anomalies don't always indicate pay dirt; they can indicate graphite and pyrrhotite, forms of iron sulphate or even pyrite, commonly named fool's gold. But there was nothing foolish about this particular anomaly located sixty miles north of North Bay and southwest of Cobalt, Ontario. Dominion Gulf wasn't interested in sending a crew down to take a look, so when the survey was finished in 1947, Keevil quietly dissolved the partnership and began staking out claims.

Keevil is a relaxed, easygoing man, but there's a sharp streak of impatience in him. He brought in Anaconda Copper Mining Company to drill the first holes. They spent $300,000 and infuriated Keevil with their ineptitude. "They didn't pay any attention," he says, still clearly exasperated. "First of all, they wouldn't pay for the geophysics, so I paid for it and did it anyway. Then they wouldn't drill the anomaly. They drilled one hole and they missed the number one ore body and went into a dyke. They missed the number two ore body by a few feet." Anaconda pulled out without retaining any interest in the site.* Keevil kept exploring, and after every major he approached turned him down, commenced his own drilling program. Of the first five holes, each drilled precisely where Keevil specified, three showed commercially significant results.

*Anaconda were entitled to a percentage but had little faith in the property, and if they'd taken an interest they couldn't have claimed a tax write-off on their expenses. To get a 100 per cent write off they would have to give up everything, which they did.

In 1955, Keevil's find became the Temagami Mine, listed on the Toronto Stock Exchange as Temagami Mining Company Ltd. Although its ore was copper, it might as well have been pure gold. The ore was so near the surface it could be simply scraped off the top in an inexpensive open-pit operation. Further, the ore was so pure—up to 34 per cent in some loads—that it could be shipped directly to the smelter, bypassing expensive primary processing. Temagami's number one ore body proved to be the largest body of almost pure chalcopyrite ore ever found in Canada. One of the drill holes assayed out at an incredible 28 per cent copper over a distance of fifty-eight feet. The mine took only six months to be put into operation after the first high-grade deposit was uncovered in 1954. In its first three months of operation, a million dollars of copper ore was scooped out. The revenue was to be the cornerstone of the Keevil empire until the mine closed in 1972.

Like many heads of large corporations, Keevil likes to keep himself above the muck. About the only way to get him agitated is to suggest that he is, or ever was, a promoter. "We don't want to be considered promoters, we're builders," he says with an evil look in his eye. In fact, he's shown a rare hand at promoting by not seeming to. Just before opening Temagami, he brought in a planeload of geologists, investors and brokers from all over Canada to view the mine. A freak of nature had exposed a 150-foot vein of pure copper to the air, so he paid $500 for a tombstone firm from Port Credit to polish the copper until it shone. It was a clear sunny day, and Keevil instructed the pilot to fly in so that the sun reflected off the vein. The visitors were awestruck. Within days, the Temagami stock, which had been languishing at 25 cents, leapt to $9 a share on the TSE.

The rock polishing was a million-dollar inspiration, but the sheer weight of his scientific eminence was Keevil's most effective promotional tool. The 1950s were a time when those who wore lab coats were considered akin to God. Children watched Mr. Wizard perform his experiments on television and hoped for a chemistry set at Christmas. Stock investors were far from immune to this reverence for science. In interview after interview, Keevil reiterated his "scientific minefinding" and his mastery of the new technology. He even went so far as to build his own instruments and a $250,000 laboratory. He subtly sneered at inefficient prospecting and denigrated "pseudo-anomaly hunters." "The geologist used to go to work after the prospector staked the claim," he told the *Financial Post* in 1958. "Now, with geophysical tools, the geologist is the prospector. Scientific precision has taken the place of costly hit and miss. We're going to apply scientific methods to a degree not previously contemplated in this country."

The media responded by playing up the scientific discoveries of the "Professors on Bay Street." "Keevil when he first came to Bay Street was a scientist competing in what was then very much a seat-of-the pants business—mining promotion and exploration," said the *Financial Post* in 1964. "Keevil has a string of scientific achievements that awed veterans of mining exploration who depended on getting a 'location bet'—nuzzling up close as possible to a discovery." Before long, Keevil had a loyal following of investors who believed that he had the key to the pot of gold, and his following eliminated the need for grosser forms of promotion. The rest of the junior mining community was thoroughly cowed, and somewhat resentful. Here was a scientist messing around in their world and doing it better than they did. Keevil seemed to have an unfair advantage.

Not only did Temagami become the basis of the Keevil empire but it also was the beginning of Keevil's persistent reputation for sharp dealing. In 1957, Quebec Metallurgical Industries (QMI), controlled by Ventures Ltd., had an option to purchase 250,000 shares of Temagami at $2. It would have represented a $1-million profit as the shares were trading at $6 immediately prior to the option deadline. But QMI was a day late with their check, and the Temagami lawyers, acting on Keevil's express instructions, refused to accept it. Keevil risked the wrath of the most influential mining man in the country— Thayer Lindsley, a man used to having exceptions made for him as a matter of course. Lindsley is enshrined in mining legend, and there are some remarkable similarities between the development of his own empire, headed by the once-powerful holding company Ventures Ltd., and the evolution of Keevil's Teck Corporation. Lindsley was associated with 185 mines in his lifetime including Sherritt Gordon, Canadian Malarctic, Frobisher and Falconbridge.* In personality, however, the two men couldn't be more different. Lindsley, shy and almost paranoid about publicity, was known to leave dinners where he was the guest of honour before the meal was served. He would spend hours talking magazines out of running stories about him.

"Some people may think that we were trying to be sharp, but the

*Lindsley purchased some Falconbridge claims that had once been held by Thomas Edison. In 1962, Falconbridge absorbed Ventures.

company acted on the best legal advice," Keevil explains. "If somebody was so negligent in my organization, he wouldn't last twenty-four hours. I still think that it is ridiculous to suggest that a transaction of such magnitude could be forgotten. The Ventures group had my full sympathy, but I couldn't have acted any other way without betraying the trust of Temagami shareholders." Keevil himself was the primary shareholder.

A portion of the Keevils' still somewhat unsavoury reputation is based on pure jealousy. The reputation doesn't really bother father or son, but they like to put the criticisms in perspective. "We both have a reputation for being fairly aggressive. I prefer to say opportunistic," suggests Keevil Jr. blandly. More than anything, the Keevils' image has to do with stunningly swift decision making and surgically precise methods of implementing those decisions—both are a result of their academic training. "As a scientist or engineer you get trained to a certain logical thought process," says Keevil Jr. "Any businessman must have it, but in science, the training starts from day one." Keevil Sr. recognizes that there is a brutality in applying scientific methods to the comparatively sentimental business world, but defends it vigorously. "When it comes to business, you must be 100 per cent businesslike. In private life you can accommodate people to your heart's desire."

By 1957 Keevil's net worth was approximately $1 million. With that in the kitty, he began his empire building, fitting one piece into another like a giant equation and disposing of those that destroyed the symmetry. Right from the beginning he intended to build a major mining company, but he wanted to do it without going the public financing route. Although he was to control over a hundred junior mining companies at one time or another, and boasts of having taken "twenty-six companies off the TSE," Keevil avoided the underwriting process until 1982. Then, he did it because he wanted to, not because he needed to.

Keevil's plan was to raise money for further expansion by purchasing or merging with companies that had liquid assets. The first step was the purchase of Goldfields Uranium in August 1957 for $540,000. Keevil then sold the shares of New Hosco Mines, a junior company held by Goldfields, for $1 million. In November 1957 he bought 23 per cent of Pickle Crow, a producing gold mine, for $704,000 and Consolidated Howey for $1.3 million. In addition to shares in Lamaque, Teck-Hughes* and other mines, Consolidated owned an additional $4 million in marketable securities. By 1960, Keevil had parlayed his $1 million into control of companies with $32 million in assets and, most importantly, $26 million in working capital.

In 1960, after several false starts, Teck bought Canadian Devonian Petroleum for $7.7 million. At the other end of the trade was Roy Jodrey, the enigmatic and publicity-shy multimillionaire from Hantsport, Nova Scotia. Jodrey, always reluctant to sell any company he owned, had been approached numerous times about his oil interests. A chance encounter at the Toronto airport was all that Keevil needed. Jodrey was upset because all the flights to Nova Scotia were booked. When Keevil used a contact at Air Canada to free up a seat, Jodrey was extremely grateful. Sensing an opportunity, Keevil accompanied Jodrey on the flight and cracked the deal over drinks.

Devonian's appeal lay in the revenue generated by the two hundred producing wells it owned in Saskatchewan's Steelman oil field. (It was to be a critical acquisition. By 1976 Teck's oil and gas profit, generated primarily from the Steelman field, was $5.1 million annually; in comparison, profits from mining were only $4.2 million.) In 1963, Keevil moved most of their assorted assets into Teck Corporation, using Devonian as the vehicle.

Acquisition followed acquisition, and by 1970 Teck had nearly a hundred companies in its stable, including some producing mines, oil and gas wells and a glut of potential mines. "We were aiming at building up a portfolio of mining properties that we could bring into production over a period of eight years or so," explains Keevil Jr. After the Windfall scandal, the junior mining market dried up in Ontario, and Teck found that more and more of its business was in Vancouver. As well, the majority of the new mines and Teck's new properties were in the West. In 1972, after years of shuttling back and forth, Teck moved its headquarters from Toronto to Vancouver. "I came here in August 1972, and if it had been a month later I probably wouldn't have, because Barrett† got in," says Keevil Sr.

The year Teck moved west was the same year that Keevil's impatience again got the better of him. His target was Afton Mines, a potentially rich copper property. Chester Millar, a local prospector,

had uncovered Afton and stubbornly wanted to bring it into production himself, even though he knew in his heart that he couldn't
raise the $90 million needed. Placer Development wanted Afton, and
so did the Keevils. "They were impossible," says Keevil Sr. of Millar
and his partners. "They'd make a deal one day and say that they were
going to meet for breakfast and they wouldn't show up. They did that
two or three times. They just couldn't make up their minds what kind
of deal they wanted to make." Fed up with the delays, the Keevils
started secretly buying Afton stock, which was listed on the VSE.
They acquired 51 per cent in a five-day blitz that still has local brokers
shaking their heads. "Only two people in the firm [Burns Bros. of
Toronto] knew what was going on," Keevil says. "The president,
Latham [Burns], and the guy who was doing the buying. He would buy
the stock till it hit thirteen [dollars] and then pull out of the market
for a few hours until it dropped to nine. The second time around, all
those who hadn't sold the first time were anxious to sell." In less than
a week the Keevils had bought the controlling block, 1.3 million
shares, for $15 million.

After their move to Vancouver, the Keevils began consolidating.
By 1975 they had reduced their mazelike holdings to thirty companies
and embarked on one of the most remarkable decades in Canadian
mining history. In ten years, they brought seven mines into production.* It was a daring expansion program, and it nearly backfired.
By 1981, when the recession began to gnaw away at the Canadian
economy, Teck was seriously overextended. That year the company
had a long-term debt of $178.5 million against shareholder equity of
only $196.7 million. As well, the Highmont mine was coming on line
at a cost of $150 million, and world copper and molybdenum prices
were collapsing. The combination could have been disastrous, but
David Thompson, Teck's vice-president of finance, devised a strategy
that not only solved Teck's recession-related problems but left it far
stronger in the long run. He began selling off Teck's excess bits and
pieces. What was particularly remarkable was Thompson's ability to
get top dollar for just about everything. Teck had paid only $30.8 mil-
lion for its share of Coseka Resources, an oil and gas company that it
sold for $85 million. Teck also began selling portions of producing

---

*Newfoundland Zinc (1975), Niobec—niobium (1976), Afton—copper-gold (1976), Yukon
Consolidated—placer gold (1978), Highmont—copper-molybdenum (1980), Bullmoose—coal
(1983), Hemlo, David Bell Mine—gold (1985).

properties: 10 percent of Bullmoose went to the Japanese for $8 million, and another 39 per cent to Lornex for the equivalent of $135 million. Metallgesellschaft, a German conglomerate, bought 20 per cent of Highmont for $50 million, and the Kuwait Investment Office later bought 29 per cent of it, also for $50 million.

Certainly Thompson's finest coup was his 1983 sale of 32 per cent of Teck's Canadian oil reserves, 40 per cent of its gas reserves and the bulk of its exploration properties to Trilogy Resources Corporation, a Calgary-based firm. In return, Teck received $24 million cash and control of Trilogy through 5 million common shares and 1.1 million convertible shares. (Teck's book value for its position in Trilogy in 1985 was $10.6 million.) It was a beautiful deal: Trilogy assumed a large piece of Teck's debt, yet Teck still controlled Trilogy and would participate in whatever strikes it made. What's more, Teck retained its most valuable producing properties in Saskatchewan and in the Bantry area of Alberta, properties that account for two-thirds of the company's oil and gas revenue. "We kept the best production but we sold the rest of it and we still control the company," says Keevil Sr. almost chortling.

Despite Thompson's heroics, Teck had its first-ever loss in 1982. "I think that's how I became president," Keevil Jr. observes, not entirely in jest. "I was made president in November 1981, and I suspect my father had an inkling we were going to have our first loss. Anyway, it was a great baptism." The first time the younger Keevil sat in for his father had been back in the 1960s, and he had a missile thrown at him for his troubles. An eccentric lady had purchased some Copperfields shares, which had subsequently gone down in price. She blamed the older Keevil personally for the drop and started attending annual meetings, harassing Keevil and writing letters of complaint to various heads of state, including Nikita Khrushchev and Harold Macmillan. She presented such a problem that Teck routinely assigned two employees to sit on either side of her during meetings, but nothing really happened until the year Norman Jr. chaired the meeting for his father. "The year before she said, 'Oh, you're such a nice young fellow. How can you have a rotten father like that?' So I figure she likes me. I'm OK. I don't have to have the guys sitting beside her. She reached into her purse and took out a piece of cement, the size of your fist, and threw it at me. I ducked, and it hit my lawyer instead." When asked about the incident later, Keevil shrugged and got off one of the best lines in the history of Canadian business: "That's what lawyers are for."

Keevil Jr. survived the rock and he survived the loss. By 1983 the debt had been pared to $100 million, and Teck was well on its way to recovery.

One of the most amazing aspects of the Keevils' evolution into a major power in the Canadian mining industry is that they have managed to retain most of the stripped-down characteristics of a small company. Far from adopting the slow-moving bureaucracy that typifies a major corporation, the Keevils go out of their way to maintain a lean and flexible organization. They do all their own public relations work, including designing and writing annual reports, writing press releases and making media contacts. Keevil Sr. is very proud of having designed the company logo. Teck's frugality extends even into their senior corporate offices, which are surely the ugliest in Canada. The top floor of Teck, accessible by staircase, houses only the Drs. Junior and Senior and their two secretaries. It's an older building with an intimate, unobstructed view of Stanley Park in Vancouver, but not even the panorama can atone for the execrable decorating job. The furniture is reproduction antique, and the carpet is a mind-snapping field of diagonal brown-and-white blocks that contrasts jarringly with the flowered wallpaper.

Despite their background in science, an area fond of fat, windy reports, the Keevils deliberately keep the paperwork to a minimum. Norm Jr. leans over his desk and points to an unassuming pile of paper. It represents Project Sow's Ear. "That's because I'm not sure that even we can turn this particular sow's ear into a silk purse," he says modestly. The pile contains two reports. One is the evaluation of a proposed takeover, the other an action plan. Each is only five pages long. Together they represent a half-billion-dollar acquisition. The research for Teck's 1986 takeover of Cominco was of similar length.

Although the Keevils bridle at being called promoters themselves, they don't hesitate to get together with Vancouver mining promoters —the kind of people who make the eastern companies shudder. "Pick any of the big companies that have been there a long, long time," says Keevil Jr. "The manager has worked in that company and built himself up to be VP of exploration or something. [He's] spent twenty-five years or so working for Bigco. You develop a certain mentality, maybe a little bit of envy for these guys who are Johnny-come-lately on the street. We started from scratch ourselves."

The result of those unions have been two of Teck's biggest and most profitable deals. In 1981 Norman Jr. signed a deal with International Corona, then controlled by Murray Pezim, that eventually resulted in Teck owning 55 per cent of the Teck-Corona gold mine in Hemlo, Ontario. As a nice bonus, Teck also got 50 per cent of the Williams mine awarded to Corona in March 1986 by the Ontario Supreme Court. In 1983, Teck invested $1.5 million in Bruce McDonald's Golden Knight Resources Ltd. for $1.5 million. Since then, Teck has become Golden Knight's largest shareholder, owning 40 per cent of Inco's Casa Berardi mine.

Teck has followed the typical Canadian formula of buying out juniors just before the development stage, when most of the risk has been taken out of the venture and the juniors are desperate for money. What distinguishes Teck, aside from their willingness to deal with the juniors, is the Keevils' policy of not annihilating them when they sign a deal. Their 1981 benchmark deal with Murray Pezim to develop the Corona properties at Hemlo is a perfect example—Teck got 55 per cent of the property, and Corona, the junior company, retained 45 per cent. "You've got to remember," says Pezim putting the deal in perspective, "that not too long ago, a good deal was 70-30 and an average deal was 80-20 or 90-10." This evenhandedness is one reason that juniors with hot properties now come to Teck first. "I've got a simple philosophy," Norm Jr. said in a 1986 interview. "I don't mind leaving something on the table, because when you do a deal thinking it will be your last, it probably will be . . . I can think of some, where the corporate culture is such that they seem incapable of doing a deal that doesn't completely grind the other guy into the ground."

Through the years, the Keevils' reputation as fast operators has clung to them like a bad smell.* It persists for two reasons: they are sharp dealers who take every conceivable advantage, and they have not forgotten their junior mining roots. Nor should they: Teck's roots are its operational strength. The memory is fading, however. In 1986

---

*Whatever their reputation, the Keevils have no trouble attracting and keeping top people. David Thompson, vice-president of finance, has become a corporate legend, and Bob Hallbauer, formerly of Placer Development, is generally recognized as the top mine operator in the business. Keevil Sr.'s lab assistant during the war, F. J. Wank, joined him in Temagami, then served through the years as a mine troubleshooter and manager before retiring in 1980. William Bergey, a geology graduate in those days, also joined Keevil at Temagami and stayed.

Teck bought a huge dose of instant respectability with the stunning purchase of controlling interest in Cominco, Canada's fiftieth largest corporation, from Canadian Pacific Ltd. Teck bought 31 per cent of the venerable company, formed in 1895, for $205 million in cash, plus $75 million in promissory notes due over four years. Teck is a 50 per cent owner and operating partner of the consortium that made the purchase. The other partners are Metallgesellschaft AG of West Germany and MIM Holdings Ltd. of Australia, each owning 25 per cent.

Teck, with a $65 million "war chest," had been publicly looking for a major purchase. No one dreamt that the target might be Cominco, a company saddled with a three-quarter-billion-dollar debt. In 1985 the company reported a loss of $92 million on $1.5 billion of sales. "If you can get into long-life, low-cost ore bodies, then that's the name of the game in this business and that's what Cominco has," explains Keevil Jr. Cominco now accounts for 10 per cent of world zinc production. Like all Teck's deals, there is a considerable "upside." Cominco's huge debt has been largely spent on exploration. Development of their rich Red Dog lead-zinc deposit in Alaska and their equally impressive Hellyer zinc-lead-silver deposit in Australia should ensure the company's position for decades. And, no doubt, there will be some sleepers among Cominco's vast stockpile of properties.

Lost in the collective corporate shock over Teck's purchase of Cominco was a little skirmish that preceded the deal. In January 1986, the Keevils were infuriated when Cominco Ltd. and Lornex Mining Corporation announced a $75-million-joint venture plan to enlarge the Valley Copper mine. It meant that ore from the Cominco mine would go to Lornex for processing, bypassing Teck's nearby Highmont mill. Norman Keevil stated that Lornex had "breached" an agreement to negotiate jointly with Teck over such changes. Not even the Keevils could have bought Cominco for the sole purpose of solving such a disagreement. Nonetheless, the swiftness of the acquisition and the sweetness with which Teck announced reopening discussions with Lornex recall the sharp knife and canny mind that Norman Keevil, Sr., used to cut his niche in the world of big-time mining.

CHAPTER 12

Morris Black:
Rude, Crude and Something Else

"I'm here to tell you that Black was the toughest little shit ever walked Bay Street, Howe Street, or any other street where there was money to be made." A LONG-TIME FRIEND AND ASSOCIATE OF MOR-RIS BLACK.

Morris Black was the maestro of Canadian stock promotion. During the 1950s, 1960s and 1970s, he converted the empty husks of junior mining companies, first on the TSE and then on the VSE, into seductive properties with little more than a wave of his hand. He combined the roles of broker, promoter and even prospector with a life and colour that makes the far better known Murray Pezim seem like a cardboard cutout by comparison. Nearly everyone who has ever met or even heard of Morris Black has a favourite story about his astounding vulgarity, his penchant for mixing up and mispronouncing the simplest names or about the superstition that governed his life. Other less told stories relate to his clever deal making, his trustworthiness and his quiet generosity.

Everyone has a Morris Black story, but no one really knew the man—not even his children. He treated his life like a jigsaw puzzle, giving friends, acquaintances and family a few pieces to look at, but no one had the full picture. As the Morris Black stories indicate, he was a mass of contradictions. He was clearly a vulgar-mouthed, unattractive and superstitious man. Yet he was a stock salesman par excellence, with an intuitive grasp of the greed that motivates the market. He was also one of the cleverest and most capable stock manipulators who ever lived. Black was poorly educated and semiliterate, yet he astonished people with his ability to absorb pages of figures, melting them down to their essence then cracking a deal wholly to his advantage. He had a large following of brokers and investors whose faith in him was almost religious. They called him predictable, dependable and honourable. "No insider ever lost putting money on Morris Black," says one long-time follower. But Black was involved in a number of blatant stock market swindles, and aside from Viola MacMillan, is certainly the best-known Canadian stock promoter to serve a jail term.

The ultimate irony of Morris Black's life was his role in the development of Endako Mines, at one time the second-largest producer of molybdenum in the western world. He loved the grimy world of penny stocks, where the game was to beguile investors with hopes and promises, never leaving them too poor to prevent them from coming back again. When Endako became a mine in June 1965, Black was transformed, almost overnight, into a "mine developer" and a "financier." At that point his paper worth, primarily shares in Placer Development Ltd., was estimated to be $30 million. He could have retired. But nothing is more unsatisfying to a dream merchant like Black than having a dream come true. He returned to his world of hustling and deal making and, eventually, he lost it all.

Black looked like a five-foot caricature of Aristotle Onassis, for whom he was sometimes mistaken: short, stout, jowly, balding and beak-nosed. But when he walked into a room, his presence overshadowed the more glamorous and famous. Born in 1906 to poor Jewish immigrants, Black was one of four sons. He had almost no formal schooling and to the day he died was barely literate. As a young boy, he sold newspapers on Toronto's Bay Street where he loved to hear romantic stories of the fabled mining camps and mining men of the 1920s—copper at Noranda, gold at Kirkland Lake and silver at Cobalt. Black was so captivated by the stories that he took to the bush, first as a miner and then as a prospector. Unlike most modern promoters, Black had mining in his blood. "I remember seeing this old guy [Black] climb the hills," says Vancouver promoter Larry Kostiak, who recalls seeing Black out in the bush many times. "It was a one-to two-day walk up to the tree line, but he did it. He probably combed the Brenda area better than most people." In the mid-1960s, the Brenda property in the Okanagan was the site of a staking rush when a huge body of low-grade copper and molybdenum was discovered. Noranda and the Japanese Nippon Mining Company put Brenda into production.

Black staked his first claim in 1928 in northern Quebec, after spending months in mining camps where he couldn't talk to anyone because he spoke no French. He prospected on and off for twenty years, never finding much of anything. When he ran out of money he would build up a grubstake by turning his hand to other things including boxing, tool and die making and operating a night club. "He was rough, tough," says his friend Peter Brown. "[He] came up through the route of gambling, almost loan sharking. He got into the investment business because he'd financed prospectors and foreclosed on a couple of shells to pay the loans. He had to promote the shells to make them worthwhile." Forced into an unaccustomed role, Black quickly realized that promoting was a more comfortable and lucrative profession than prospecting, and by the early 1950s he was promoting shells full time. Still, it wasn't until he met Sam Ciglen that he got his first glimpse of the big time. Ciglen was a Toronto lawyer who, in the late 1950s, had a remarkable presence in the junior mining market. It's now estimated that more than half of the eight hundred mining companies then trading on the TSE counted Ciglen as either an owner, shareholder or company lawyer.

The chemistry between Ciglen, the cunning, well-educated, well-connected lawyer and Black, the crafty, street-smart promoter, produced a series of stock deals. But it was the infamous Sweet Grass promotion of 1957 that first brought Black to public prominence. There were actually two companies involved, Great Sweet Grass Oils Ltd. and Kroy Oils Ltd., both controlled by Black and Ciglen and listed on the American Stock Exchange. Sweet Grass was a beautifully orchestrated promotion, done with the kind of panache and innovative flair that makes deal makers today sigh with admiration.

A key element of the promotion was chanced upon while Black and Ciglen were in New York recruiting phone men and briefing tout sheet writers. (Black's associates insist that he would always pay top dollar to hire the most prominent newspaper financial writers to write his tout sheets. And, if one of Black's stocks should be favourably mentioned in the writers' columns, that was a nice bonus.) Black was already priming the market, using forty-six different accounts to buy and sell the shares. One evening they had dinner at a Manhattan restaurant, and Black discovered that the waiter's last name was Rothschild. Vastly amused over the idea of a Rothschild waiting on his table, Black had an inspiration. He, Ciglen and the waiter formed an investment company called F. J. Rothschild & Company, then opened a tiny office on Park Avenue, across the street from the moneyed Rothschilds. Impressive letterhead was printed up, and Black started a phone blitz, something he did better than almost anyone. The phone crews, working in shifts, heavily emphasized their bogus Rothschild connection to sell the Kroy and Sweet Grass stock all across the U.S. and Canada. Doubters were usually hooked when they received the followup literature bearing the famed name and address.

At the height of the Sweet Grass promotion, Black and Ciglen were netting $1 million a week. Their run ended when the U.S. Securities and Exchange Commission delisted the stocks in April 1957. Four years later, the SEC charged Black and Ciglen with defrauding the American public of over $15 million through Sweet Grass. Also in 1961, the RCMP charged Black and Ciglen with evading income tax on $8 million in market profits from the same promotion. The case dragged on for six years, culminating in the longest income tax trial in Canadian history, 115 days. At the end of it, in 1967, Judge William Rogers tersely acquitted the pair.

Sweet Grass and Kroy gave Black a stage for his consummate and irresistible salesmanship. "Morris was always laughing," says John Black (no relation), a Vancouver accountant who kept the books for Black's companies. "He'd stop you in the street and sell you stock. He'd take the money right out of your pocket if he had to. He'd sell you so well, it would make your day." But Black had one major flaw. He was so adept at manipulation that he could never believe that the promotion was over when the public or circumstances turned against his stock. In 1957 he was worth a fortune, between $4 and $8 million depending on which court case you read, but he lost it in a hurry. Although the SEC had halted Sweet Grass from trading, the securities rules at the time allowed a stock to trade on the over-the-counter market after it had been suspended on an exchange. Sweet Grass opened at $5 over the counter. Black immediately ordered a purchase of 100,000 shares to support the price, but his purchase didn't stem the heavy selling, so he ordered another buy of 100,000 shares. Within twenty minutes the stock had bottomed out at 10 cents, and Black had flushed away $1 million.

Black was still rich. He had his Toronto mansion in Forest Hills and his summer home on Lake Simcoe. But between 1957 and 1960, the money dribbled away as Black plunged into one promotion after another, coming out of each with less than he started. By 1960, Black had lost his Forest Hills home, the phone company had cut him off and his wife Rita even had difficulty feeding their four children, Alana, K. C., Mark and Jeffrey. "We moved to our summer home on Lake Simcoe," recalls Jeffrey Black, who was four at the time. "We lived there for several years, but I had no idea why." The same year, the Ontario Securities Commission and the TSE, aware of the American and Canadian investigations, blackballed him, letting it be known that they were going to walk with heavy boots over any deal associated with Morris Black.

Sam Ciglen saved Black from penury. In 1961 he phoned mining engineer Andy Robertson in Vancouver and asked him to bring Black west. Knowing that Robertson needed financing for some mining property he was working on, Ciglen framed the request so it appeared that Black, with his selling skills, would be indispensable to Robertson. "I paid his telephone bill, gave his wife money to buy food, paid his way out to Vancouver and paid his phone bill here," says Robertson.

The development of Robertson's property is a classic serendipitous mining tale. Located west of Fraser Lake in British Columbia, it first attracted attention in 1927 when Charles H. Foote and Alfred Langdon stumbled across a richly mineralized area while stalking a deer. They staked twenty-six claims and prospected the site on and off for thirty-two years, even sinking, with a pick and a shovel, a twenty-seven-foot shaft that led them to a rich twenty-four-inch vein of quartz molybdenite. But molybdenum was almost as cheap as sand, and no one was willing to put up money to find it, much less mine it. Finally, after nurturing the area for three decades, they gave up.

That year, Dr. Christopher Riley, a Vancouver mining engineer, hired Foote's son to guide him to a nearby property that showed signs of uranium. When Riley examined the yellow oxide, he found it was molybdenum, not uranium. Foote perked up immediately and dragged Riley over to the other side of the mountain where his father's claims were languishing. Riley optioned and then took over the claims. One day he happened to be in the B.C. Chamber of Mines in Vancouver doing some research. Peering over the shoulder of the man next to him, Riley noticed he too was researching a molybdenum property. The man was Andy Robertson, one of the most astute mine managers in the country. Riley pestered Robertson for a week until he agreed to fly to Prince George and take a look.

"I did some surface work, but Riley wouldn't let me put a drill on it," says Robertson. "He said if I didn't find anything he wouldn't be able to sell it to anyone else." Robertson, excited by what he found from scratching the surface, convinced Riley to sell him the claims for $15,000. "I put a drill on it in May 1960, and after the first drill hole I knew I had a big mine." Robertson spent another $67,000, which he'd raised privately, to drill ten holes and prove up the area.

By this time Black was in Vancouver, and the two of them formed Endako Mines Ltd., which paid Robertson 750,000 escrowed shares for his property. It is here that the legend and reality of Morris Black separate and become muddy. Bernie Nayman, Black's personal accountant in Vancouver, maintains that the promoter also owned some claims surrounding Endako and that he showed his usual flair for deal making by selling them to Endako for $100,000, which he took in the form of one million Endako shares.

Robertson calls the story "eyewash." He says he gave Black the one million shares to sell privately through several of his companies. (Black never bought or sold in his own name, but always in the name of companies like Key Trading, Fleet Trading and Bayshore Investments.) Black was to give him $100,000 when the shares were sold. "He kept the million [shares] and he never gave me the $100,000," complains Robertson. "It was no good trying to take a lawsuit out on him. It would be like trying to fight a shadow." It is impossible to sort out the facts because the VSE has virtually no documents prior to 1965, and what they have between 1965 and 1975 is scanty at best.

Certainly Black did end up with at least one million Endako shares, whatever the source, and he was responsible for raising the money, through private placements of Endako stock, to drill the property. Just days after Endako was listed on the VSE in 1963, Placer Development Ltd. phoned Robertson and Black and made a deal to take over Endako. The agreement was heralded as one of the simplest and neatest buyouts in mining history. Placer was to get 60 per cent of Endako in return for building a 10,000-ton-per-day, $20-million mill. If the plant cost more than $20 million, Placer's share would rise to 70 per cent. But Robertson believes that he and Black were taken. "They made darn sure it cost more than $20 million," he growls.

Molybdenum became the metal of the 1960s. Extracted from molybdenite ore, its primary use was as an alloy in the steel industry. It was scarce, and more than 60 per cent of the western world's production came from one source, the Climax Mine in Colorado owned by American Metal Climax Inc. In the early 1960s, producers could only get $1.67 a pound for the ore, but by 1965 the spot price was up as high as $22 and the bulk price $14. Endako stock, which was selling at $5 in 1963, hit $17 in 1965; and when the Endako shares that Placer hadn't already purchased were eventually traded for Placer stock, the price reached $45. Black could not pronounce the name of the metal that made him his second fortune, but any effort to correct him was met with: "[I] couldn't give a shit how you pronounce it. It makes money and sells."

Robertson and Black crossed swords once again when Robertson found a solid little mine, called Horn Silver, in the southern Okanagan. Although angry at Black, Robertson again turned to him for fund-raising help. Black vended the property into one of his shells called Utica Mines Ltd., and Robertson thought he had come up with a perfect ploy to keep the promoter under control. Black's shares in Utica were the escrowed vendor's shares, so he couldn't do a thing with them until some work was done on the property and the superintendent of brokers released them for sale. Robertson's Utica shares were held in trust for him by a Vancouver trust company, but were fully tradable. Somehow, Black was able to surreptitiously trade his escrowed shares for the tradable stock without Robertson's knowledge. Black got to work promoting, and by 1964 the price of Utica had eased up to $2.35. That year it traded 10 million shares, the third-highest volume on the vse.

In the years between 1965 and 1972, the Black legend swelled to monstrous proportions. He was toasted, feted and honoured by the same community that had tsk-tsked when he had come west. Admired or derided, he fascinated people with his coarseness. Eating, in particular, seemed to bring out the beast in Black. Disdaining knives and forks, he would often dig into his food with his bare hands, talking all the time—or rather, bellowing at the top of his lungs—spewing out words and stray bits of the hamburgers, hot dogs and steaks he preferred. "He had an awful mouth, vulgar," remembers George Cross. "[He] makes Pezim look like a choirboy. Morris used to live in the

Bayshore. You didn't dare go near there for fear that he'd catch you and drag you in for dinner and embarrass the hell out of you." When friends ate with Black, they manoeuvred to get a seat facing the window or the wall so their backs would be towards the other tables. The Hotel Vancouver, where Black lived for four years, always provided him with a pad and paper in the dining room, but he scribbled on the linen anyway.

Black's speech was so salty that reporter George McBurnie credited him with "peeling the paint in the back rooms of every financial street in the country." John Black once bought him a dictaphone so he could dictate his correspondence, but he was never able to hire anyone who was willing to transcribe the tapes.

Morris Black is fondly remembered for what friends call Blackisms, his unique mangling of English. "Butchering the language was too kind a word," says John Black. " He couldn't pronounce most words over one syllable and couldn't remember anyone's name if it wasn't John or Jake." Two Blackisms are recalled with particular fondness. One day he called in an engineer to chew him out for overspending. He told the man that "he sure as hell didn't have cash blanche down in Arizona." On another occasion, Black was having dinner with Ed Scholz, an old friend and then Placer's chief of exploration. Black was commiserating with him because Scholz had expected to be named president of Placer Development but had been passed over. At the table with them was Jack Wasserman, the West's famed columnist. Black thumped his fist on the table and told Scholz the reason he had not made president was because he wasn't "an Anglo Saxmon and a Grasp." Wasserman, well used to Blackisms, snorted his wine all over the table at this new high mark. When he recovered, he tried to explain to Black the error in his pronunciation. "I don't care a fuck," Black shouted in response. "If you're not an Anglo Saxmon and a Grasp, you'll never become president of Placer."

Black called everyone by his or her first name, because he seldom remembered the second. On business trips to Mexico, he would be introduced to various officials with names like Don Miguel and Don José. Thereafter, he would invariably call them all Don despite their polite efforts to inform him that Don was not a name in their country, but an appellation of courtesy. Company names gave Black a lot of trouble too. He solved the problem by giving them all simple names, often associated with something familiar. Bayshore, one of his holding companies, was named after the hotel where he was staying at the time. Black Giant was so named because BG were Bernie Nayman's first two initials.

Black was also extremely superstitious. He would only stay in a hotel room that ended with the number four. If he accidentally knocked a file folder containing a deal off his desk and didn't like the look of the way it fell, he might not work on it again for years. And, during his high-rolling days in Vancouver, prospectors would hang around the lobby of his hotel like backwoods beggars because Black, fearful his luck would run out, would never pass them without stuffing $20 bills into their pockets.

In contrast to his idiosyncrasies, Black's stock promotions were exercises in methodical patience and restraint. He kept only five or six companies in his stable, concentrating his energies on one at a time, using the others as support. Black's stratagem was to control the market utterly when a company was under promotion. Almost every trade found him on the other side of the deal. In addition, when a promotion was running, he either daily called or saw every broker who handled the stock, buying drinks for as many as possible and often having a group up to his room at the end of the day. Black always worked out of his room during the fifteen years he lived in Vancouver. Sometimes he wouldn't get dressed until 4:00 or 5:00 P.M. Once his lawyer called him just after lunch to tell him there was a problem and to come over to the office right away. Black put on his overcoat over his pajamas and hustled down to the astonished lawyer's office. "You told me to get down here right away," said Black in explanation.

Brokers knew they could count on Morris Black. They knew that he would run his market up carefully and that he wasn't too greedy. They knew he'd never blow off his stock right at the top instead of selling $20,000 worth here and there as the stock was rising. When interest waned, he would ride the market down slowly, buying shares back again at successively cheaper prices. Black prided himself on never letting a market collapse—at least not too quickly. When he was asked at the height of the Slocan promotion/manipulation, which earned him his jail sentence, if there was any chance of his "pulling the plug" or withdrawing his support of the market once he had made his profit, he scoffed, "What, and run like a thief? If I was going to do something like that, it would have to be for fucking millions."

In short, Black was trustworthy. Insiders could make money riding his back, knowing that he'd take his bite but it wouldn't be a trencherman's feast. Even the public, usually the least likely group to make money out of any promotion, had a chance. "Morris believed in giving the public a fair shake," says Bernie Nayman. "Not too much of a fair shake, mind you, but something."

Even though Black couldn't pronounce it, he also believed in psychology, the psychology of numbers. He taught Nayman his magic numbers. "If you see a stock laying there at 60 cents for a long time and it goes to 90, then buy because you know it's gonna run. The $2 market is a very important market. If your stock gets stuck at $1.95 you know you're in trouble." In 1963, when Endako stock was starting to climb on the VSE, Morris flew to the Bahamas for a holiday at his favourite Nassau Beach hotel. He left strict instructions to his trading crew in Vancouver not to let the stock get above $5. He feared that if the stock topped $5 he'd never be able to hold it down to a steady increase. For three weeks demand kept escalating, and the stock hit $4.50 and went on past $5. Black, in a fury, was on the phone from Nassau almost daily, screaming at his traders to keep selling to hold the stock down. He wasn't afraid of making too much money but rather of losing it all if the market crashed and he was forced to step in and start buying to support it. "He knew that stock that goes up fast will come down even faster," says Nayman. "He never wanted to have the market run ahead of the news." Black was also loathe to attract the attention of the authorities. Markets that danced up and skidded down tended to provoke unwelcome observation by the media and the regulators.

When Endako was merged into Placer and its stock exchanged two-for-one, Black owned half a million Placer shares. His dividend income alone in 1968 was over $1.2 million, and his net worth was estimated at $30 million. "I told him to go home and enjoy life, but he wouldn't go," says Nayman. "I would see him in his hotel room, and he would be crying, 'I can't go home, I've got all this and I've got no one.' He couldn't go home because he couldn't spend five minutes with his wife and they'd be screaming their heads off at each other.'

Black was hardly an orthodox Jew, but he held firmly to some religious tenets and regarded marriage as a sacred trust. Despite the well-known rancour between him and his wife, Rita, he would never consider divorce. He chose, instead, to live almost the entire year in Vancouver hotel rooms. Black returned to Toronto for religious holidays and special occasions but from 1961 on Vancouver was really his home. "My mother used to go out every once in a while and hated the rain," says Jeffrey Black. "I don't think my dad wanted us there. He wanted to do his business and then come back home."

None of the Black's four children really knew or understood what their father did for a living until they became adults. "Dad never discussed business with us," remembers his daughter K. C. "Every year when I had to fill out 'What does your father do?' on my school forms, it was a real problem. I had to keep asking him because I didn't know. One year he would tell me financier, and the next promoter." To his long-distance children, his short, thick presence was always a powerful influence, even in absentia. "He was always a larger-than-life figure to us," recalls K. C. "We had some good screaming matches, but you certainly knew where you stood with him."

Although Black thought nothing of manipulating (he called it "supporting") a market, he was a curiously ethical man. It was a point of pride with him that he made his money trading stock, not living off the company treasury, which he considered to be stealing. Black never took a commission on a sale, preferring to put the money directly back into the company. Nor would he ever charge his hotel or food bills against the company. "We told him that it was legitimate," says John Black, "but he didn't think it was right." Had Black been a complete rogue, his children would be far richer today. By the late 1960s, he had accumulated an $8 million trust fund for his four children. Black, who was one of the first promoters to systematically tap the European market, had salesmen in Germany flogging a variety of VSE stocks. One salesman was selling one of them at ten times its listed value. Jeffrey Black remembers his father getting an angry phone call late one night from a German securities official, who told Black that there was going to be a terrible scandal over his man's activities. Black could have walked away, and it's doubtful that any extraditable action would have been taken. Instead, he wiped out his children's trust fund to buy back all the stock.

After Endako and Utica, Black restlessly searched around for a new challenge. Between promotions he had very little to do to occupy himself, so he spent a lot of time just hanging around, talking and making something of a nuisance of himself. Peter Brown devised a unique method of getting rid of him. Although Black could read better than he let on, Brown knew he had great difficulty deciphering wordy legal documents. When Morris dropped by, Brown would end the visit by hauling out a prospectus and asking him for his professional opinion. Black, unwilling to display his ignorance, would disappear for a couple of days, presumably to have someone read it to him, and come back with his verdict.

In 1971 Black took control of Slocan-Ottawa Mines (later renamed Slocan Development) when the stock was trading for a few cents. Officially, he bought 1.2 million of the 2.3 million shares outstanding, but it is certain he owned a considerable portion of the remaining shares through nominees. Black's cost for Slocan was no more than $150,000. The company owned a small silver mine that produced "a bag of dimes in profit whenever the silver price was right," according to one newspaper report. The VSE mining market was depressed and became more so as the NDP government moved in and slapped a mineral royalty tax on mining profits. Black, unable to sit still even in a bad market, and perhaps believing the press reports that described him as a "developer" and "financier," used Slocan to become an entrepreneur. He explored a raft of oddball investments of the sort still called "industrial deals" on the VSE. The first was Fantastic Fudge, endowed with a miracle "plastic milk" ingredient that gave it an indefinite shelf life. Black, who didn't know how to manage a mining company much less an industrial, couldn't figure out how to adapt the bulky dispensing machines to the corner stores where they wanted to sell it. The 34,000 pounds of fudge, as fresh as the day it was made, sat in a Vancouver warehouse until it was sold in 1977 to a Seattle salvage broker for cattle feed.

Next came Banish, an antihangover pill. When the government objected to the medical implications of calling it an antihangover pill, the name was changed to Trixx and it was sold as an antiflatulent. No one knows what happened to the million pills stored in a Toronto garage. In fast succession came Kleen-Air (a deodorizer), polyurethane foam furniture and a movie about the stock market, *Another Smith for Paradise*, which was shown to poor reviews at the Cannes Film Festival. Black also investigated a ski resort/hotel purchase, the importation of wafer-thin roll-on metal roofing from Australia and a slot machine that dispensed lottery tickets. All were commercial failures, but the carefully timed announcement of each helped to boost Slocan Development's price during 1972. It was one of the happiest periods of Black's life, and he thoroughly enjoyed playing with his industrial ideas.

In 1975 Black became one of the few stock promoters, East or West, ever to go to prison. In October, he pleaded guilty in a Toronto court to thirty-four counts of wash trading in Slocan, then listed on the VSE and MSE. Black used to refer to wash trading as "Jewish budgeting." It is one of the most nebulous, most common and most difficult to prove stock market infractions. The term refers to the practice of buying and selling to yourself and not to the public at large, thus giving the false impression of activity in a stock. Black was a master at it, but he was far from alone. Stripped of the technique, many speculative companies, then and now, would remain rooted in the nickel and dime range. Wash trading is excruciatingly difficult to prove because promoters use nominee accounts to disguise their activities. Nominee accounts—trading accounts in the name of friends, relatives, fictitious people or companies—are the vehicles used to buy and sell stock.

With five companies as the buyers and sellers of record, Black manipulated the price of Slocan until by the end of the 1971 it had climbed from pennies to $2.90 per share. The charges of wash trading were focussed on the period from April to May 1972, when the stock rose from $1.15 to $1.40. (It is a common police tactic to simplify prosecutions by confining charges to a relatively narrow time period.) Trading reports for April show Black's typical market-making pattern. One of his companies, Fleet Trading Ltd., bought a total of 200,000 Slocan shares and sold 202,000 shares. Another Black company, Key Trading Ltd., bought 380,400 shares of Slocan and sold 337,000. Essentially, the shares were just moving between companies.

Black claimed to have lost $2.5 million in the promotion, citing, as proof, the fact that he officially owned more stock—1.8 million of 2.3 million outstanding—at the end of the promotion than at the beginning. "I bought it all back, knowing it was no good; I didn't steal it," he said at the time. Newspaper reporters swallowed his explanation whole. But, at the end of a successful stock manipulation, a "good" promoter always tries to buy his stock back on the way down. That way, a total crash of the share price is avoided, and the promoter still controls the company for use again, with a name change. The fact that Black ended up with most of Slocan's shares wasn't evidence of innocence, but a clear indication of the end of a successful promotion. Black would have had to buy virtually all his shares at the peak of the market to have lost anywhere near his claimed $2.5 million. "My heart was in it, but not my head," Black mournfully told the press during the trial. "Slocan was my first big loser. I was a novice."

At the trial, Judge William Rogers, the same one who had acquitted him of tax evasion, wasn't having anything to do with Black's touching tale of naiveté. "There seems to be a penchant for nostalgia in this case," he said during his presentence summation. "I think it would be appropriate to say to Mr. Black, 'Hail and Farewell.' I think there must be a legion of stockbrokers and accountants and lawyers who are indebted to you for keeping them in business for years. Hopefully this is the end of an era. In this case, I think the Mounties have got their man. Only the greedy have been involved." Rogers sentenced Black to six months in jail and levied a $50,000 fine. When he heard the sentence, Black stood up and left the court without turning to face his friends in the gallery. He simply raised his hand in a backward farewell. Just before he was banished to Beaver Creek Correctional Institute in northern Ontario, he offered an insight into his market philosophy to a Vancouver writer: "Promoters in Vancouver are in this business to make $50,000 to $100,000, I'm in it to make $15 to $20 million."

The embarrassment and shame of his arrest deflated Black for the first time in his life. "There wasn't any bitterness," recalls his daughter K. C. Black. "But he said to me, 'I have just given up.' " At the age of seventy-two, Morris Black went to jail. He served four months in a minimum-security prison. "He was able to come home some weekends," says K. C., "and I used to ask him how he was, and he would say, 'I'm fine, I'm fine. I'm trading—pants for cigarettes, books for food.' " Black, a three- or four-pack-a-day smoker, quit cold. He used his $1.90 a day spending money and his trading savvy to corner the prison cigarette market and emerged from prison with a huge box of cigarettes. He was just as proud of this trading feat as he was of his stock market accomplishments.

When Black was released in 1976 he had regained his spirit but had lost his obsession with the market. He dabbled with his companies but never again became interested in a major project or promotion. In 1978 he was diagnosed as having intestinal cancer and on September 10, 1979, he died. Black's estate was smaller than one might have expected. His Placer shares were long gone, and the main tangible asset was the $2.5-million Forest Hills mansion he'd bought with some of his Endako fortune. He still had substantial stock holdings, but his key companies had lain dormant while he was dying and there was little real value in them. Without Black's sure hands, they were just so many empty shells.

Rita, Black's widow, still lives in the Forest Hills palace. An utter contrast to her squat husband, she was a beautiful, head-turning blonde as a young woman. Even today her face and body seem to belong to a much younger woman. Of their three children, K. C. understood and got along better with her father than the others. Precocious and smart, she wanted to become a promoter, but Black refused to let her inside his empire. He believed it was the wrong sort of life for a girl. Still, K. C. persisted, and today she is a vice-president with Merrill Lynch in Toronto.

Judge Rogers was right. When Morris Black left the stock market, it was truly the end of an era. He was the last, and by far the most successful, of the old-style promoters. He was hard, tough and remorseless when it came to getting the best of a deal, and he had little compunction about bending VSE rules into pretzels. But he cared for his markets with a passion that was personal. They were alive for him, not just empty numbers.

CHAPTER 13

Murray Pezim:
Making and Losing It,
Making and Losing It

"The thing you have to ask yourself about Murray Pezim is, has he done more good than bad? I don't know the answer." A LONG-TIME FRIEND AND ASSOCIATE sizing up Murray Pezim's career.

Murray Pezim personifies the best and the worst of the Vancouver Stock Exchange. During a thirty-seven-year career that began on the TSE, he has promoted more than five hundred companies and personally generated billions of dollars in trading. The cockamamie ideas and companies Pezim has promoted read like a Canada Council grant list from the 1960s: Vita Pez rejuvenation pills, Minnie Pearl of Canada Ltd. (a fast-food chicken franchise that lost him $850,000), the Pez chocolate bars, a three-wheeled Pezmobile called the Rascal, monogrammed Pez apples, The Pez Brand B.C. Salmon and Chateau Pez (a $40-million hotel and golf course to be built outside Victoria, designed to make the exclusive La Costa health club "look like a peanut stand"). Yet, he has been integral to the exploration and financing of such important resource properties as Stampede Oil's piece of the Strachan-Ricinus gas field and Hemlo, one of the largest gold discoveries in Canada.

Pezim has made and lost several fortunes, and along the way has lined the pockets of brokers, other promoters and occasionally a few investors. The brokerage commissions on his trades routinely run to several million dollars a year and, depending on whom you believe, account for between 15 and 20 per cent of the VSE's total volume. He has also left behind him more shattered and burned-out wrecks of companies than George Patton did tanks on his pell-mell rush to beat the Soviets to Berlin.

Pezim has been called everything from a crook to the Jewish Howard Hughes. He is alternately adored and vilified by the Vancouver brokerage community, half of which calls him "sweetheart" while the other half says, "He's so hot he should be wearing an asbestos suit." The media commonly portray Pezim as a genial gnome with a big heart and a rare knack for having fun. In fact, he's short, ugly (his face bears all the marks of sixty years of hustling, punctuated by sybaritic peaks and manic-depressive troughs), paunchy and crude (he boasts about blowing a police whistle into the telephone to end unwelcome calls). His ego drives everything, and it is so big it seems to have physical dimensions; he surrounds himself with flunkeys and sycophants to feed it. He refers to himself as "the Pez," as if speaking of a completely separate entity. Underlining it all is his undeniable and magical ability to sell stock. That, more than anything, has enabled him to make more money on the VSE than any promoter in the history of the exchange. But the money has never given him what he wanted. Each time he has had the chance to fulfill his dream—to make the jump from penny stock hustler to international financier— he has pissed it away.

Murray Pezim was born in Toronto in 1920 of Roumanian immigrant parents. "My mother was the strong one," he says. "Boy, was she tough. Father was a very good-natured guy—liked to gamble but couldn't afford to." Initially, the Pezims prospered, owning two drugstores that did a brisk business in medicinal alcohol. They lived well in those pre-Depression years in an upper middle–class neighbourhood. "This home on Palmerston was *the* street. We had guards on the street, would you believe it? I remember he used to bring home the silver from the drugstore and throw it on the carpet so we always knew there was money."

The Depression affected the Pezims as it did millions of others. The drugstores became unprofitable, and his father opened two butcher shops to replace them. The big house eventually went and, at the age of fourteen, Pezim left school to help his father sell meat. The shop was unheated to preserve the meat, and one of Pezim's clearest memories is periodically unthawing his tingling hands in a bucket of warm, bloody water. The Pezim's Rogers Street shop was located in a poor neighbourhood, right next to the packing houses. The hours were long—the shop was open until midnight on Friday and Saturday—and the work tedious, but Pezim was already honing the selling ability that was to become the basis of his fortune. Many of the shop's clients were forlorn, beaten people whose lot had been made even worse by the Depression. "They'd come in in the morning, looking like the wrath of God," remembers Pezim. "I'd kibitz with them— 'How lovely you look today, Mrs. McGuire.' It got so that they'd [let] only me wait on them because I gave them a bit of a spark in a terribly drab life."

Pezim left meat to join the Canadian army during the Second World War. He never saw combat and recalls working at a POW camp in Kingston, Jamaica. "I was a truck driver and used to run the crap games. We'd win the money, then spend it on a big party for all the guys. I enjoyed it, but it scared the shit out of me many times. The Germans were huge bastards from the Afrika Corps—one little Jew looking at them . . . if they ever [got] loose here, you know? I'd be chopped liver." He returned to butchering after the war, and by 1950, when he was thirty, Pezim had saved between $12,000 and $15,000. It was the year he lost it all for the first time. "A chap walked into my store and ordered four centre-cut pork chops. When he said centre cut, I knew he was rich." The man was a broker, and he sized Pezim up as an easy mark. He told Pezim the market could make him rich and talked him into investing all his savings in a junior company called Duvay Resources. "I kept buying the stock as it went up. I was lying at home dreaming. Geez, I'm going to be the bull of Wall Street, you know, I get these crazy visions. Boy, I'm really going to be something."

Pezim lost all his savings, but the sting of his first financial crash pushed him out of meat for good and into the market: "I figured if I'd lost it, somebody else had made it." And Pezim was determined to be the one who made it. It took a while to learn that, on the street, the unschooled are shark bait. In 1951, his first year selling stocks, he made $100,000 in commissions and lost it all for the second time when a number of his clients refused to settle their accounts. "I was so green," he says, "accepting orders from just about everyone. There were a lot of sharpies in the business looking for live ones like me."

Between 1950 and 1953 Pezim worked for several brokerage houses and in 1953 joined Jenkins, Evans and Company, now defunct but then a thriving penny stock trader. Surprisingly, considering the fact that Pezim the promoter now jumps from company to company and from project to project like an epileptic flea, he stayed with that firm as a broker and later director for fourteen years. He became the backbone of Jenkins, Evans and, like many of the Bay Street hustlers in those days, was part broker and part promoter.

In 1953 Pezim met his first partner, a young, sharp-eyed promoter who had most recently been a janitor. His name was Stephen Roman and, unlike Pezim, he was soon to ascend the corporate ladder to respectability and status. Roman had been approached by three mining men to help them raise money for exploration near Quirke Lake on Lake Superior's north shore. Over 1,400 claims already crisscrossed the area with no major find, but Roman, convinced by the fervent belief of the three, agreed to help them finance the operation. He brought in Murray Pezim, who was already making a name for himself as a man who could sell anything. In November 1954, eight drill holes were sunk on the property, and all but the first struck commercial-grade ore. Denison stock soared to $85 from 40 cents, and though Pezim sold out at $17 he made so much money even he was overwhelmed. It was Pezim's first big hit, his first million—and it was to be the third time he lost it all.

Actually, it was more like squandering, as the thirty-three-year-old Pezim embarked upon an eighteen-month party. He bought a twenty-two acre estate with three houses near Ocho-Rios, Jamaica. "It was a wild scene," he said in 1982. "In those days, sure, I loved to screw. Jamaica is a great island—your pecker goes up as soon as you get off the plane."*

Pezim rarely speaks of his one-time partner Steve Roman, whose current stature as a member of the eastern establishment clearly irks him. Roman and Pezim are alike in some ways: they are both opinionated, colourful, straight-talking, working-class characters who started with nothing. There the similarity ends. Roman has become a pillar of the business elite. Roman did what Pezim has spent his life trying to do—he made something and he hung onto it. He is now chairman and majority owner of Denison Mines, and his Roman Corporation has, over the years, successfully run enterprises ranging from cement to

---

*"He came here with an erection at the age of forty-three," says one of Pezim's friends of his arrival in Vancouver in 1963. "And he's still got one."

shipbuilding. In most accounts of the financing of Denison, Pezim's name isn't even mentioned.

Earl Glick was Pezim's next partner, and between 1957 and 1967 the duo was known as Glick and Pezim. History, and Pezim, have switched the emphasis. After Denison, Glick and Pezim embarked upon a spree of promotions, most of them disastrous for investors, though the two of them always seemed to walk away with slightly fatter wallets. The list included Delta Electronics, a Toronto company that made coaxial cable; Spartan Air Services, a firm that owned forty fixed-wing aircraft and thirty helicopters; Leland Publishers, and Phantom Hosiery. By the early 1960s, Glick and Pezim were major players on the TSE. In 1964 they, along with hundreds of other proximity hounds, were flogging dozens of companies riding on the copper-lead-silver bonanza of Texas Gulf Sulphur's huge discovery in Timmins, Ontario. "I remember one day the TSE traded 28 million shares," says Pezim. "Of that volume, 14 million was ours. One of our companies traded three times its issued capital in one day."

Like every other promoter who fled Toronto in the mid-1960s, Pezim says he wasn't part of either the dirty dealings rampant on the TSE at the time or the Windfall scandal. "Which I had nothing to do with, by the way. That was [a] heartbreaker," he laments. "She [Viola MacMillan] was so respected. But she out-and-out lied to us. The day before it dropped, Earl and I dropped a fortune—$450,000—that was a big loss. She phoned and told us how great it was and then—a sad thing. Hated to see it."

Even before Windfall and Pyramid, Glick and Pezim had been scouting the Vancouver Stock Exchange, realizing that the once sleepy little market was starting to wake up. The value of the exchange's trading had increased from $40 million in 1960 to $113 million in 1962. Looking back at those days, Pezim likes to relate how he single-handedly hauled the VSE into the big time. One of his favourite stories about the VSE's insignificance has to do with his 1963 takeover of National Explorations. "I told someone, 'Buy me a hundred.' He came back and said, 'Okay, I got you a hundred at ten and a half.' I thought, hmmm. Came pretty easy." Pezim instructed the broker to buy him another hundred and another, and each time he was told the price was ten and a half cents a share. When he noticed on the tape that the stock was selling for ten cents, he got suspicious. "I said, 'How come I see on the machine it's ten cents, and I'm paying ten and a half?' He says, 'Well, you're buying an odd lot.' I say, 'What do you mean?' He says, 'Well, I bought you three hundred shares so far.' I said, 'Wait a minute, I'm talking 300,000!' What I'm trying to stress to you is the mentality of the place. But I saw the potential."

No one man was responsible for the VSE's coming of age, but Pezim did bring a certain, previously absent, savoir faire to the exchange. In 1963 he rented the Lord Stanley suite in the Hotel Vancouver and began a three-month party. Howe Street had never seen anything like it. George Cross is still bemused by the competition for Pezim's attention during his big bash. "The strangest people would turn up; senior financiers, presidents of companies, senior bankers and cabinet ministers. They didn't have to go home for a month. What you didn't see, you just asked for. Booze, broads—anything you dreamed of." Pezim's flash made it seem that he was worth millions; in fact he now admits that he was worth barely a few hundred thousand.

The magnitude of everything he did impressed even the most seasoned traders. When he was promoting Galaxy Copper Ltd., just one of the horde of location shots during the Pyramid staking rush, he would walk onto the trading floor, ask who the Galaxy sellers were and tell them he would take 100,000 shares. A few years earlier, total daily trading might not have amounted to that much. Pezim told anyone who would listen, "I'm going to make you rich. Anyone who doesn't believe me, just watch."

In 1966 Pezim was still with Jenkins, Evans, which had purchased a seat on the VSE. He was wearing several hats, including running the promotions and trading on the floor. Almost forgotten in the Pezim myth is the fact that he was as solid and skilled a floor trader as any who had ever worked on the VSE. In January, two months after the Pyramid excitement had sagged somewhat, Rolling Hills, a company controlled by Glick and Pezim, landed in the headlines with rumours about its Thubun Lake property in the Northwest Territories. The street was buzzing about a find, and the stock zoomed from $1 to $3.05 in a matter of days, coincidentally reaching its peak on the very day that 50,000 shares were released from escrow.

It was an odd situation. Thubun Lake was not known as a mining area, and despite abundant rumours of mineralization, no other companies had moved into the region. Asked if they really intended to make a mine, Glick retorted, "Are you kidding? We sacrificed some of our own stock this morning to keep an orderly market." The sacrifice consisted of selling the released escrowed shares at the market's peak.

The report on the property turned out to be false. Pezim asked that the stock be suspended, and after an eighteen-month investigation, Superintendent of Brokers Bill Irwin announced there was no basis for any charges against the directors or promoters. This was the last profitable deal that Glick and Pezim were in together. According to the newspapers, they parted "arch enemies." Pezim says they are still friends, though he claims that Glick cheated him: "The partnership was totally one-sided. The losses were mine, the profits were his."

Pezim left Jenkins, Evans in 1966 and immediately bought into another VSE seat holder, H. H. Hemsworth (later Canarim Investment Corporation) for "a couple of hundred thousand" dollars. That same year William Somerville, then a vice-president of the TSE, summoned Pezim and told him if he was going to work the VSE he wasn't welcome in Toronto. Apart from the ignominy of it, the ultimatum didn't bother Pezim since he was heavily involved in the West Coast market. It took him less than a year to bring Hemsworth to its knees. He did it with his promotion of Bata Resources Ltd., an inconsequential oil and gas company. Only 2.3 million Bata shares had traded in 1966, but in the first month of 1967, under Pezim's stewardship, 6.7 million shares changed hands. The volume meant that the outstanding Bata shares (about 2 million) had been bought and sold three times in that period. The mystery was that there was nothing to base the activity on, save a few vague statements from Pezim regarding an exploration program and the hiring of two geologists.

Short sellers sensed Bata was sitting on hot air, and they attacked, driving down the share price as they sold. (Pezim eroded Hemsworth's capital by absorbing the shares as they came on the market.) He had to support the price because he had pushed the firm into taking a dangerously large position in Bata. In the end, Pezim couldn't buy enough stock to keep the price up and, when it started to slide, he couldn't make good his margin. He was forced to sell his house in Toronto and his interest in Hemsworth. "He suffered the worst case of stock-eating indigestion in the exchange's history," Bill Fletcher wrote in the *Sun* at the time. Pezim reacted to the crisis by disappearing for months. He spent four weeks of his sabbatical cloistered in a Toronto hospital.

A few people thought that Pezim was finished. More than a few were surprised when he surfaced in 1967 to underwrite Stampede Oil and Gas. It turned out to be a great cure for depression. Pezim did the underwriting for Adam Kryczka, a young Calgary geologist, and his partner, Ken Bottoms, who had originally incorporated the company. A year after the underwriting the pair were searching for sulphur when they hit gas. It was part of the massive Strachan-Ricinus gas field, one of the largest in the country. Stampede's shares jumped from 50 cents to $27. Ironically, Bata, Pezim's nemesis, which had been languishing in disgrace, jumped with it, simply because it had properties in the vicinity.

Despite the Stampede bonanza, Pezim was still hurting from Bata. When the 1968–69 oil and gas market fizzled, he was left with millions tied up in the market. Then came the 1971–72 slump, and he watched as $6 million was flushed away. At the same time he was having to swallow the costs of a failed takeover attempt of a meat-packing plant. While all this was going on, he was searching around desperately for something to prop up his fading fortunes. He turned, not to the market, but to a carny hustler with a taste for grand opera and champagne, Nick Zubray.

Zubray, a profligate wrestling and boxing promoter, was infamous in the West for his sulphurous language, highbrow tastes, and phenomenal ability to lose money. When he travelled he ensconced himself in a hotel, stuffed the fridge full of champagne, ordered in some caviar, cranked up his portable record player and began listening to the stack of opera records he always kept with him. When his money ran out, as it inevitably did, he stayed in the hotel until the debt he ran up was so large that the manager didn't dare turf him out for fear of losing all chance of collecting. "If Runyon had seen him, there would have been no Harry the horse. It would have been Nick," chuckles *Province* sportswriter Jim Taylor. Just before he died, Zubray bought some land in Edmonton, planning to set up a nudist colony there. After Zubray's funeral, Taylor asked a friend how the event had been attended, and the friend replied, "Great, great! It outdrew his last three promotions."

Zubray was a powerful persuader, and when he suggested that Pezim bankroll a fight between Muhammad Ali and George Chuvalo, the nearly insolvent Pezim couldn't resist, even though a year earlier his and Zubray's attempt at promoting an event—the closed-circuit TV airing of a heavyweight match—had ended in disaster. They'd sold tickets at $75, but just before the event, Pezim discovered the same fight was being broadcast live on channel five in Vancouver—a little detail his partner Zubray had forgotten to mention. As a result, the crowd at the fight was barely larger than Pezim's entourage.

With two propaganda artists like Pezim and Zubray behind it, the buildup to the Ali-Chuvalo fight was enormous. Pezim promised a long list of beautiful people and announced a ninety-hour prefight party. Well-placed stories about stars like Frank Sinatra promising to attend fed the rumour mill. But hyperbole can't sell a product without intrinsic appeal. No one wanted to see Ali turn Chuvalo into hamburger for ten rounds, as he had done two years before in Toronto.

Paid and paper attendance at the boxing match was less than 50 per cent of the Coliseum's capacity, and the ninety-hour party lasted less than twenty-two. *Sports Illustrated* called the whole business one of the biggest failures in fight history. Pezim lost at least $200,000. After it was over, sportswriter Jim Kearney happened upon Pezim sitting dejectedly in the Georgia Hotel lobby, "looking as if he'd just been shot through the head."

The market slump, the takeover failure and finally the fight; it was all too much for Pezim. In 1972, he declared bankruptcy. Once again, he retreated from sight to apply salve to his punctured ego. But as before, he rose out of the ruins, this time lying low until he rebuilt his shattered business. By 1975, despite the almost stagnant market, Pezim was back at the top. The loud, opinionated, self-serving statements, which had been missing from his colourful vocabulary, returned. That year he paid $2.5 million for an Arizona limestone plant purchased through a VSE-listed shell called BX Developments.

His comeback ended catastrophically again on January 28, 1976, when the RCMP raided seven of Pezim's companies and seized records in the offices of his brokers, lawyers, accountants and several business associates. (The RCMP sergeant who led the investigation was Rupert Bullock, who later became superintendent of brokers in 1980.) It was an unprecedented investigation; more than 5,000 of Pezim's phone calls had been recorded between October 1, 1975, and January 28, 1976. The allegations crushed Pezim and his ten companies, which collectively lost $3 million on paper as their share values plummeted. The most impressive loss was to BX Developments, the only revenue producer, whose shares fell from $2.10 to 90 cents on the news of the raid. "Right now, I've been effectively put out of business," Pezim moaned. "Brokers are afraid to call me unless they really have to. I'm like a pariah." He then disappeared to Arizona.

Police investigations increasingly centred on the activities of BX

Developments, and in January 1977 charges of fraud and theft were laid against Pezim, Arthur Clemiss* and three others. Pezim didn't return to Vancouver until May 1978, when he pleaded not guilty to the charges. In the previous two years, Pezim had concentrated on running BX, an unusual feat of management perseverance for him. The company actually reported an after-tax profit of $166,077 U.S. in 1978. Pezim's lawyers exhausted the appeal procedure, and he was forced to go to court. He chose the trial date to announce his latest project, a device called Porta-Tel, which allowed deaf people to communicate by sending typed messages over phone lines. He promised the world that the future of the new gadget would "just drive you nuts." Porta-Tel came to naught, but so did the charges against him. For the first time in several years, Pezim was free to go to the bathroom without fear of someone or something recording the event.

Murray Pezim prides himself on never giving up and boasts about his mongooselike tenacity in dealing with failing companies, doubters and detractors. But the fact is, Pezim rarely learns from his mistakes. In some cases, it's a fortunate omission in his character. Pezim distinguished himself as a wretched fight promoter, but he loved mixing with the famous, even if it cost him his shirt, and he wanted more of it. Charity fund raisers were his ticket. Not only were they fun but charity work was great for business, raising his profile immensely, improving his credibility and giving him access to scores of rich people eager to take advantage of stock tips from a real live promoter. "Charity work is another form of promotion," he says. One of Pezim's favourite projects over the years has been the Variety Club. In a grand gesture, at a 1980 charity roast for Vancouver restaurateur Hy Aisenstat, founder of the Hy's chain, Pezim gave 5,000 shares of BX Developments, worth $42,500, to the Variety Club in honour of an old friend, Joe Cohen, who was just recovering from surgery.

Pezim was determined to go one better than the Hy's roast, and on March 21st, he hosted a gaudy and excessive seventy-eighth birthday dinner for retired Vancouver judge Angelo Branca, to raise $1 million for charity. The event mesmerized the gossip columnists. Pezim prom-

---

*Arthur Clemiss was Pezim's partner at the time, and the only one he has been able to stick with. Clemiss, the quietest man around the VSE, never grants interviews and few have even seen him, much less know him. He's also one of the richest men on the street, and he and his wife, Marion, are invariably the most active traders listed on the VSE insider trading reports.

ised the dinner would make the Aisenstat roast seem "like a bagel breakfast in comparison." The bigness of things is Pezim's way of assessing his worth, whether it involves charitable contributions or friendships. He hired John Francis, who produced one of Frank Sinatra's charity specials, to stage the show, and he pulled up all his Hollywood buddies to headline the entertainment. The list included master of ceremonies Joey Bishop, Red Buttons, Dick Shawn, Milton Berle, Henny Youngman and Jan Murray. Tickets went for $200 each. It was Pezim's kind of evening: stars, money and conspicuous display. He got his million, and the money went to the Miriam Camp for underprivileged children. The toilet humour at the event was so raunchy that several people walked out in disgust. Pezim himself may have the foulest mouth in Canada. George Cross remembers introducing Pezim to John Harvey, who had been president of Noranda for a long time. Pezim greeted him with "Hello, you fucking old asshole." Cross laughs, "Murray wanted Harvey to know that even though he was the president of Noranda, he was his equal."

In 1982, Pezim's salad days came to an end once again. For the rest of the world, it was the beginning of a recession. For many brokers, speculators and promoters, grown fat on the incredible markets of 1978—81, it was the beginning of ruin. Some stocks dropped as much as 90 per cent, and Murray Pezim was one of the hardest hit. Pez Resources slid from $4.10 to 48 cents, and International Corona, then the favoured child in his stable, went from $8¼ to 80 cents; both were key Pezim companies. The year before, Pezim, caught up like thousands of others, had plunged into the real estate market with a $630,000 condominium overlooking Vancouver's English Bay. The price dropped 25 per cent even before he moved in.

Things got so bad for Pezim that in February 1982 he was forced to call a press conference to announce, as Mark Twain had done, that rumours of his death were greatly exaggerated. At the time he confessed to paper losses of $15 million and a debt of $1 million for margin calls. "But I'm not bankrupt and I'm tired of all the rumours," he said of persistent stories that he'd had a heart attack. "Everyone has been hurt in this market, everyone's been killed, but the fact is, I'm not dead."

A lot of people think they have got Pezim's ebbs and flows charted well enough to invest in his wake, but if you're not a true insider, the only sure-fire gauge of his level of success at any given time is the size of his offices. At one point in 1981 they covered 3,000 square feet. In early 1982 he sublet a third of the space and cut some of his $40,000-a-month overhead, a painful procedure because Pezim's offices are really an extension of him. They are his security blanket, his statement to the world. At the height of his power in 1983, Pezim's command centre swelled to 14,000 square feet. As he lost control in late 1984 of Pezamerica, International Corona (the company primarily involved in Hemlo) and Tri-Basin, his offices shrank to 1,400 square feet, and some irate shareholder or creditor gouged his name off the door.

Pezim's office has often been described as a cockpit, but in reality it is a bizarre combination of theatrical agency and the waiting room of a patent attorney. The atmosphere in the football-field-sized room is electrified by persistently ringing phones. People heedlessly wander in and out. One day in 1984, Joe Capozzi, a typical visitor, lurked patiently at the back of the room. There was a lull in the action, and Capozzi pounced, flapping his hands for Pezim's attention. Talking as fast as an auctioneer, he made his pitch, trying to interest Pezim in a pair of flimsy-looking spectacles with tiny flashlights on the sides, to be used for reading in bed or changing spark plugs in the dark. "Okay, okay, so you wouldn't wear 'em yourself, then forget that," Capozzi said when Pezim didn't immediately bite. "You're a numbers man," he urged, trying a little flattery and waving his arms so much he looked as if he might take off. "You know numbers, so let's forget everything but that. These'll sell. It will make you seasick they'll sell so fucking fast." But Pezim wasn't in a buying mood. "You think you've got a good thing," he taunted. "I've got a better thing! Want to see my thing?" From out of his desk he hauled a long, phallic, multipurpose flashlight, with more bells, whistles and lights than a Rube Goldberg invention. It was an abandoned pet project of last week, or last month. Pezim's desk drawers are full them, gewgaws and gadgets that look more like the inventory of a trick and joke shop than the industrial ideas of a promoter.

Whatever else you might say about Pezim's organization, buttoned down and corporate it is not. Even the most momentous conference is stopped dead when his girlfriend, Susan, marches in to argue with him about whether she will take home the Rolls or the Mercedes. The two of them are an interesting combination. Pezim habitually looks like he needs an oxygen mask. Susan, a streaked blonde in her thirties, is aerobically attractive. She looks like she gets out of bed in the morning bouncing and clapping. She's not high class, but likable because of it. There's an earthy naturalness about her. She is, however, aware of her position as girlfriend to the Pez, and it doesn't take much provocation to elicit from her a harangue about writer Matthew Hart,* who obviously got the wrong idea. "He wrote that I was his secretary in that book of his about Hemlo," she says in disgust, jabbing her finger towards Pezim who apparently gave Hart the mistaken impression. "I'm certainly not and never was. I'm his girlfriend."

At the mention of Hemlo, Pezim is ready with stories. He has always hungered for the big score, the one that would transform his image. "You start off as a stock hustler," he said in 1984. "Then you're a promoter, then you're an entrepreneur and last year Toronto called me a financier." But just when he hooked the really big one, the Hemlo goldfield in western Ontario, he threw it all away.

Even Pezim has trouble exaggerating the Hemlo goldfield. In 1983, Bache Securities Inc. estimated that the site contained 14 million proven ounces of gold, making the ore body worth $5.5 billion at today's prices. In comparison, the Campbell Red Lake field, formerly the largest in the country, has extracted 1.5 million ounces in the last thirty-five years and has proven reserves of only 3 million ounces. International Corona's piece of it with high ore content turned the company into a blue chip. In 1986, Theodore Rhenius, Corona's chief financial officer, estimated pretax profits of between $75 and $100 million.

The way Pezim likes to tell it, he alone made the mammoth discovery, battling valiantly all the while against stupid Torontonians. "We spent a couple of million bucks before discovering hole number seventy-six in May 1982. That took a lot of guts," he brags. "Everyone was against us. There were a lot of major companies who explored this ground, and they walked away after a few holes. It was stubbornness and the bombing that I was taking from the East that kept me going."

It's a nice little homily about the persistence of one man winning out against long odds and entrenched eastern interests. In truth, two of Pezim's associates in Vancouver, Doug Collingwood and Nell Dragovan, first brought Hemlo to Pezim's attention as early as October 1980. He wasn't the least bit interested. By the time they badgered him into getting involved, there were already sixty-five holes drilled

---

*Hart wrote *The Golden Giant*, published by Douglas & McIntyre in 1985. The paperback edition published in 1986 was retitled *Hemlo*.

184 RIPE FOR THE PICKING

with decent results. From there, Pezim's story has some truth, and
there's no question that his canny money raising was vital during the
critical stages of exploration.

In 1983, Pezim was so inflated by Hemlo's success and feelings of his
own invincibility that he travelled to Toronto where he kindly offered
Bay Street some ideas about how to improve the Ontario Securities
Commission. "The osc should copy the rules of the B.C. regulators,"
he advised in a dinner speech. "Put a lock on the TSE doors and forget
it, or get another Murray Pezim." When Pezim is on a roll, he's insuf-
ferable. But this roll, like the others, was to be short-lived. He was
already fouling his own nest.

He had publicly stated his fear of losing control of International
Corona, the listed company that owned the Hemlo claims, as far back
as May 1983. Privately, he had worried about it even earlier, and the
fear gnawed at him like an ulcer. He knew that Corona was an attractive takeover target for the big mining companies, and he had to do
something to keep them at bay. The ownership of International
Corona was a complex web, with many of Pezim's other listed companies holding share positions in it. His strategy was clever. He
bought shares of Corona through his stable of sixty companies, keeping the price up and gradually increasing his control, thus making a
takeover difficult and expensive. Pezim's companies, used in concert,
gave him considerable latitude to buy shares and control the market.
With so much buying power he had enormous influence in the
market. His strategy would have worked, but Pezim, instead of concentrating on Hemlo and sticking to his plan, got carried away with
his fame. He flung himself into a madcap orgy of gimmick hustling and
deal making, dissipating both the time and money needed to protect
Corona.

One of his most inexplicable projects was a Don Quixote-like
crusade to buy control of B.C. Resources Investment Corporation in
June 1983. In just two days, he bought, personally and through his
companies, 750,000 of the 96 million shares issued.* This activity,
coupled with his announcement that he intended to purchase five million shares of BCRIC, drove the price up to $4.75 from $3.45. Pezim
could provide no rational explanation for his actions. BCRIC, created
by the provincial Socred government, had gone public in 1979, and

*At the time it was possible to use so-called "unallocated funds," up to $150,000 for develop-
ment companies and $250,000 for resource companies, to buy into other companies.

every B.C. resident received five free shares, a good move for the stock market but little else. Within four years the company had become a huge white elephant with shrinking assets, obsolete equipment and ineffectual management. "I'm a total character," Pezim said to the *Financial Post*. "I like tweaking the big boys once in a while but they need that. There's nothing like a good street fight." The street fight was comprised of such tactics as calling BCRIC president Bruce Howe a "snotnose" on television. It was all over quickly. At the end of February 1984, the fight was finished. Pezim, who had purchased more than 2 million shares, was apparently satisfied with a minor concession by the BCRIC board. "I felt before that they were too aloof, they were not listening," he explained. "Now, they've promised to set up a committee of small shareholders and listen to them." It was surely the most expensive shareholder committee in history. Pezim's takeover attempt generated a scrapbook full of headlines but cost him and his companies over $2 million.

While Pezim was tweaking the noses of the big boys, he was pioneering another industrial enterprise—cassette greeting cards. It was to be a happy marriage of his promoting skills and his long-time association with Las Vegas stars. The dimestore "Greetings from the Stars" came complete with tacky, semifunny messages recorded by stars from another era. Each tape featured an introduction that began: "Hi, I'm Joey Bishop (or whoever). A friend of mine asked me to tell you a story." Four minutes of tired jokes later, there was sufficient blank tape for the sender to include a personal message. The tapes were to retail for $4 to $5. It was just the kind of scheme that might make it—after all, someone bought all those pet rocks. But Pezim chose his contemporaries and friends to be the stars. Instead of sexy drawing cards like Eddie Murphy, Joan Rivers, Steve Martin and Lily Tomlin, he chose the likes of Norm Crosby, Buddy Hackett, Jan Murray and Don Knotts. Many of his intended audience had never even heard of them.

Pezzaz Productions, a wholly owned subsidiary of Pezamerica, was the vehicle to take the "cards" to market. At first, everything looked rosy, at least according to a flood of press releases and glossy come-ons that spoke of a $7 billion annual North American greeting card business and marketing plans that included supermarkets and convenience stores. "One major firm, with over 2,500 outlets has expressed its intent to place an initial order valued at $2 million," was one forecast. Even as this cheerful statement was issued, the cassette venture was falling to bits. In the fall of 1984 the sheriff nailed Pezzaz's doors shut. The company had lost over $4 million in manufacturing and promotion costs including $250,000 to renovate a warehouse to produce the cassettes, the costs of hiring ninety staff to assemble the product and production expenses of $10,000 apiece for four minutes of tape from forty celebrities. The day before Pezzaz went under, the Vancouver management was issuing business-as-usual statements, but inside Pezim's office the atmosphere was stretched tight with tension as employees scuttled about packing up files and making cryptic phone calls. Pezim had already departed for Arizona, leaving his nephew Larry to face the questions. An unknown amount of Pezim's own money went down the drain with Pezzaz, but it was a disaster for Pezamerica, his flagship company. As the major unsecured creditor, it was owed $2.6 million. The company's shares tumbled from a 1984 high of $8 to $2. At the same time International Corona stock dropped from $13⅞ to $5¾.

As the cassettes sank out of sight, Pezim was fighting a desperate battle to prop up his empire and to keep the takeover vultures away. He was using the treasury of one company to buy shares in another. While he was chairman of Tri-Basin Resources Ltd., he used that company's funds to buy Pezamerica shares and traded Tri-Basin's $4-million holding of International Corona for Pezamerica shares. The transfers and share purchases were all legal under VSE rules, but they made a rat's nest of his companies' treasuries. Pezim's hijinks had depressed the share prices of his various companies, and he was left frantically trying to meet margin calls.

On October 22, 1984, Royex Gold Mining Corporation of Toronto announced that it had purchased control of both Pezamerica and International Corona. In December, Royex and Pezamerica merged under the name of Royex. It was all over for Pezim once again. He admitted to losing between $7 and $8 million in cash, though his true losses, including the decline in value of the shares he still held, was three or four times that amount. Pezim's paper worth in 1983 was estimated at $40 million; by the end of 1984 it was down to $9 million. It was the first time Pezim admitted to being solvent after a crash, but he lost control of International Corona, his ticket to becoming a big-time financier. It was a once-in-a-lifetime opportunity for a hustler who was already a very old sixty-three.

In November 1985, Pezim emerged once again, ready for another public debut. He had a new play, the La Ronge claims 220 kilometres north of Prince Albert, Saskatchewan. "The discovery is frankly spectacular," Pezim told reporters. "La Ronge could prove up more ounces than Hemlo." Despite the pessimism of analysts and geologists, Pezim's enthusiasm for the drill hole results worked wonders on the share prices of three companies controlled by him and his associates. Canadian Premium jumped from $1.10 to $4, Mahogany Minerals from $1.15 to $4.35, and Goldsil Resources from 55 cents to $6.75, all amid a flurry of releases and promotion.

In February 1987 Pezim had one more tilt at the windmill with a bizarre takeover attempt of his lost baby, International Corona Resources Ltd. Again, the veteran street fighter chose the perplexing tactic of publicly announcing his takeover intentions. One day, he was questioning the competence of Corona's management, and the next day, he was lauding the senior officer for having done "a fine job." Analysts calculated that any bid for Corona would require at least $400 million. In the end, Pezim's attempt failed, as two of his supporters on Corona's board of directors were defeated for re-election at the company's annual general meeting on February 11, 1987. Pezim stalked out of the room, vowing, "I will return."

Each time Murray Pezim returns to the vse, having purged himself with a bout of depression in Scottsdale, Arizona, there are always more people waiting to empty their bank accounts for his companies. Part of the reason lies in the myth he has carefully cultivated over the years of going to the wall for his shareholders. It's an old promoter's line, but Pezim says it better than most: "If people lost on my stocks, I was always the biggest loser. I've never sold anything I didn't buy myself." Even the most cynical observers of the stock market swallow the posture whole. "Every time Murray's clients suffered, Murray went down with the ship," affirms Peter Brown. "And if anybody lost, he'd be the biggest loser. Ask anyone. If he wasn't honest, he wouldn't have gone broke so many times." But Pezim tacitly admits that the myth has reached unbelievable proportions. "When I went broke [in 1972], I was really broke. I was stripped of everything. But I've learned. I've made sure I always have some liquid assets set aside."

Pezim may not lose his shirt when he goes under, but what does fall apart are the essential elements of his ego. Long-time friend, employee and gofer Sam Rosen calls Pezim "the greatest egomaniac I've ever met." The ego is a theoretical construct of Sigmund Freud, to explain the intangible self. But Pezim's is so monumental it has a life of its own. Sandy Ross put it best in his book *The Traders:* "His voracious ego seems to swell like a barrage balloon, until his mere physical presence can dominate entire ballrooms." Vancouver *Sun* columnist Denny Boyd once suggested that this aspect of Pezim "belongs in a lead box in the Smithsonian Institute, where they keep the stuffed whales and other huge things."

Murray Pezim still refers to himself as "the Pez" and is still an important player on the VSE. He still trots out the old, once-outrageous, self-serving statements: "I ain't going to change. I'm still the same old Pez. And, by the way, I am the greatest promoter that ever lived." Brave words, but now there is an ineffable sadness about Pezim, the sadness of a man who knows, deep in his heart, that he has had rare opportunities to fulfil his dreams. It's the sadness of a very old, worn out man who has been granted one more chance at that really big one and again allowed his massive ego to kick it all away.

CHAPTER 14

Bruce McDonald,
the Golden Boy

Murray Pezim still gets more publicity, but R. A. Bruce McDonald is now unquestionably the most powerful promoter in Vancouver. Four years ago, McDonald was virtually broke. Today, everything he touches seems to turn to gold. In 1983 and 1984 McDonald's company, Golden Knight, was instrumental in financing the exploration of the rich Casa Berardi goldfield in Quebec, and he has twenty-five junior companies hot on the trail of precious metals. At the same time, McDonald has been in the forefront of the transformation of the Vancouver stock promoter's image from that of sleazy hustler to corporate executive. Once the most colourful of promoters, today's public Bruce McDonald is reticent and almost never quoted. The original McDonald is still there, of course, and slips out in unguarded moments, but to anyone who didn't know him a few years ago—and doesn't look too closely now—McDonald is virtually indistinguishable from big money's grey denizens.

McDonald, born in 1941, has been totally immersed in the stock business as a clerk, money trader, currency trader and broker since the age of sixteen when he quit school to mark the boards at the Toronto Stock Exchange. Right from the beginning, he loved the market. "It was like being at a baseball or football game all day long," he says. In 1978 he became a full-fledged stock promoter and moved to Vancouver. "I was bored, the markets were poor. I took a hard look at other promoters, and I decided I could run a company as well as anybody out there," he says. McDonald (then worth about $100,000) and several partners took control of a nearly dormant company, buying 800,000 shares at eight cents. He changed the company's name to Liberty Petroleum and underwrote the stock at $1.50. Within six months he made his first million when he sold his 300,000-share position for slightly more than $5 a share.

Today, McDonald's net worth bobs between $50 and $75 million depending on the market. He enjoys it and lives well—vacations in Hawaii, a $2.5-million house in Vancouver's prestigious West Point Grey that's so large and opulent the word "mansion" seems to belittle it and a fresh, new wife whom one friend describes as "a young '10.' " It's a nice life, and one he's acquired in just a few years.

Unlike most promoters, who can look back on a career pockmarked with perilous dives into misfortune, McDonald has weathered only one real crisis. In 1982, McDonald was on the ropes. He, like hundreds of others, had been caught in the recession. A combination of market losses, the bitter dissolution of a partnership deal ("one guy had an out-and-out conflict of interest, the other guy, he was great on holidays") and a divorce from his first wife ("Christ, I didn't have any money when my old lady was through with me") left him scrambling just to pay his office rent. Ironically, three thousand miles away, Inco Ltd., McDonald's corporate bride-to-be, the solid matron of the mining industry, was having a few troubles of its own. The recession and falling metal prices dug deeply into the company's profit. Everything got cut, from disposable frills to the vital exploration budget, which dropped from $30 million in 1981 to $15 million by 1984. As with most majors, Inco had a vast reserve of unexplored and partly explored mineral properties. One of those was the Casa Berardi claims in northwestern Quebec. Inco had already sunk $1.5 million into it, staked 882 claims and drilled eighteen holes yielding 15,000 feet of bore. The company had actually been looking for base metals, though nearly every hole it drilled turned up signs of gold. But what remained of Inco's exploration budget had to be devoted to projects that were closer to completion. Inco's chief of exploration, Terry Podolski, estimated that another $3 million was needed to complete the work "You don't walk away just because money is hard to come by," he says. The emaciated budgets offered no help in the short term, so the company was forced to take to the streets. "We decided to go out and see if anyone wanted to join us," explains Podolski. "I spoke to nineteen groups and individuals. When you talk to exploration people you don't talk to pessimists, but very few had that kind of money to spend." None, in fact.

One of the first people Podolski spoke to was a mine financier by the name of Getties Baxter. Baxter told Inco that his plate was full but dropped the name of a Vancouver promoter who had impressed him, Bruce McDonald. The Inco brass had never heard of McDonald, but the mention of a VSE promoter sent shivers through the ranks of the sixty-five-year-old company. The idea of Inco dealing with a VSE promoter was as preposterous as the Pope endorsing Dr. Henry Morgentaler.

Inco's senior officers admit that, even more than the other big mining companies, they had assiduously avoided any contact with the junior market. In the history of Canadian mining, Inco has written its own tradition—a tradition born out of a once-awesome power in the industry. In the 1950s, for example, the company controlled 80 per cent of the nickel being mined worldwide. Nickel prices weren't negotiated, they were proclaimed. Furthermore, it was major companies like Inco that, smeared by the promoting burlesque in the 1960s, had encouraged the Toronto Stock Exchange to run junior mining promoters out of town. Truckling to one of the banished, even if he hadn't been promoting then, stuck in Inco's throat. Resistance to the idea polarized the company, but eventually pragmatism won out over tradition.

The unlikely marriage between McDonald and Inco consumed several months of discussion over the summer of 1983. McDonald's bombastic ways confirmed Inco's worst fears. The most liberal minded and progressive of the company's officers disliked him on sight. Others described him as an "asshole," a "pitch man" and a "mouth organ."

The stories circulating about McDonald certainly didn't help. One such escapade occured in June 1983, immediately before the onset of negotiations. In that month, one of McDonald's stockbroker friends was ejected from London's prestigious Park Lane Hotel at 2 A.M., for trying to sneak a hooker into his room. McDonald was also shown the door when he tried to mediate. The real trouble began when the night manager delivered a lengthy lecture—in a loud clipped voice—on the disgustingly low level of Canadian morals while holding McDonald's credit card hostage to ensure an audience. In a fury McDonald seized a can of white paint from a man who was painting the ceiling during the hotel's off-hours. "I threatened to throw it if he didn't give my card back," remembers McDonald. "He said that I wouldn't dare. I said yes I would. [I] took a run at it and really doused him." The manager was white from brogues to collar. One of the painters laughed so hard he fell off the scaffolding and broke his leg.

The police laughed too when they frogmarched McDonald off. "[I] ended up spending the night in the Old Bailey with murderers and thieves," he says with a trace of pride. The next day he was fined 10 pounds for his behaviour and 2,000 pounds for damages. "I am a little impetuous," he admitted when confronted with the incident in 1984. Another Bruce McDonald from Vancouver, no relation, had the misfortune to check into the Park Lane Hotel with his wife a few months later. While they were out shopping, their bags were taken out of the room. They thought he was the Bruce McDonald of the paint episode and "threw him right out of the hotel," says McDonald laughing uproariously.

McDonald is a big-faced, handsome man, immaculately groomed and erect, but even a $1,000-suit cannot hide his sly, street-tough aura nor his barroom bravado. There's an animal magnetism and confidence about him that still astonishes long-time friends. Alastair Dow, a Toronto financial analyst who has known McDonald since his early days on the TSE, remembers going out to dinner with him at one of New York's most exclusive restaurants. "Don't worry about a reservation," McDonald told him. "The Queen of England couldn't get a table without a reservation," responded Dow. McDonald prevailed. "He got the best table in the place. I don't know how he did it. He didn't flash any money," says Dow, still amazed years later. It was with the same confidence that McDonald assured Inco—amid depressed market conditions and his own poverty—that he could easily raise the $3 million in two or three months through his VSE-listed company, Golden Knight. "I committed to it, but didn't have the money," he now admits with a chuckle. In return for the $3 million, Golden Knight would receive 40 per cent of the property.

Inco may have found it difficult to face up to the prospect of dealing with McDonald, but he immediately recognized the opportunity for what it was. "It was a chance in a lifetime for us," he says. "I'd always wanted to get involved with the majors, but they wouldn't have anything to do with juniors." McDonald believed he could ride the back of Inco's prestige to a new level of respect and credibility. What's more, the arrangement made tremendous sense. "Inco will stop something when they think it isn't worthwhile to spend any more money on it," he says. "When you see them that excited about it, you know you're not going out trying to catch lightning in a bottle. Staking claims, drilling holes, doing all that stuff we're not equipped to because we're not engineers, we're not geologists. We're strictly in the money business."

Junior mining companies in Canada, some listed on stock markets, some not, have found more than half the mines discovered in this country. Almost invariably, at some point in the exploration process, a major company takes over the junior company and develops the mine, using its expertise and financial resources. An early marriage between a junior and a major could maximize the strengths of both; the junior's ability to raise the risky early exploration money, and the major's exploration and operating expertise. "The majority of those guys," says McDonald of other junior operators, "are going out on a location bet, just because there's been a discovery in the area. In some cases, fifteen miles away. It's a fucking long walk, and geologically it's a huge, huge difference. You've got people who don't even know the mining business running the companies, in most cases. What chance does the investor have?"

Despite McDonald's confidence, raising $3 million wasn't easy. To meet the first instalment of $1.5 million, Golden Knight made an offering of flow through shares in Quebec at $1.00 in September 1983. Juniors cannot offer the appealing flow through shares without the cooperation of a major like Inco, because they lack sufficient income. The Canadian exploration expense provision of the Income Tax Act permits subscribers who buy flow through shares to deduct from personal income 133 per cent of the money they invest that is spent on exploration. And the Quebec exploration account allows residents to claim an additional 33 per cent. Still, in 1983, when people were scrambling for income, not write-offs, the initial offering came perilously close to collapsing. Late in October, McDonald, in a panic to sell the issue before Inco's deadline cancelled their deal, flew to Montreal for three days of frantic knocking on brokers' doors. He squeezed out every ounce of charm to place the remaining $1.2 million.

By 1984, McDonald's controlling position in Golden Knight, which had cost him $45,000 to acquire, was worth $3 million. Preliminary drilling results on the Casa Berardi property were promising, and McDonald had thoughtfully staked 1,500 claims in the surrounding area. "What they've found so far looks good," said Bill McWilliam, formerly of Canarim Investment Corporation. "But they need extensive drilling before they really know if they've got anything."

McDonald, then still the old McDonald, flung himself enthusiastically into promoting Casa Berardi. He told people that Inco was working for him and generally treated the promising goldfield with the promotional hype of a stock hustler trying to unload moose pasture. Inco was uncomfortable to the extreme. In the first months of the partnership a thick file was accumulated documenting countless times Inco phoned or wrote to McDonald urging him to cut the hyperbole and flackery. The company was accustomed to letting a mine speak for itself and was horrified and embarrassed by McDonald's approach. While Inco was carefully considering the merits of the property, McDonald was already touting the mine's size and profitability as if it were an established fact.

McDonald's sudden wealth didn't make it any easier for Inco executives to deal with him. "It's tough when you are talking to a guy who is an instant millionaire," explains one Inco manager. Many "old culture" Inco people resented the fact that a man who didn't know quartz from slate walked into a major discovery.

Terry Podolski, large, big-fisted and possessing a laugh that fills a room's corners, represents the core of Inco's strength. He has been with the company for over thirty years, and though he is a well-educated geologist, he still looks like he just exchanged his prospector's garb for a sombre suit. He shoots words out like bullets and has no time for the medicine show of stock promotion. Nonetheless, painful though it is, he gives McDonald his due—but no more. "Bruce is a promoter. He wouldn't be doing his job if he weren't tooting his horn. He brought $3 million to the party. Full stop."

Bruce McDonald's feat in raising the money elevated his status to mythical proportions within Inco and on the street. Even those who had never met him knew he was the man who made Casa Berardi possible. The property would have been developed eventually anyway, but without McDonald it would have sat on the shelf until Inco's balance sheet improved. Mixed with the antipathy toward him was a certain grudging respect and admiration: "He's pure dynamism. Even if you don't like him, when he walks into a room you know something has changed."

McDonald is quick witted and has a prodigious memory. Organized, however, he is not. His desk, pristine at 7 A.M., is a welter of papers, scraps of envelopes used as notepads and overflowing ashtrays by 8:30. The rest of his Noramco office, the parent company controlling McDonald's twenty-five or so juniors, is, therefore, a complete surprise. The rooms are quietly and tastefully decorated. Everything purrs with efficiency from the meticulous computer-generated monthly financial statements to the friendly and obliging staff. Until December 1986 the man behind it all was McDonald's partner, Ray Cottrell, who owned 20 per cent of Noramco. "I'm there to balance Bruce," he said before he left, "and to provide the back-up that will make him more effective." Ray Cottrell was to Bruce McDonald what Brian Harwood is to Peter Brown. McDonald may have provided the promotional genius, but Cottrell was the man who funneled it and who ensured that all the little administrative details, the things that are so often the downfall of promoters, got done.

In the four years of their partnership, Cottrell provided the calm counterpoint to McDonald's verbosity and flamboyance. When things went awry, Cottrell straightened them out. Early in 1986, McDonald and Cottrell were en route to a meeting with a VSE executive. McDonald was sputteringly furious, twitching and bobbing like a boxer before a bout, his face as red as an overripe tomato. Cottrell quietly soothed McDonald, patting him on the shoulder like a child, and told him to leave all the talking to him. "It'll be all right, Bruce," he said repeatedly. By the time the elevator had reached the VSE's executive floor, McDonald, who minutes earlier looked like he might go up like a Roman candle, was under control.

During the honeymoon stage of McDonald's link-up with Inco, he was like a man possessed, on the phone constantly to Toronto, asking the company when a press release would be ready, chivvying them into announcements they weren't ready to make, phoning brokers and asking if any orders had been made, then placing one himself "just to get things going." He couldn't keep still. Riding high on Casa Berardi, he threw himself into more ventures. In 1985 he made a deal with another major, Teck Corporation, to explore the claims of Golden Triangle Mining, a company he financed with $20 million raised in Quebec. Also in 1985, McDonald's Golden Hope Resources,* with

---

*Golden Hope represented a tidy profit for McDonald. He had purchased 1.2 million shares, then worth $12 million on paper, all at less than $1.15 a share; 750,000 escrowed shares, granted in return for McDonald's claims, had cost him 1 cent each, and he'd bought another 250,000 founder's shares at 15 cents. The rest he had purchased on the market at prices ranging up to $1.15.

some of McDonald's claims in the Casa Berardi area, leaped past $12 a share by June 1986 on the strength of reports showing a substantial ore body. Golden Group, another McDonald company with claims in the Casa Berardi, also traded near $10, and others in his Casa Berardi stable prospered too. The companies had all purchased property from the 1,500 claims McDonald had staked around the Golden Knight site. Suddenly, McDonald was rolling in money.

In August 1986, McDonald began to branch out. He announced a deal to buy a home video distribution company from Coca-Cola for $85 million U.S. It was the biggest deal of its kind in the VSE's history. McDonald used Nelson Entertainment Inc. of Los Angeles, a wholly owned subsidiary of the VSE-listed Nelson Holdings International Inc., to buy Embassy Home Entertainment from Coca-Cola. It was a rare VSE deal in that Embassy has considerable revenue: $72.2 million U.S. in 1985 and $14 million profit. The agreement called for the production of twelve films over a three-year peiod in conjunction with Coca-Cola. The other principals in Nelson Holdings were Barry Spikings, producer of the 1978 Oscar winner *The Deer Hunter*, and Richard Northcott, a British financier. This was just the kind of deal to gladden hearts on the street and inside the VSE. It positively reeked of the big time—Hollywood names, big money and international corporations.

As McDonald got richer and more powerful, he peeled more off more and more of his former stock hustler image. Newspaper accounts called him "publicity shy," and Peter O'Neil, Vancouver *Sun* business writer, spent months in 1985 trying to get an interview. When O'Neil finally got inside the door, Cottrell all but assaulted him for mentioning McDonald's champagne episode. In 1984 McDonald had attended a Toronto champagne reception with a bunch of other brokers. Everything was peachy until a man who managed an institutional investment account and was a pillar of the British financial community ("a real gentleman sober, but nasty as a snake drunk," says McDonald), insulted the mild-mannered Cottrell and their companies: "Why should we look at your piece of shit mining company?"

The man could have been important to McDonald and his shareholders, but McDonald quietly ordered a bottle of Dom Perignon and dumped it over the man's head. Just a few months later, McDonald, who had chortled proudly over the incident, suddenly retreated from the public eye. The baring of this and other escapades in an otherwise favourable 1984 *Canadian Business* magazine story had sullied the financier-about-town image McDonald was striving to project. At first McDonald and Cottrell had liked the article enough to want to know where they could get five hundred copies of the magazine. Then they began to get reactions from others. "Some people were asking, 'Who is this asshole?' " said Cottrell.

The first thing McDonald told Inco negotiators in 1983 was: "I want to become for Inco what Pezim is to Noranda." He used to be flattered by statements calling him the next Murray Pezim. No longer. "I don't know how many people make money with Pezim. Everybody around us makes money. Murray's from the old school. You won't find me on the phone yelling and screaming at anyone to buy $10,000 in shares. . . . You've got to remember Murray is well into his sixties. I'm only forty-six."

The new McDonald persona has come equipped with a growing sense of his own invincibility. He talks of his holding company, Noramco, started in 1982 with $30,000, being worth $500 million by 1995. He plans to get involved with more diverse deals like the Nelson Holdings home video purchase, and he is aiming for the top in mining. "I'd like to take over Inco," he said recently. If there is a problem with the rocketlike progress of McDonald's career, it is that he seems to be following in the steps of Morris Black and Murray Pezim, moving far afield of what he really knows—raising risk money to explore junior mining properties. Although McDonald now disdains comparisons with Pezim, he could learn a valuable lesson from the older promoter. If Pezim had stayed with mining, he would be a far wealthier and more respected man today. Perhaps in an omen of what is to come, McDonald made his first serious mistake in nearly four years in December 1986, when, in an act shrouded in mystery, he cut loose Ray Cottrell, the man who had held it all together.

The Money Machine: Into the 1980s

The 1980s have been a period of bureaucratization and sanitation at the Vancouver Stock Exchange. The exchange's paper is shuffled more efficiently than ever before and great effort is expended to promote the exchange's image as the premier locale for raising venture capital. But no amount of attractive packaging will forever disguise tainted contents. As a result, the 1980s have been punctuated by a series of evermore virulent scandals that the exchange seems helpless to contain. Unscrupulous promoters and brokers, briefly neutered from 1976 to 1980 while Bob Scott was president of the VSE, are running wild again. Greed and expediency seem to be the overriding ethics of the players.

CHAPTER 15

Scandal:
New Cinch, Black Friday
and the Underworld

"Oh shit no, this is too good to give the clients." A BROKER discussing various speculative stocks.

The decade started auspiciously for the Vancouver Stock Exchange with the continuation of the powerful bull market that had begun in 1978. The price of gold hit its peak of over $800 U.S. an ounce in 1980, and the Canadian government's efforts, through tax incentives and surcharges, to "Canadianize" the oil industry had made vse junior oil stocks popular. President Ronald Reagan had announced his intention to deregulate the U.S. oil and gas industry, adding further impetus to the rush for junior oil and gas companies. If the market needed a final push, it was the entry of many first-time speculators into the Vancouver market. The western housing boom that had started in 1978 doubled the value of many homes, giving people thousands of dollars of unforeseen equity. The equity wasn't cash, but it was all the incentive people needed to dabble in the market, which was making headlines with record-breaking trading and price volumes.

On Wednesday, November 20, 1980, vse records were set when 12.9 million shares, valued at $47.5 million, were traded. The average price per share was $3.69, vaulting the vse well out of penny stock status. All during that week, friction was high on the VSE's cramped trading floor as the more than two hundred traders pushed and jostled, forming and reforming their trading scrums. Fistfights broke out, and brokerage house presidents began paying visits to the floor. "I guess you could say that we're here to see how the boys are doing and to sooth their ruffled nerves," said Brink-Hudson president Brian Graves. During that period, top-producing salesmen commonly grossed $300,000 annually just from commissions.

The public threw itself into a market feeding frenzy. Ron Stanaitis, then a B.C. government employee, was caught up in the excitement too. In 1980 he took the money he'd been saving to buy a house and acted on a hot tip he'd heard from a broker at a party. (The broker is now tuning pianos.) "I sold the stock a week later and made $300. "I thought, oh my God! I'm really onto something." He picked up two more tips and laid down some more money. A broker assured him over the phone that the stock was "going over the top, but one company sank out of sight almost immediately, the other is now hovering at 17 cents with negligible trading. Stanaitis's little incursion into the market cost him $1,200, and he never even got to look at his stock certificates for his money.

The boom began to peter out in June 1981, and by July 1982 the average price per share of VSE stock had plummeted to 83 cents. In mid-1982 trading volume had declined by nearly 50 per cent over the previous year, and share value by 81 per cent. As usual, many Vancouver brokerage houses had overextended during the good time. One of them, Rademaker, MacDougall and Company, went under in August 1982.

The recession numbed the optimism of the West, and its effects—unemployment, slow growth and high bankruptcy rates—are still being felt as the 1980s draw to a close. For the VSE, however, the downturn was brief and quickly forgotten. Soon, the market began to rally. Volume in 1983 was triple that of 1982, with a record 3.1 billion shares traded. The next year the exchange announced the beginning of options trading.* In 1985 another record was broken as financing rose to $348 million, topping the 1981 high of $218 million and wiping out the dismal memory of only $50 million in 1982. As this

---

*An option is the right to buy or sell a given stock within a certain time period, and can itself be bought and sold.

frenetic activity was going on, the internal rot, which the vsE had
supposedly cut out in the 1970s, was eating away at the exchange. The
rot broke out three separate times with the New Cinch affair, Black
Friday and the Ultra Glow scam. Even more sinister were hints that
organized crime was taking an increasing interest in the Vancouver
Stock Exchange.

NEW CINCH: SALTING AN ASSAY

Remarkably few public scandals arose from the trading free-for-all of
1980–81, but one that did, the New Cinch Uranium hoax, affected
the vsE as none had done before. It actually cost the exchange
money. Most importantly, in the aftermath of New Cinch the vsE af-
firmed its philosophy that it had little responsibility for the affairs of
listed companies. New Cinch was also an eerie reprise of the 1937
Hedley Amalgamated scandal: both of them involved salting a gold
property.

The promoter of New Cinch Uranium Mines was Albert Applegath, a loquacious individual known on the street as a fast-talking
stock hustler. In later years, Applegath chose to call himself a natural
resource broker, though most knew him as a promoter. "Usually one
gentleman provides the funds," he liked to explain when describing
his role. "Another gentleman provides the idea, and I provide the corporation who would be interested in buying the property." Applegath
was a successful Toronto securities salesman until the combination of
tax problems and a divorce left him penniless in 1975. In 1976 he
approached the highly respected Toronto financier Arthur White,
who was also the godfather of Applegath's child, and spilled out his
problems. Arthur W. White is one of Canada's outstanding mine
financiers. By 1966 he had raised $15 million to finance such mines as
Red Lake Camp, ViolaMac, Cobalt Mining, DeCoursey-Brewis Minerals, Taurcanis and United Cobalt. In 1976 at the age of sixty-five,
Arthur White, along with his son Vance, had a controlling interest in
the Dickenson Group, which included Dickenson Mines and Kam-
Kotia Mines of Toronto. Also in White's portfolio was New Cinch
Uranium Mines, of which he was president.

"To be totally blunt," Applegath testified in 1984, "I was at that
particular time in my life without funds. What he [White] was doing

was resurrecting a human being in the financial sense." He convinced White to finance exploration of several New Mexico mineral prospects and to lease an estate in Albuquerque as the headquarters for the project. In return, Applegath brought to White the Orogrande property, a number of claims staked in the Jarilla Mountains, seventy kilometres north of El Paso, Texas. Between July and December 1979, an intensive drilling program was conducted and core samples from the first hole were analyzed by Chem-Tec laboratories in El Paso. According to a New Cinch release, the samples contained "gold values." These promising results were flatly contradicted by a concurrent analysis done by Vancouver consulting geologists W. G. Stevenson and Associates Ltd., whose tests showed "negligible gold-silver content." Meanwhile, Applegath, at a cost of between $250,000 and $300,000, had staked a seventeen-mile belt five miles wide around the New Cinch property. A number of Applegath's VSE companies including Brass Ring Resources, New Beginnings Resources, Tundra Gold Mines and Villeneuve Resources began negotiating for the rights to this staked land.

Exactly why the VSE allowed the disputed Chem-Tec results to stand is one of the great mysteries of the New Cinch affair. The pessimistic W. G. Stevenson report was relegated to the VSE's green confidential files and reappeared only in 1981 after the stock had crashed. In 1985, VSE president Bob Scott defended the exchange's actions in the pretrial hearing: "In this case, they [the Dickenson Group] were experienced operators and had been around a long time. Their reputation had a bearing on the way the case was handled by the VSE." Scott gave no reason why the results of testing by unknowns from El Paso were favoured over those of experienced analysts from Vancouver, but the VSE must have been suspicious, because in December 1980, the exchange sent engineer James Mackie to check up on the Orogrande site and Chem-Tec laboratories. By this time, however, the Chem-Tec results were already enshrined in a press release campaign.

In August 1980 the VSE had cleared a statement of material facts (SMF) allowing New Cinch to raise money through a public offering of shares and warrants. The SMF, which claimed significant gold values in the holes in question and made no mention of the conflicting assays, was signed on behalf of the underwriters—Continental Carlisle Douglas, McDermid Miller (now McDermid St. Lawrence) and Canarim Investments—by Peter Brown. As part of the underwriting deal, insiders received warrants* entitling them to purchase 200,000 shares at 50 cents and a further 100,000 shares at a slightly higher price. These shares, which cost less than $150,000, would have a paper worth of nearly $9 million at the peak of the market.

On November 10th the results from hole twenty-nine, an excellent 0.21 ounces of gold per ton over 589 feet, were revealed with an aura of great secrecy. "We're not announcing who did the assaying for us," stated New Cinch vice-president H. I. Tony Miller. "And we're not saying who did the drilling. There's a lot of people standing around the property." But the information had leaked out hours before, setting the VSE afire. Between November 10th and 25th, the share price of New Cinch leaped from $3.80 to $27, and the price of warrants correspondingly jumped from 75 cents to $12.50. The assay results released November 24th from hole thirty-one—0.13 ounces of gold and 0.22 ounces of silver along 443 feet of the core—bumped the stock to its peak of $29.50. "It's still an exploration project, but the results are starting to have the earmarks of a major gold discovery," enthused Peter Brown.

This was where Willroy Mines, controlled by Little Long Lake (later Lac Minerals) of Toronto, jumped in. The company began buying up New Cinch shares, eventually amassing 16.7 per cent of the 6 million common shares and 57 per cent of a series of warrants, for $25.7 million.

Late in December 1980 and early in January 1981, rumours began to circulate on the street about the discrepancies in assay results. The gossip came to a head in January, when Willroy Mines issued a press release stating that independent tests had come up with substantially lower values than New Cinch's assays. Willroy punctuated their concern by dumping all of their New Cinch shares on the market, at a staggering loss of $21 million. The VSE briefly suspended trading, as share prices dropped first to $7 and then $3 by the end of January, and instituted a review of the previous assay results to be conducted by the well-known international consulting firm Davy McKee Corporation.

Incredibly, a brisk trade was still being conducted in New Cinch shares, the demand ebbing and flowing in relation to rumours about when the McKee study would be finished and what it would find. On

---

*A warrant is a certificate that gives the holder the right to purchase stocks at a set price within a set time. Warrants are traded in much the same manner as stocks.

February 5th, for instance, the price climbed back up to $7 from $3.10 on the strength of rumours that McKee's results would be favourable, but immediately dropped to $4.55 when New Cinch denied that the review was finished. On Friday, February 13, 1981, Willroy Mines Ltd. filed a multimillion dollar writ in Ontario Supreme Court, seeking damages of $21,396,000 against New Cinch's controlling shareholder, Dickenson Mines Ltd.; Kam-Kotia Mines Ltd.; the VSE; Chem-Tec, and various individuals including New Cinch's president Vance White, vice-president Tony Miller and Albert Applegath. A week later Davey McKee published a preliminary review of their results. To prevent tampering, they had instituted rigorous security procedures on the Orogrande site. New cores were taken from the controversial holes, and samples were taken every five feet over the six hundred feet drilled. The gold values ranged from 0.005 to 0.1 ounces of gold per ton over ten feet in one hole and 0.035 to 0.1 in another hole. Both results were far below those found by Chem-Tec. McKee admitted for the first time that they were also looking for "any deliberate or inadvertent salting of drill core pulps."

Des Harrison, the VSE's new vice-president of listings, was asked at a press conference why trading hadn't been halted during the review period instead of being briefly halted whenever the stock reacted to rumours about the review. He replied: "As far as the exchange is concerned, all of the available information is available to everyone. And there's no doubt in our minds that everyone knows about the uncertainty: in this instance, the drill results. Therefore, we feel we should continue to provide a market for the shares."

New Cinch shares continued to trade on the strength of rumours until December 11, 1981, when the company formally announced that Chem-Tec's November 1980 assays had indeed been contaminated. Gold had been added to one of the flux ingredients used to test the assays. No one had any knowledge of how it got there, but having gold in the test materials ensured that there would be gold in the test results.

At this point the New Cinch story turns from a stock swindle to something considerably more. On November 14, 1982, Michael Opp was found murdered in his Phoenix, Arizona, apartment. It was a cool and professional execution: the killer had kicked in Opp's door, shot him once in the head and disappeared into the night. A Phoenix resident, Hoyt Trujillo, was subsequently charged and acquitted. The prosecutor maintained that the murders involved a dispute over a small drug sale and a $25 television set.

Opp's father found an eighteen-page letter, allegedly written by his son, detailing his knowledge of the New Cinch affair. Michael Opp's letter, really a confession of a failed life, describes his homosexual tendencies, his criminal record and various drug binges. In the letter, young Opp claimed that he was an employee of Chem-Tec, the firm that had done the first assay, and lived in the home of the firm's owner, Robert Simon. Opp further claimed that Simon had bought Chem-Tec with money advanced by Applegath and Vance White. Michael Opp's parents said that their son had expressed fear for his life: "He could be killed over the salting of the Orogrande assay. He knew the assays were being salted by someone higher up."

On August 2, 1984, Lac Minerals began a new $21.4-million suit in B.C. Supreme court against the Vancouver Stock Exchange; former VSE officials Des Harrison and Jeremy Wise; Peter Brown, president of Canarim Investment, and Gus MacPhail, chairman of Continental Carlisle Douglas. "The main reason we have taken the action in B.C. is that the VSE would not appear at the suit we launched in Toronto in February 1981," said Lac's lawyer Trish Jackson, of the Toronto firm Tory and Tory.

In June 1985, the VSE announced in a press release that it would contribute $275,000 in legal costs towards a $4 million out-of-court settlement with Lac: "The key factors that influenced the exchange in agreeing to the settlement were the significant legal costs and executive time which would be expended in defending the case if it were to continue." New Cinch would put up a further $1.3 million towards the settlement. It is not known who among the defendants paid the remaining $2 million.

The New Cinch Affair is one of the most confusing and mysterious scandals ever to hit the VSE. It is clear that the Chem-Tec assay was salted, but who benefited from the salting other than the obvious underwriting brokers and other VSE insiders? Everybody claims it wasn't them, and as the years go by, it appears that there will be no criminal charges relating to the case. "It's a travesty beyond description," summed up Bert Applegath. "It will go down in the annals of this country we live in as one of the most infamous cases ever to come to court. . . . Perhaps the greatest tragedy of all, other than the human frailty, is that none of us in this room, or any room, might ever know who concocted this whole thing." Today Applegath is a paper millionaire several times over, and his companies, New Beginnings and Tundra Gold Mines, are still actively traded on the VSE.

Of the tragedies associated with the New Cinch hoax, the effect on the VSE is one of the greatest. During Bob Scott's tenure as president, the exchange had made considerable strides in taking responsibility for listed companies by vetting releases and keeping a close eye on promoters. After New Cinch, instead of being challenged to even greater heights of vigilance, the exchange chose to retreat into a very narrow definition of its role. On the bottom of press releases issued by listed companies now appears this disavowal: "The information contained herein has neither been approved nor disapproved by the Vancouver Stock Exchange."

BLACK FRIDAY: THE SCANDAL TO END ALL SCANDALS

On October 19, 1984, VSE president Don Hudson and the rest of the Vancouver Stock Exchange were skating placidly along, enjoying a return to record-breaking trading volumes and grandly pronouncing the VSE as the leading venture capital exchange— not only in Canada but the world. New Cinch was out of the headlines for the time being, and the future was glowing. Yet, beneath the surface, was roiling a smelly mess that erupted into a nightmare of international proportions. "Like the end of a cracking whip, it was heard before it was seen," wrote Mike Macbeth in *Canadian Business* magazine. "And by the time it could be seen, by the time it lay still and lifeless, it was over." In the space of only two hours, six VSE resource stocks—Beauford Resources, Champagne Resources, Rencon Mining Company, Shiloh Resources, Amazon Petroleum and Marathon Mines—crashed with an impressive finality. The event generated headlines around the world, the likes of which hadn't been seen since the bucketing scandals of 1929. Friday, October 19th, came to be known as Black or Bloody Friday.

Stocks falling out of bed on the VSE are hardly news. They are a fact of life. What distinguished Black Friday was that it was the culmination of a blatant stock manipulation—one that the VSE bureaucracy could neither cope with nor apparently understand. The exchange's failure to halt trading before and during the crash, and its befuddled reactions after the fact, allowed the culprits to become the accuser. "The one thing that the Beauford gang did very well, they made fools of the stock exchange after the event," observes John Woods. "The swindlers who ran that operation screamed long and loud about 2,600 shares that ruined their market.* Now if 2,600 shares ruined their market, their market was no good to start with. And if they were the market makers, why the hell didn't they buy the shares [themselves]? Now that's my retort to those liars."

Friday, October 19th, was "sheer hell," according to Doug Garrod, the VSE's respected vice-president of listings. "Don Hudson and I wondered if we were going to live through it. There were charges, countercharges and accusations flying all over the place. Hudson and I went to the washroom at the same time, and we looked at each other in the mirror, and said, 'This is awful. We'd better go out there and do it for the old lady.' "

One of the ironies of Black Friday is that until the crash, the promotion was well run. The president of Beauford was Ross Dion, age forty-seven. Behind the scenes were promoters Erich Brunnhuber, forty-nine, and Bert Roosen, fifty-seven, who were eventually charged and convicted. All three were relatively unknown on the VSE. What *was* known wasn't altogether favourable, but that hardly set them apart from numerous other hustlers.

What the promoters of Beauford so brilliantly constructed was a reverse pyramid, perched point first on their own initial purchase of stock that gave them control of Beauford. The building blocks of the pyramid were purchases of stock on margin, the amount actually paid by a customer who is buying with credit. The balance is advanced by the broker against acceptable collateral, in this case stock in Beauford and its related junior companies. Standard practice varies, but generally blue-chip stock is good for 50 per cent of its stock value and juniors 25 per cent. As the purchases of Beauford and its companion stocks brought the price up, the value of the collateral stock also rose, allowing even more market purchases with the same shares.

To facilitate trading, Brunnhuber and Roosen opened more than forty nominee accounts at different brokerage firms. Trading back and forth among these accounts steadily increased the stock prices. In all, more than fifteen shell companies were formed to support the Black Friday stocks. These companies opened more than 150 nominee accounts at nearly half of the forty-six Vancouver brokerage houses. On

*Woods is referring to the slightly more than 1,600 shares of Beauford that sent the share price tumbling on Black Friday.

some days Brunnhuber and Roosen personally accounted for all of the trading in Beauford. From the trading of this pair alone, brokers collected nearly $200,000 in commissions.

Beauford Resources Ltd., the pivotal stock in the fiasco, was listed on the VSE on November 25, 1983. In February 1984, Beauford's $1 million in assets consisted of a variety of unproven mining claims and oil and gas leases. Through the first six months of 1984, the stock steadily climbed from $2.50 to $4. Promotion of the Beauford stock over the summer of 1984 was routine, with periodic optimistic news releases about the state of affairs. Announcement of the purchase of additional oil leases helped bump the price from $4 to $5. On August 9th a statement containing a geologist's report pegged the value of Beauford's oil and gas properties at $16.9 million—making Beauford theoretically worth $17 a share. The VSE rejected the report, but not before the stock rose to $8 under heavy trading. The report that the VSE finally accepted valued Beauford at $1.09 million. Nonetheless the stock kept climbing; in the six weeks leading up to the crash it reached $11.25.

Black Friday started out like any other day. Between 7:00 A.M., when the VSE opened, and 12:30 P.M., more than 10,000 Beauford shares changed hands in the $10 to $11 range. By lunchtime it was clear that the sell orders could no longer be matched by equivalent bids. No one was supporting the market: no promoter was buying when investors wanted to sell. A whiff of something desperate crept into the air, and by 12:30 there was a flood of sell orders. Beauford proceeded to drop like a bowling ball down a flight of stairs. A tiny board lot sold at $9, another 100 shares at $8, 500 at $7, 600 at $5, 100 at $4, 200 at $3.50. Within twenty minutes the trading of a paltry 1,600 shares pushed the price down to $2. As Beauford's stock thumped downward, a traders' mob formed in front of the marking board. The five other associated stocks became unhinged too, and in the final thirty-six minutes of trading nearly 250,000 shares in the group changed hands at successively lower and lower prices. When it was all over, the six companies had traded more than 2.5 million shares. Paper losses were estimated as high as $40 million. Brokers alone lost $5 million on margined accounts.

That day VSE officials blundered blindly about, and a minor official was quoted in newspapers, speaking vaguely of looking for a common link among the companies. Meanwhile, the president of Beauford, Ross Dion, was telling everyone who would listen that the crash was the VSE's fault. "It was not what you'd call an orderly market," he said. "Normally, when a stock moves up a certain percentage, we ask for a halt in trading. But when we asked for our stock to be halted, they told us they didn't want to do it."

Don Hudson, the VSE president, wouldn't speak at all until the following Monday, and even then he wouldn't comment directly on the events of Black Friday. "If we halted trading at every company's request, it would stop the market," Hudson said to explain why the VSE hadn't put a lock on Beauford. "We have to say why, and they have to have some answers. We'll only halt if there's a reason, or if we believe there is something wrong. In most cases, halts are done to make disclosure of information to the public that is not previously known." Hudson then shrugged the whole thing off by offering up the traditional "you pays yer money and you takes yer chances" line: "For every seller, there is a buyer. It's a marketplace after all." What slipped past Hudson was the fact that it hadn't been a market in any sense of the word. The promoter or promoters were creating the activity, and when they pulled out, it all fell apart. The five associated stocks disintegrated with Beauford because they were unhealthily connected, each relying on the other to keep the prices up.

Six days after Black Friday, the VSE held a press conference starring exchange chairman Tony Hepburn, past chairman Peter Brown, president Don Hudson and vice-president of listings Doug Garrod. Hepburn admitted that the VSE was reviewing its rules and regulations. "We have learned by this," he stated. He went on to issue an incredible warning to the stock-buying public, saying that if investors had examined the companies and their assets, they would have found no reason to buy. No one asked him why the VSE had listed the companies if there was no reason for investors to buy their stock. Nor did they ask why the VSE had not become suspicious when the stock, which investors had no reason to buy, had risen so steadily. On September 2, 1985, about a year after Black Friday, Don Hudson added insult to injury by telling a *New York Times* reporter that "no thinking person would have bought stocks on that basis." Again, no one asked why a thinking stock exchange had listed them, or why twenty-three of the forty-six VSE members had held margin accounts for the promoters.

Peter Brown claims to have been leery of the Black Friday gang long before the fateful day, refusing to give them margin accounts: "The three guys in Black Friday had known problems from way back." Just why Brown, a former VSE chairman and a board member for ten years, didn't pick up his phone and call his pal Don Hudson is rather perplexing. It would have prevented a lot of problems.

Not only was Ross Dion unapologetic for Black Friday, he indignantly claimed that his company had been victimized by the exchange. He announced his intention of removing Beauford from the VSE because he wasn't happy being involved with "an exchange where it is possible for the events of October 19 to happen."

On July 17, 1985, after a laborious nine-month investigation, the superintendent of brokers announced that Erich Brunnhuber and Engelbert Roosen had been charged with defrauding West German investors of $1.3 million. They were accused of making unrealistic promises to West German investors about the future performance of Beauford and its related companies, and of not using the money raised to buy stock. Instead, they had put $600,000 into their own pockets and spread the remainder over forty different brokerage accounts to help keep the Beauford market moving upward. No charges were laid against Dion.

Brunnhuber and Roosen's trial, which began in December 1986, proved to be a continuation of the public relations nightmare for the Vancouver Stock Exchange. Day after day during the seventeen-day trial, Roger Cutler, the defence lawyer, described the activities of the defendants as normal business practice around the VSE. "They were playing by the rules of the game, and they didn't make those rules. . . . The impression being portrayed is that this was an isolated situation." On January 9, 1987, ironically a Friday, Roosen and Brunnhuber were found guilty of two counts of fraud, one of theft and one of stock market manipulation. They were sentenced to seven years in prison. The sentence was one of the harshest in the history of Canadian stock promotion.

The Vancouver Stock Exchange saw the verdict as some kind of exoneration. "The exchange feels confident that the public will understand that if this sort of situation occurs, the exchange will not hesitate to act," said Marc Foreman, the VSE's vice-president in charge of trading. The Vancouver *Province* stock market reporter covering the trial, David Baines, had a different view: "As far as the system is concerned, it's more of a censure than a vindication. Certainly anybody who sat through the trial would be wary of the Vancouver Stock Exchange." The judge, Mr. Justice John Bouck, had the final word in the matter: "Ladies and gentlemen, I don't know how many of you are going to rush out and invest in the stock market after this. I suspect not many."

ORGANIZED CRIME AND THE VANCOUVER STOCK EXCHANGE

There have been whispers about organized crime's activity on the VSE since the 1950s, but the first public airing of the suggestion didn't come until March 28, 1969, after four highly profitable years sparked by Pyramid and Dynasty. During a testy marathon legislative debate that lasted until 4:00 A.M., NDP leader Robert Strachan said, "The Vancouver Stock Exchange is a local legalized Las Vegas," insinuating that the exchange—like the casinos of Nevada, which were very much in the news at the time—was controlled by the underworld. Later that year, a Vancouver interviewer asked author and junior mining expert Ivan Shaffer if he believed that the Mafia was involved in the VSE. "The Mafia will never take over the market, but they have a great influence," he said, and went on to tacitly accuse the brokerage houses of complicity as they were aware of "the undesirables" but had made no move to rout them out "because of greed." Jack Van Luven, the VSE president, rose to do battle, stating that "to the best of our knowledge any Mafia affiliation with the exchange that we are aware of has been eliminated." In other words, he was admitting that organized crime had been, and perhaps still was, involved with the VSE and, what's more, that the exchange had known about it.

Not until 1972 did any real evidence show up to indicate the Mob was indeed around. In December of that year, William "Fats" Robertson and Archibald Robb were prohibited from buying or selling securities in B.C. pending an investigation into the trading of Attilla Resources and Bonus Resources on the VSE. Robertson and Robb were the most notorious of a West Coast drug-dealing ring and had strong connections to the Mafia. They were charged with deceitful stock distribution and with paying secret commissions and bribes to salesmen across the country.

Paradoxically, the Fats Robertson case was the best thing that could have happened to the Vancouver Stock Exchange on the subject of the Mafia or organized crime. Because Robertson was charged and Attilla Resources suspended from trading, the VSE is able to point to the case as an example both of its ability to combat organized crime and the failure of the Mafia to infiltrate the securities industry: "They tried it, by God, but we stopped 'em!" The proponents of this reasoning neglect to mention the fact that Robertson was not convicted. Also unspoken is the fact that Fats, while a clever and violent drug dealer, had no experience in the securities industry, much less in the speculative market. He was simply taking a casual dip into the warm, inviting waters of the VSE.

The subject of organized crime came up again in 1974 in a report on commercial crime by the Co-ordinated Law Enforcement Unit (CLEU) in Vancouver:

> Associates of organized crime syndicates from the East have attempted to engage in activity in the Vancouver market. In addition, a number of known local criminals, including drug figures and gambling promoters, are, or have been, involved in the market. It has been estimated that there are about 25 to 50 people with criminal records involved in some way or another. The Securities Commission knows of people with long criminal records who associate with major criminally-oriented promoters.

That is a quote from the shortened public version. The more detailed report with names and cases was never released.

Despite CLEU's assertions about criminals being involved in the VSE, few were convinced. "The market isn't really a fruitful area for organized crime because they have to get too many other people in with them. And they don't know the business either. It's not as simple as prostitution or drugs. The few attempts they have made have been caught fairly early," says Bob Scott. His sentiments have been echoed by various superintendents of brokers, exchange officials, brokers and a large number of the RCMP. Another old saw about the market and the Mob is that any incursion by the underworld into trading can be handled by shorting them to death. One broker was betting heavily against a stock controlled by Fats Robertson. Robertson paid a visit to the man one day, and the shorting attack stopped immediately. The broker also took the midnight plane out of town and hasn't been seen since.

The attitude that organized crime isn't smart enough to play the market elicits guffaws from the experts. "Listen, they can count as well as anyone else can," contradicts Stu Allen, a special investigator with the U.S. Securities and Exchange Commission division of enforcement. "They may not have the expertise themselves, but they will go out and buy it." The experts point to the subtle and sophisticated control of union pension funds in the U.S. and Canada, the operation of dubious offshore banks, and the infiltration and control of legitimate businesses like garbage collection as evidence of the Mafia having moved beyond the simple basics of drugs, numbers and prostitutes. (When pressed, SEC officials admit that there are major ongoing operations specifically designed to prove the involvement of organized crime in American stock markets.) Additionally, the Mob has never worried too much about the involvement of outsiders in their business. Hundreds of lawyers, accountants, politicians and corporation heads who provide services for the Mafia are not made men or bona fide family members.

One of the reasons the VSE is not seen as a Mafia target is because everyone assumes that organized crime would move in only if they could reap the kinds of rewards they do in their traditional areas of interest. In fact, the mob doesn't need another illegal profit vehicle nearly so much as it requires some means of laundering money. In 1983 alone, illegal drug sales in Canada totalled $9.65 billion: heroin $2.8 billion, cocaine $875 million, various chemicals $375 million, with the remainder attributed to marijuana. It is often easier to make money out of crime than it is to find ways of spending money without drawing unwanted attention. As a result, there is a large and experienced industry dedicated to cleaning dirty money.

The VSE could have been designed for organized crime. Since 30 per cent of the heroin and 50 per cent of the marijuana sold in Canada passes through B.C., a money laundry in Vancouver is geographically convenient. Further, the securities industry in the province is no longer the parochial little institution that it was in the 1950s, and any buying or selling that crosses international boundaries logarithmically increases the difficulty of tracing trades to real people. It is not uncommon now for listed companies to boast many directors from other countries. Even the promoter community, once largely confined to people from Vancouver and Toronto, has recently been fleshed out with a host of characters hailing from Australia, the Bahamas, West Germany, Holland, Italy and elsewhere. Since big money and an international presence are now commonplace on the VSE, any Mafia presence is comfortably diluted.

It is not only the nature of investment and where it is coming from that makes the VSE, next to offshore banks and dummy corporations, the perfect laundering vehicle. Anonymity, as long as accounts are paid on time, is a way of life in the brokerage community. Nominees, proxies, strawmen, call them what you will, are a recognized and common way to do business. Accounts can be opened with little or no identification, and if it is a big account, margins are extended without pressing too hard for bank references. Some Vancouver brokerage houses rigorously enforce the golden rule of the industry, Know Your Client, but many others just pay it lip service. "We are a big firm and well respected," says the senior member of one of the VSE's largest member firms. "But if someone comes in here and opens an account with $100,000 and starts trading, the shit will fly from above if I hold him up because of a few unanswered, dumb-assed questions. Face it, there's lots of people trading through middlemen on the VSE, and it's not my job to find out what they do for a living."

There are many ways of laundering money on the VSE, but the simplest may be the best. First, register one master trading account to the person who is to receive the laundered money. Only clearly legal funds will enter that account, possibly money borrowed from a bank. (In a nice twist, overseas banks owned by organized crime may make the loans.) Any profits taken out of that account will be pristine and even eligible for tax credits.

Second, buy a substantial interest in a listed shell (there are people who specialize in shells) or in a new underwriting with cheap stock. The shares can be acquired over a long period and held until needed—that way, there is no quickening of market interest. Nominees then open a multitude of trading accounts with the dirty money at a host of brokerage firms. As long as each nominee holds less than 10 per cent, no insider trading reports need to be filed.

Third, the master account slowly makes blocks of stocks available. They are picked up by the nominees through their various trading accounts. The aim of the master account is to remove a dollar of clean money for every dollar of dirty money used by the nominees. A one-for-one trade between clean and dirty money is considered excellent in the laundering business, and profits are a bonanza.

Finally, with any luck, a real market will be generated by this buying and selling activity, and public buying will elevate the stock further or keep it up long enough for the master account to make a profit. Even if the master account is selling as the price is declining, it won't be too difficult to make a profit since the stock was purchased for pennies. The system is open to many embellishments, and obviously any number of stocks could be used to launder money, not just one.

Not only does the money get laundered, but the nominees aren't in any real danger. It's not uncommon to buy and sell stock for years without ever meeting the broker you're dealing with. If the authorities suspect some illegal activity, the nominees can simply disappear with no one the wiser. This kind of laundering can be easily done without the co-operation of brokers or promoters, though their involvement certainly makes everything a little smoother. Police market specialists are convinced that laundering is happening on the VSE. To what extent, no one knows. But it's an easy logical step to envision organized crime going from a little laundering now and then to controlling the market in a big way.

When organized crime is mentioned, most people think of the Cosa Nostra or Chinese tongs. However, there is another group, with unlikely antecedents, that has definite interests in the Vancouver Stock Exchange—motorcycle gangs. The leather-jacketed gang members have metamorphosed from the 1960s "good ol' boys just raising hell" subculture to a high-powered, internationally connected criminal organization, second only to the Mafia.

According to the Criminal Intelligence Service of Canada, motorcycle gangs are a major organized crime threat, and in fact, have become the dominant organized crime force in some Canadian cities. Many gang members are now millionaires thanks to a superstructure so sophisticated that counterintelligence against police is a matter of course. According to the RCMP, Satan's Angels, the dominant gang in British Columbia, promotes rock concerts, owns ranches in the interior of the province and is active on the VSE.

Gang expert Sergeant Kenneth Reid (in 1981 head of the Modesto, California, task force on motorcycle gangs), erases the Hunter S. Thompson image most people have of the gangs and their hangers-on: "It's an organization which has expanded to the point that its members have become, in many cases, wealthy businessmen. They own property and businesses on a grand scale. They have been so successful that well-educated, well-respected businessmen who have never before become involved in criminal activities have invested hundreds of thousands in quick-profit criminal activities. Businessmen, teachers and even attorneys have become part of this organization, some even becoming members."

A report released in 1984 by the RCMP confirms that these gangs have the same laundering needs as other elements of organized crime:

> The manufacturing and distribution of illicitly produced chemical drugs in Canada, tend to be dominated by outlaw motorcycle gangs operating throughout the country with strong links to similar gangs operating in the United States. Money laundering through real estate and legitimate business investments will enable these groups to further consolidate their power base and to diversify their operations.

Organized crime in a number of different forms is without doubt involved in the VSE. The influence of organized crime on legitimate business is one of the most pernicious problems facing the police today, and its presence on the VSE is no exception. Regardless of the extent of infiltration into the market in the past, the VSE is becoming a more attractive target every year. Not long ago a $10 stock was a very big deal, but now $25 and $30 stocks are unremarkable, and some, like Chopp Computers, sail up close to or even past $100. The profits to be made on such speculative issues are fantastic. The VSE is also becoming more international every year, and, with the introduction of interlisted stocks (listed in Hong Kong and Vancouver), the Asian influence will become larger. Any criminal organization with strong international connections, a multitude of obscure hiding places for money and a limitless supply of cash is bound to view the VSE with increasing favour, not only as a place to clean money but also as a place to make it.

As long as the VSE members pretend that organized crime does not and could not possibly exist on the exchange, they will be providing a fertile breeding ground for a group that pays little attention to policy manuals.

CHAPTER 16

Beverlee Claydon and Ultra Glow Cosmetics

"People keep throwing money at her." A CLAYDON ASSOCIATE explaining her persistence in promoting Ultra Glow.

The story of Beverlee Claydon and Ultra Glow Cosmetics Ltd. illustrates the ineffectiveness of the VSE when it is faced with someone who has little regard for the niceties of regulations. Far more money, at least $9 million, mysteriously disappeared from Ultra Glow and its related companies' coffers in 1983, 1984 and 1985 than was lost during the infamous manipulations that culminated in the internationally publicized Black Friday scandal of 1985. Yet, the principals of Ultra Glow are to this day actively involved in promoting stocks in British Columbia. An exotic creature, Beverlee Claydon flaunts her mystique and wears the turbulence of her career like a badge of honour.

Thursday April 18, 1985, was a day of contrasts. Outside, it was a clear, crisp spring afternoon, and the long azure horizon invited optimism and renewal. Strangers smiled at each other in the street, and the relentless momentum of a city at work was slowed. Inside, in the commercially plush confines of a conference room in the Four Seasons Hotel, any generosity of spirit was strangled by tension. Fifty people—prosperous and middle-aged—sat trying to look at ease. But their expressions showed a combination of muted anger and despair, and their conversation, devoid of pleasantries, was limited to tight-throated enquiries about the time. Around the group swirled a subtle aura of fear—that special variety you feel when you wonder, deep in your soul, if you've done something very foolish with your money. It's not the kind of feeling you get after blowing a small fortune on a whimsical present, but the bowel-knotting doubt that comes after—always after—buying a used car from a really nice young man, without first searching the title.

The fifty were stock investors, and they were waiting for Beverlee Claydon, president of Ultra Glow Cosmetics Ltd., to tell them why they had lost millions on the collapse of her company. Just two short years ago, their stock had been the toast of the Vancouver Stock Exchange, one of the heaviest traders on the floor and the envy of everyone not savvy enough to get in at the beginning. But on that April day, the company was disgraced, permanently delisted for securities violations, and the stock hadn't traded in six months. The meeting that Claydon called wasn't even recognized under VSE or public incorporation act rules.

Promptly at 3:30 P.M., Madame President wafted into the room, enveloped in scent and lit by a halo of excitement and promise. She was flanked by the two young principals of her most recent auditing firm, Corcoran and Company. The sober mantle of their profession couldn't hide their delight in being part of a larger-than-life-world—its glamour authenticated by the presence of actress Margot Kidder in the entourage. Kidder, lean and strikingly severe in a dark man-tailored business suit, was so deeply bronzed and radiant she appeared almost radioactive. Part of her sheen came from the Hollywood sun, but the rest was bestowed by the cosmetic around which the fortunes of Ultra Glow turned.

Claydon easily matched Kidder glow for glow. She was forty then, a stunningly crafted blonde who looked like a Barbie doll grown up—slick, streetwise and chic. Her personality and penchant for the harsh flash of diamonds have earned her the nickname "Sparkle Plenty" among friends. The atmosphere in the meeting room lightened palpably as she dispensed bon mots and cheery hellos to acquaintances and strangers. Subtly, even in the first few seconds, Claydon took the temperature of the audience. With each smile she made penetrating eye contact with someone, charming and assessing at the same time. As she moved to the front of the room, fifty pairs of eyes glued themselves to the pale, flowing garments she favours, and even with her back to the investors, she sensed their truculence beginning to melt. When she turned to face the room, wide-eyed with candour, she projected utter confidence.

You'd never guess that the woman standing there had a lot of explaining to do. More than $5 million had passed through Ultra Glow's treasury: $3 million to Charles Blair International Inc. (a now-defunct New York cosmetic company), nearly $1 million paid to Claydon and her two private companies in the form of loans, advances on inventory and deferred start-up costs, and a further $1 million lost in an inexplicable welter of expense accounts and convoluted financial statements. Lawsuits and creditors were everywhere, sales unsubstantiated and the whereabouts of Ultra Glow inventory a mystery. To top it off, an ominous investigation by the superintendent of brokers office, in co-operation with the RCMP fraud squad, was advancing on both Ultra Glow and Claydon.

Turning up the volume of her sincerity full blast, Claydon began her remarks with pathetic, wrenching descriptions of selling her jewels and furs to keep the company going while her mother, an unpaid volunteer, manned the company switchboard. She then switched channels in an eyeblink, assuming the gentle, optimistic manner of an instructor teaching climbing to a group of vertigo-prone adults. "Ultra Glow is doing very, very well," she said. "What we're going to do today is ratify the financial statement. It's all very straightforward where the money went."

In truth, very little about Ultra Glow is straightforward, and the verifiable facts are few. In 1981, Ultra Glow Cosmetics International Ltd., a private company, was registered in British Columbia (incorporation certificate No. 226514). Fifty-two percent of the ownership was held by Claydon herself, the rest by her brother, Robert, and mother, Joyce. The company's sole product is Ultra Glow (also sold as Le Glow), a rust-coloured, loose facial powder that, when applied, imbues even the most pallid complexion with the lustre of sunnier climes. "I've used it for four or five years," endorses actress Margot Kidder, Superman's girlfriend and, in 1985, a director of Ultra Glow. "My sister would come down from Vancouver and visit me, and she had this stuff. If she had a hangover she would look immediately healthy and young." By March 1981, Claydon had managed to convince the Hudson's Bay Company department store in Vancouver to stock her miracle powder. Shortly after, the glossy, tortoise-shell box began showing up in other major retail outlets: Woodward's department stores, London Drugs and Shoppers Drug Mart. The price varied but was most frequently between $17.95 and $19.95.

In 1983, Beverlee Claydon launched a second company, a public one this time, called Ultra Glow Cosmetics Ltd., which was listed on the Vancouver Stock Exchange in June. Claydon's private company retained manufacturing rights to the powder and distribution rights throughout western North America. In return for 800,000 class "B" escrowed shares, Claydon signed over to the public company the right to sell the product in the big markets of eastern Canada and the U.S. east of the Mississippi. The escrowed shares gave Claydon complete control of the public company.

Even as it was being listed, the public company was swinging into action. On June 30, 1983, it purchased 20 per cent of Charles Blair International Inc., a fragrance distributorship with troubled finances but a sexy French connection and a good New York address. The price was $100,000 U.S., plus 25,000 class "B" Ultra Glow shares to be paid to the company's president, Isidore Capelouto, with an option to acquire another 60 per cent. The stated purpose of the purchase was to provide Ultra Glow with instant, hard-to-acquire shelf space in stores where the Blair product was sold (the number of outlets touted ranged between sixty and two hundred, depending on whom you talked to). At the same time, the powder was renamed Le Glow—"for the woman who wants nothing short of everything," stated the company's sophisticated promotion material. "When we changed the name, it went from $16.50 to $24.50 [retail]," Claydon boasted at the time.

On paper, the relationship among the three companies was simple and plausible. Claydon's private company would manufacture and package Le Glow and sell it to the public company, which, in turn, would ship it to Blair in New York for distribution and sale in the stores where Charles Blair already had shelf space.

While all this was going on, four of the biggest Vancouver brokerage houses—Odlum Brown, Bache Securities, Pitfield MacKay and Paine Webber—were pushing Ultra Glow shares, which had opened for trading at $2. Claydon, never idle, embarked upon a media blitz.

Beverlee Claydon could have been designed as press media copy. She is photogenic. She is entertaining. She is high-spirited. She has a warm throaty laugh, lots of colourful anecdotes and an engaging line of ingenuous, uncensored chatter. She told one interviewer that morticians loved Ultra Glow because of the lifelike sheen it lent to corpses. She told anyone who would listen about how she'd burst into the Hudson's Bay Company store in Vancouver in 1981, "dusted everyone in sight" and landed Ultra Glow's first placement. She told about blowing into Bloomingdale's main store in New York and convincing the cosmetic industry's toughest customer to give the product an unprecedented seven sales locations (including three for Ultra Glow's masculine counterpart, Brava Bronze). As Claydon told a writer for Vancouver-based *Equity* magazine, which featured her on its November 1983 cover:

> Fortunately, thank god the gal who was in charge of the cosmetics department was one of those little pasty, white ladies—she looked perfect. We couldn't have picked a better one. She was one of those gals that Ultra Glow made a 400 per cent difference. We couldn't drag her away from the mirror.

Numerous other interviews and stories appeared in such diverse publications as *Executive Magazine,* the *Financial Post, Colorado Magazine* and twice in the prestigious American fragrance industry newsletter *FDC Reports.* There were countless newspaper articles, and dozens of radio interviews and television appearances. Claydon was an ideal subject, and she was always available. She predicted that Le Glow would become a staple "just like lipstick and eye makeup" and was quoted as expecting sales as high as $17 million and earnings as high as $1 per share in the coming year.

The cosmetic industry is one of the most savagely competitive in the world, but winners are inevitably big ones. In 1982, Indian Earth, a U.S. product similar to Le Glow, had achieved more than $10 million in sales, and in 1983 Revlon's lookalike, Pure Radiance, had racked up $20 million. It isn't uncommon for successful cosmetic firms to achieve share values of ten and sometimes up to twenty-five times their earnings. Fuelled partly by this knowledge and partly by Claydon's inimitable hype, the price of heavily traded Ultra Glow Cosmetics Ltd. stock rose from $2 to $7 in less than a year. Then in June 1984, the shares were split two-for-one.

"Claydon is on a roll," enthused Vancouver *Sun* columnist Denny Boyd, "a hot roll that has the yeasty smell of success." There were notably few dissenters along the Ultra Glow path. "I have a basic healthy skepticism when a stock as appealing as that gets so heavily promoted," says Henry Huber, a Vancouver broker and publisher of the market newsletter *Uptrend.* "I warned a couple of my clients to get out of it. They wouldn't; they liked the story."

To understand the turn that the story took in 1984, it's useful to know a little of the tangled web that is Beverlee Claydon's past. Her life history has the verve, colour and melodrama of a prime-time soap opera. Unfortunately most of it is just a script. Born in Vancouver around 1945, her mother a professional dancer and her father a professional musician, Claydon moved to the U.S. when she was five. Her business career began just after high school, and she tells a charming tale of crashing the male, tradition-bound stockbroker enclave in New York, lying about her age and becoming a broker at the age of eighteen for Merrill Lynch, Pierce, Fenner and Smith. "The first thing I did was get a limo and driver," she bubbles. "I figured having your own limo—not a rented limo—boom, you've got their attention." In fact, Merrill Lynch has never heard of her nor has she ever been registered as a broker in the state of New York.

In 1966 she went to California "to get a little experience as a floor trader." The California State Department of Corporations, broker/dealer division, has no record of licensing her as a broker. She also lays claim to a degree from UCLA, but the university files show she did not attend, let alone graduate. In 1969 she and her mother, Joyce Claydon, opened California Professional Colleges, a school for training medical and dental assistants. She says her colleges merged with Blair Schools (no connection with Charles Blair). "By 1970, we had the largest chain in California." The "chain" consisted of seven schools of 2,700 then registered in California. She has said the schools closed because of changes in the federal student loan plan. She has also said that she sold the outfit to International House of Pancakes, a California public company. In fact, her operation came to an abrupt halt in 1975 when the state filed charges of misrepresentation against her Blair Schools partner, Steve Martin. Martin gathered up the secretary and the money and simply disappeared. He was later charged with fraudulently collecting tuition fees, but since no one knows where he is, the case has never gone to court. "It was a long investigation," says Herschel Elkins, attorney for the city of Los Angeles, who remembers Claydon well. "We had a number of complaints from people who went to those schools."

Claydon then turned to real estate. "I had homes in Bel Air, I had homes in Beverly Hills. I couldn't do anything wrong. Everything was perfect," she chortles. "The Arabs were coming in, prices were going up." In one transaction she spent $60,000 redecorating Caterina Valente's lush residence and within three months sold the place, netting $697,000. "It was fun," Claydon adds in her come-hither laugh. Unfortunately, the only record of her real estate career is a 1980 Los Angeles Department of Real Estate cease-and-desist order against her for selling Colorado property from California without a licence.

In the midst of renovating and flipping property—so the tale continues—Claydon discovered Ultra Glow on a Hollywood movie set. "I used to see this product that made everyone look great. I thought, why don't they use this commercially? I started taking samples home, and my girlfriends would borrow it and we'd be splitting up the baggies like the local drug dealer. I took it to a chemist and went through fifty-six formulas to arrive at what we have now." The research and development, she claims, cost her $300,000.

While she was discovering Ultra Glow, Claydon was also busy elsewhere in California. In 1979 she and three others, including a notorious con artist, Attila "the Hungry Hun" De Agh, were arrested in a joint Los Angeles–Newport Beach–Orange County dragnet. California police describe De Agh as a "very heavy shooter" with an FBI rap sheet four pages long. He boasts of being arrested thirty times and convicted only twice. His 1979 Cadillac bore the licence HUN 1. De Agh was nicknamed "the Hungry Hun" when he won a bet by eating ten hamburgers, four orders of french fries and two malted milks in an hour.

The charge against Claydon and De Agh was conspiracy to commit grand theft. The scam was a classic gambling sting, in which wealthy marks were relieved of millions at a bogus casino staffed by forty shills and set up in a house rented from actor George Montgomery. When one of the marks admitted to losing $250,000 and his Rolls, the police moved in.

Claydon's explanation of the event is typically charming, typically Claydon. "What had happened was that I was doing the movie rights for a con artist . . . he's done maybe $100 to $200 million worth of deals, maybe more than that—Attila De Agh, Attila the Hun. The people that I knew in Hollywood wanted to do a movie about his life, so I said great. We had Paul Newman ready to go because he hadn't had a success since *The Sting*. Now while I'm up doing an interview with him [De Agh], one of the neighbours came in by the name of Steve Schwartz. They go out and decided to do a crime together, and they arrested me for conspiracy. Figure that one out!"

Although Claydon passes off her association with De Agh as a quirk of fate, a brief encounter, L.A. criminal court records reveal otherwise. Several felony warrants were issued against her and De Agh in 1979. In 1980, at the same time as the charges related to the gambling sting were proceeding, Claydon was again linked with De Agh. This time, they were charged with grand theft involving a Newport Beach art dealer. De Agh was again convicted, and Claydon's charge was "set aside" when she made restitution. When asked if he had any doubt that Claydon and De Agh were associates, the L.A. deputy district attorney and prosecutor at the time, Michael Brenner, categorically states, "None." It's interesting to note that the California police—who also know her as Beverlee Black, Beverlee Purcell, Beverlee Seacan and Beverlee Mack—speak of Claydon with amusement and something close to fondness.

Claydon moved to Victoria, B.C., in 1980. "Things were getting too Beverly Hillish. It became a joke; you had to have a Mercedes 450, had to have silicone breasts and your tubes tied, tummy tucked. I didn't want my daughter [Joanna, then thirteen, from her first marriage] to grow up like that. I thought it [Victoria] is a nice cooling out place. Within two weeks I was ready to climb the walls." She got to know the authorities there too when the local Oak Bay police investigated the theft of jewellery and furs valued at $140,000 from her Beach Drive home. They have her name recorded as Beverlee Claydon-Mack.

When asked for an explanation of that name, Claydon furrows her brow and ponders: "There must be some mistake. That doesn't mean anything." There is however a Dr. Ralph Mack, a prominent Orange County surgeon who, when pressed, admits to dating her in the late 1970s. Claydon-Mack is also the name that appears on the 1981 incorporation certificate for Ultra Glow Cosmetics International, her original private company. As well, Claydon and Mack's names are linked in a series of liens and counterliens in a dispute over a piece of property in Victoria, B.C.

By 1984, when Ultra Glow was nearing its trading peak, Claydon had set up a third company, International Glow Cosmetics Ltd., for which $750,000 seed "preprospectus" money* was raised. (More

---

*An unknown amount of money was raised for another preprospectus stock touted by Claydon, Sundae's Slender Sweets and Gourmet Treats Ltd., which had a revolutionary low-calorie dessert. The preprospectus document indicates that the projected amount raised would be $2 million.

would be heard of this company later.) That year too, she married a Denver, Colorado, stockbroker and ex-Green Beret, Richard Kamerling, in an intimate New Year's ceremony attended by "two hundred of my closest friends." Kamerling, tall and lean, has a rough-hewn handsomeness that makes the whey-faced inhabitants of the brokerage community look effete in comparison. He met Claydon at the lush and expensive La Costa resort outside Los Angeles. Claydon now refers to Kamerling as a gold digger and says he is the real culprit in the Ultra Glow story.

Kamerling, though hardly an innocent, was smitten by Claydon's almost bewitching charm and girlish enthusiasm. He ruefully admits falling into the marriage and being dazzled by the pace and promise of Claydon's life. At one of her parties, which became minor legends in Vancouver at the time, he turned to Claydon's secretary and mused, "Is it all real?" The secretary merely shook her head sadly and wondered how long he would survive. When Kamerling moved into his wife's mammoth home (rented from Dr. Norman Keevil, Sr.) in exclusive West Point Grey, her former lover, broker Ed Kirby, accommodatingly moved out, but only to the guest house. "I used to call myself guest house Eddie," Kirby now jokes. At the same time, Kamerling became president of Ultra Glow, though Claydon remained its chairman. Then, around the end of May or the beginning of June, before leaving on a trip to England, she became pregnant.

Shortly after marrying Kamerling, Claydon was forced to deal with a looming deadline: under the B.C. Company Act, the public company owed the superintendent of brokers a set of audited financial statements, and they were due January 31. Claydon did produce a statement dated January 31, 1984, but it was prepared by management and was not audited. On February 6, 1984, Robin Levasseur, the statutory filings clerk in the superintendent of brokers office, sent a formal letter to Ultra Glow requesting the overdue audited statement. A second financial statement popped up, dated February 29, 1984, but it too was unaudited. At that point the superintendent of brokers office quietly began to investigate Claydon, along with her various companies.

That summer and fall, Ultra Glow stock continued to hang encouragingly in the $3 range (after the stock split). The SOB's scrutiny centred on three puzzles. The first concerned $604,000 lent by the public company to Claydon's private company and then apparently recycled through her private trading account for purchases of Ultra Glow stock. She had a ready explanation for the stock purchases:

"What I did through this series of companies was keep the stock alive . . . that block of stock I took down [bought] at $3.50 I sold it for $3¼, $3, $2.90, whatever I could get for it to keep putting the money in the treasury." Claydon dismisses this manoeuvre as a minor infraction worthy only of a $300 fine. But even on the VSE, a director can't just take money from a public company and then turn around and use it to buy that same company's stock.

The second puzzle concerned the exact relationship between Ultra Glow and the Charles Blair company in New York. Although there is no record of payment by Blair beyond the original $100,000 plus 25,000 shares, one of the Blair principals, Louis Giusto, was listed as executive vice-president of Ultra Glow, and the other principal, Isidore Capelouto, was listed as a director. To add to the confusion, the record of actual product having been shipped to or received by Blair—when and in what quantities—was as sketchy as the record of Blair's having remitted any payment.

The third and by far the biggest puzzle was the whereabouts of the Ultra Glow inventory. Claydon had valued it as high as $3 million U.S. and from 1981 onward had variously claimed it was located in a secret California laboratory, a packing house in Burnaby, a little warehouse in Vancouver, in Blaine, Washington, and in the Fairlawn, New Jersey, warehouses of Charles Blair International. The superintendent of brokers office, which had been trying to confirm the inventory's existence since January 1984, found itself playing a game that increasingly resembled find-the-pea-under-the-shell. "You ask a simple question, 'Where's the inventory?' and we get back a six-page letter," growled one exasperated official. "We still don't know where the inventory is."

On October 29, 1984, the superintendent of brokers filed a temporary cease-trade order against Ultra Glow for failure "to provide timely disclosure of material information to the investing public" and because "Ultra Glow Cosmetics Ltd. has filed financial information with the Vancouver Stock Exchange which is false or misleading with respect to material facts or which omits to state material facts the omission of which makes the information false or misleading." Elaborating on the cease-trade order, Superintendent of Brokers Rupert Bullock took pains to point out that his investigation did not centre around the company Ultra Glow but Beverlee Claydon's "Ultra Glow activities," her control of the company and the mystery surrounding the whereabouts or the existence of inventory for which the public company, Ultra Glow Cosmetics, had paid Claydon's private company hundreds of thousands of dollars. Underlining the entire matter was the persistent absence of an audited financial statement.

On November 26th, the superintendent of brokers office convened a hearing to give Ultra Glow an opportunity to "show cause" why the cease-trade order should not be continued. At the hearing, the company submitted a corporate reorganization proposal but did not submit an audited financial statement. Bullock subsequently extended the suspension for ninety days. "I just don't see public trading going ahead when the shareholders don't know what's going on," he said.

In December 1984, less than a year after his marriage to Beverlee Claydon, Richard Kamerling resigned as president of Ultra Glow and quietly left Vancouver, $200,000 poorer; his losses were mostly purchases of Ultra Glow stock. An acquaintance described him as a "broken man" who left with "only the shirt on his back."

After her husband's departure, Claydon began elaborating her big conspiracy theory. The main plotters whom she identified were Kamerling himself, along with the principals of Charles Blair International, Giusto and Capelouto. But there were various other bit players, cast in ever-changing roles, including auditors, ex-employees and ex-business associates who were all accused of dipping into the company till, and a jealous and vengeful ex-boyfriend (Ed Kirby) who was supposed to have shopped her to the superintendent of brokers on a trumped-up insider-trading charge. The various conspirators were in New York, Vancouver, Paris, London and Denver. (Claydon never mentioned that she personally had brought them all into the company at one time or another.)

The plot was to steal the company from her. Claydon maintained that she unwittingly had handed over control to the conspirators by naming Kamerling president: "If you are going to be married to someone, you've got to trust them. Else why get married?" Thereafter, she claimed, she was in the dark about what was going on. She blamed her husband and his cronies for the never-appearing audit: "Between May 31 [1984], which is our year end, and November 31, $700,000 went through that company and they couldn't pay $25,000 for an audit. Why? Because they [Kamerling, the Blair people, her lawyer and the auditors] didn't want an audit. Because if you don't have an audit, the company can't trade. If the company can't trade, then Charles Blair can say the shares you gave me—that was the scheme—don't have value, therefore our contract is null and void. Good-bye."

In this scenario, Claydon was alternately the trusting victim ("To the end, I was really, really stupid") and the shareholders' plucky champion ("I had to go out and sell the cars to keep putting money in the company. I called up my friends and I said, 'Look, I've got four fur coats, a diamond ring, you can take a chattel on the Rolls' "). Even after Rupert Bullock made the temporary cease-trade order permanent, Claydon was still touting the company and dangling the possibility of takeovers and partnerships. "There were companies crawling out of the woodwork," comments a former Claydon colleague. "You could never keep it straight who was doing what." The putative list of benefactors included two separate pension funds (one in Illinois and one in Florida), an unnamed associate of Gucci's, Allen Oil Corporation, the Bank of Micronesia and a junior mining company, Telstar Resources of Vancouver. An irate Bob Sim, vice-president of Telstar, admits his company spent $147,000 on Ultra Glow and Charles Blair before pulling out of a takeover bid.

Claydon also announced that the company would work hard to produce a financial statement and that Ultra Glow shareholders, on March 8, 1985, would be asked to approve the sale of one million preferred shares, at $5 each, to the First Republic Bank. When asked the location of the bank, Claydon responded, "I don't know. One of those little countries."

On March 4th, Claydon gave birth to a son, Nicholas Alexander. The March 8 meeting was not held, and the First Republic Bank was never heard from again. Claydon did summon her shareholders, but the meeting consisted only of a home movie showing her playing with her new son. No business matters were discussed by the lawyer who chaired the gathering. Claydon also hired new auditors (her fourth set), and the young men from Corcoran and Company finally produced an audited financial statement for Ultra Glow. For shareholders who had been promised $17 million in sales, who were supposed to hold $3 million in inventory, who might (or might not) own Charles Blair outright and who had been stuck with untradable shares for the past six months, the financial statement had to be a significant document.

The document reported sales of $1,051,648 for the twenty-one months ending February 1985. Over half of the money was paid to Claydon's private company. Inventory on hand was valued at only $1,190. Another $212,280, paid to Claydon's private company for advances on undelivered inventory, was written down to $1. The statement further showed a loan to Claydon's private company of $604,000, of which $400,230 had been paid back (it didn't say how). The rest had been written off, "due to the fact that the company does not have title to the inventory and its collectability is uncertain." Finally, the statement showed transfers totalling $3 million to the Charles Blair company. Current assets were set at $7,720, and current liabilities at $441,389.

The auditors admitted to never having seen any inventory and to not knowing if Ultra Glow controlled Charles Blair. They also stated, "We are unable to express an opinion as to whether or not the accompanying financial statements present fairly the company's financial position as at February 28, 1985."

At the April 1985 shareholders meeting, Claydon sadly described the conspiracy. "I was advised by my lawyers, my husband, etc., that I should sign over all my shares to particular shareholders. And I was going to get a 2 per cent royalty, and the company was going to be given to the Charles Blair people, who were conspiring with my husband. And I did that, I signed that agreement." Then she introduced Margot Kidder, who said, "I know all too well from movies what happens when you start out with a group of people who have an idea with some integrity to it and get taken over by a large studio and the whole thing goes haywire."

At the perfect psychological moment, Claydon proffered the carrot, a takeover bid by an unnamed American company. "Your shares will be exchanged for an amount that was taken off the board or higher. The book value of that company will be higher than the book value of the company we have now," she announced triumphantly. "When it is fully disclosed who these people are, it's another star-studded cast." The announcement seemed like a miracle to the now-smiling shareholders. Relief turned to excitement as Claydon added that Ultra Glow would be sold in duty-free stores, px's, the largest drugstore chain in the U.S. and Sears—to name a few. "We've got people all over the place, turning product and turning cash."

The shareholders meeting lasted only forty minutes. Not one question was asked of Claydon or the auditors. Nothing had changed: the company was still broke, still in a shambles and still under investigation. Nonetheless, shareholders stayed after the meeting to tell her they were buying Ultra Glow by the caseload to bolster the company. Claydon thanked them heartily but neglected to mention that B.C. sales benefited only her private company. Other shareholders pressed their business cards on her as they volunteered to help at the office.

Nothing further was heard of Claydon or Ultra Glow until April 17, 1986, when a little-known mining company named Liberty Bell Mines announced "an agreement in principle to acquire the North American manufacturing and marketing rights to a photo-cosmetic product." It was the first public sign that an eerie rerun was already well underway. In May, Liberty Bell announced that the product was called Photoglow. The product rights and 100,000 units of initial inventory were purchased for stock and a royalty. Liberty Bell had entered into an agreement with International Glow Cosmetics Inc. of Palm Beach, Florida, to market and distribute the Photoglow product. International Glow was to provide Liberty Bell with an "established network of 23,000 outlets. Photoglow is the only product of its kind for this lucrative and highly visible market," Liberty Bell enthused. "Negotiations on Glow related product lines are continuing."

By June 1986, Liberty Bell was already behind in submitting financial statements to the superintendent of brokers. That didn't stop the company from publicizing another interesting acquisition, "Carnival Enterprises Ltd., of Vancouver, yet another privately held cosmetic distribution company, for $150,000 cash and 500,000 common shares of Liberty Bell." The acquisition gave Liberty Bell access to additional cosmetic lines including Ultra Glow, and an established distribution network in B.C., Alberta, Saskatchewan and Montreal. On June 25, 1986, Liberty Bell announced that they were no longer in the mining business, but were taking "a new direction for the company from a mining exploration and developer . . . into a marketing and distribution company specializing in cosmetic product lines." (At this point neither the vse's compliance nor listing departments realized that Ultra Glow and Claydon were once again involved with the exchange.)

In August 1986, now calling herself Beverlee Karling ("I took the 'me' out of Kamerling"), Claydon and Ultra Glow, like persistent boils, erupted once again. She issued a press release saying that International Glow had struck a deal with American Express to sell a *Romancing the Stone* gem and perfume combination. There were to be at least six mailings, and profits from just one were forecast to be between $2.35 and $7.85 million. An American Express spokesman firmly stated that the company was only considering a proposal made to it and pointed out that the profit figures were "a figment of someone's imagination."

Undaunted, Claydon fired off a notice to shareholders asking them to approve a plan to swap their worthless Ultra Glow shares for shares in International Glow, which was trading in the United States on the over-the-counter market. On August 29th a dispirited group of shareholders trooped into a Four Seasons meeting room to await news of their fate. Only nineteen shareholders were there in person; the remainder of the capacity crowd were thrill seekers and funeral followers. A small group of young men, clearly brokers, sat with their heads together, giggling over some Claydon joke. At the front of the room was the usual coterie of supporters, hardy shareholders and Claydon's mother, a Beverlee look-alike, thicker around the middle but with hair bleached to the colour of a champagne bubble and swathed in an almost identical pale, flowing muumuu-style dress.

Margot Kidder had long ago joined the Ultra Glow/Claydon celebrity discard heap—a heap that includes Vic Damone and Cathy Lee Johnson (former cohost of "Good Morning America"). Both at one time or another purported to be spokesmen for Ultra Glow. "We wish her well in her Tab commercials," Claydon said of Kidder, as if speaking of someone whose prospects have dimmed. She announced a new front man, Joseph Soloman, a chisel-faced Marlboro type who had been involved with the start-up of the Vidal Sassoon product line. Claydon introduced him as a very rich man who had retired from life to his hundred-acre farm in Thousand Oaks, California, to raise thoroughbreds. Claydon claimed that Ultra Glow, plus the fact that "he felt a little sorry for me," brought him out of retirement. Soloman described himself as president and CEO of Fuji Electricell and spoke a little of Fuji's potential, especially when it and International Glow were merged.

Claydon, soft-spoken and a little fluttery, was a perfect foil to the virulent masculinity of her new partner. When she called for a vote to approve the share exchange, the motion passed easily. The shareholders had nothing more to lose. "What do you know," observed one man as he filed out of the room, "she got away clean as a whistle."

In the background, the wheels of justice were turning, albeit excruciating slowly. On October 16, 1986, Mr. Justice A. G. MacKinnon of the Supreme Court of British Columbia ruled against Beverlee Claydon in a civil suit relating to the $750,000 raised in preprospectus shares for International Glow Cosmetics Ltd., way back in 1983 and 1984. One of the plaintiffs was Margaret Mott, a lead broker in the original share offering by Claydon's public company, Ultra Glow Cos-

234 THE MONEY MACHINE

metics Ltd. Mott purchased $10,000 worth of International Glow shares directly from Claydon. The company has never been approved for trading by the superintendent of brokers, and no shares were delivered until after June 1985 when court proceedings were initiated. Justice Mackinnon awarded $10,000 plus interest for "a breach of the contract" to Mott and flayed Claydon in his judgement.

> The most flagrant breach, is that with respect to the use of the funds raised by the defendants. Although there is no evidence as to the particular reason why the defendant company's prospectus was not approved by the superintendent of brokers, one need not look too deeply into the affairs of the defendant company to understand why the approval was not forthcoming . . . the statements disclose that some $750,000 was raised in the sale of shares in the private company. In the Statement of Expenses for the year 1984 $105,000 was paid for consulting fees, $48,000 for salaries, and about $30,000 for travel, hotels and promotion. The most horrendous item, however, is the advance made of $464,158 to a company called Ultra Glow Cosmetics International Ltd. These moneys were "advanced" for inventory. However, the inventory has never been delivered to the defendant company. Ultra Glow Cosmetics International Ltd. is a company controlled by the defendant Beverlee Claydon, and is described by her as her "private company." What the defendant company is left with in exchange for the $464,158 is a non-interest bearing promissory note by the defendant's private company Ultra Glow Cosmetics International Ltd.*

Also in October 1986, Claydon was charged with defrauding Ultra Glow Cosmetics Ltd. and with theft of $604,000 from the same company. The hearing was set for April 1987 and stayed until September 1987.

At this point, most VSE stories end with the promoter quietly disap-

---

*Justice Mackinnon's judgement, which centred on the 1984 period, included a financial statement (which had not previously seen the light of day) for International Glow Cosmetics Ltd. As usual, the statement is unaudited, but it contains a bombshell. Listed under revenue for the 1985 period was $3 million for the sale of Class "B" shares. Under expenses $3 million was paid for "license rights" to an unidentified party. The nearly $4 million missing from International Glow Cosmetics Ltd., coupled with well over $5 million missing from Ultra Glow Cosmetics Ltd., makes it at $9 million the largest mysterious disappearance in the history of the VSE. In comparison, the theft charges relating to Black Friday involved only $1.2 million.

pearing into the sunset. Not Claydon and Ultra Glow. In May of 1987, Claydon, this time calling herself Beverlee Carling, surfaced once again when a number of flattering profiles appeared on local television stations. The stories centred on her new crusade to help indigent women. In one interview, Beverlee blamed former husband Richard Kamerling for all her personal and Ultra Glow—related problems, intimating that all would soon be set to rights. The message was clear: Claydon and Ultra Glow were back in business.

Somewhere, Phineas T. Barnum must be chuckling. The story of Beverlee Claydon and Ultra Glow Cosmetics and the Vancouver Stock Exchange—all of which Phineas would have adored—gives indisputable proof of his famous saying: "There's a sucker born every minute."

CHAPTER 17

Adnan Khashoggi
Drops in for a Fast Buck

"The great unbillionaire. . . . He owns very little. Everything is mortgaged—except his wife." A CLOSE BUSINESS ASSOCIATE OF ADNAN KHASHOGGI at the height of his VSE stock play.

When Adnan Khashoggi's wealth-encrusted name first became associated with the VSE in 1986, it seemed that the exchange had, at last, reached the pinnacle of its ambition. Finally, here was tangible evidence that the VSE truly was the world leader in risk capital. Khashoggi's presence was big, none bigger, and appropriately enough, his VSE entrance had a suitable warmup act in Sir James Goldsmith.

Goldsmith, a maverick European financier, moved his company, General Oriental Investments Ltd., from the Hong Kong exchange to the VSE for the purpose of bidding a reported $4.71 billion U.S. for Goodyear Tire and Rubber Company. Goldsmith, a fierce entrepreneur, corporate raider and media baron, delighted the VSE. *The Wall Street Journal* describes him as "one of the world's richest and most influential people, not by hewing to convention but by systematically defying it. He ignores constraints, whether they be intellectual, political, economic or in the case of his personal life, social." Tales of his mistresses and wives regularly juice up scandal sheets and business gossipmongers frequently speculate on what he will be up to next. Goldsmith denied that his choice of the VSE was related to its relatively lax public disclosure requirements and comfortable regulatory atmosphere. He gave his reason for listing on the exchange to Vancouver *Sun* reporter Peter O'Neil: "In my view it [the VSE] is not full of self-righteous, pompous stuffed shirts." Eventually, Goldsmith was bought off by the Goodyear management for $618 million plus expenses—$90 million clear profit—but while the proposal existed, the VSE basked in reflected glory.

Exciting as Goldsmith's cameo appearance was for the VSE, the real stir of 1986 came with the announcement in June that Arab arms dealer and middleman Adnan Khashoggi would join the board of directors of an insignificant and largely dormant VSE-listed company, Skyhigh Resources Ltd. The exchange nearly wet its corporate pants with joy. Khashoggi was then still described as the world's richest man, and his reputation was such that he is commonly credited with being the model for his pal Harold Robbins's lurid best seller, *The Pirate*, which details the exploits of an Arab who is an international middleman.

Those impressed by Murray Pezim's entourage of personal masseuse, tired celebrities and gaggle of yes men were awestruck by Khashoggi who travels with a platoon of servants including a masseur, valet, barber, chiropractor and chef. In 1987, his lifestyle alone cost $250,000 a day to maintain, what with his twelve estates (including a 180,000-acre ranch in Kenya), his 282-foot yacht *Nabila* (outfitted with a helicopter), three commercial-sized jets, twelve stretch Mercedes limousines and a stable of blue-blooded Arabian steeds. Khashoggi cheerfully admits to sybaritic tastes and calls himself "an artist" with wealth. What even the richest people could not envision, Khashoggi had, like a ten-foot-square bed covered with a $200,000 Russian sable spread and a wardrobe so vast he required a warehouse in which to store it. "We're seeing a whole new class of major players on the VSE," solemnly declared Peter Brown. "There's something happening here. If we keep attracting these kinds of deals, the whole complexion of the place is going to change."

Adnan Khashoggi's fortunes are inextricably linked to the Saudi Arabian royal family. His father, Dr. Muhammad Khashoggi, was one of the personal physicians to Abdul Aziz, the man who founded the Saudi kingdom early this century. Young Khashoggi, born in Saudi Arabia in 1935, mingled with Aziz's sons, making the contacts that would bring him his future wealth. In Egypt, he attended the highly prestigious English private school Victoria College, where two of his classmates became King Faisal II of Iraq and King Hussein of Jordan. His entrepreneurial career began in the 1950s when he served as an agent for Muhammad Binladen, one of his father's patients. It was common practice for Saudis, including the royal family, to use intermediaries to ease their deal making in western nations. Binladen, a contractor, asked Khashoggi to find some trucks for him, and the $500,000 deal, which took Khashoggi less than a month to set up, netted him $50,000. This happened right at the beginning of the Saudi development boom, and Khashoggi personally purchased the Saudi agencies for Rolls-Royce airplane engines, as well as the local agencies for Fiat, Marconi and Chrysler. By the mid-1960s Khashoggi was a leading arms merchant, simultaneously representing such giant competing firms as Lockheed and Northrop, as well as a host of ancillary suppliers. "He collected commissions like the sixteenth-century quartermasters in Europe who shared their spoils with their monarch," wrote Anthony Sampson in his book *The Arms Bazaar*. By the mid-1970s, Khashoggi had been paid over $100 million in commissions from Lockheed alone.

At that point Khashoggi was well advanced on his own empire building, the tentacles of which reached into the far corners of the globe, and the momentum of his progress gradually overshadowed his involvement in the arms business. He bought ranches in Arizona, meat-packing plants in Brazil, fashion companies, chains of hotels, shipping firms and of course invested extensively in Saudi Arabia, often in partnership with the royal family. The list is endless and eclectic, and often quite fantastic. In Sudan, for instance, he negotiated with his close friend President Jaafar Nimeiri a half-ownership of the new national oil company, with oil and mineral rights to the entire country. When Khashoggi made Salt Lake City, Utah, his base in the U.S., he stunned the city with his largesse and grand plans. In 1979 he announced that the Triad Center, a billion-dollar redevelopment of the city's downtown core, would be built by his American holding company, Triad America Corporation. The five blocks between the Mormon Tabernacle and the Union Pacific station would eventually contain at least three huge hotels, apartment and office buildings, shopping plazas, condominiums and a theatre. "My initial reaction is one of complete delight," declared Scott H. Matheson, the governor of Utah at the time.

Far more important to Khashoggi than his business possessions was the image he created for himself by the simple expedient of spending with lavish abandon. Short, oily, paunchy and balding, he could easily be mistaken for a particularly gracious maitre d'. He overcome these physical handicaps with a talent for selecting the kind of expensive accoutrements that become the stuff of legend. His $50-million yacht *Nabila*, with its five decks, swimming pool, space-age communications centre, helicopter landing pad and heavily armed escort boats could have been designed by writer Ian Fleming for one of James Bond's arch-enemies. Khashoggi's airplanes, his estates, and especially his parties, were always the most. For his fiftieth birthday, his cake was a gooey replica of Louis XIV's coronation crown, and he flew the chef to the Louvre to study it so every detail would be post-card correct.

Of particular pertinence to the business world was the fact that some of his financial coups were based not on canny number crunching but on information supplied by well-placed hookers. It was a strategy he used frequently and to great effect. What titillated followers of the wealthy, however, was his unashamed admission of the tactic. Not only did he hire women to cozy up to important contacts at parties but he paid out large sums to recruit the "hostesses" of others. Women surrounding the Shah of Iran fed him a regular stream of information about Iranian military affairs. "The Shah was timid with women and liked to impress them by telling them exciting secrets," Khashoggi told *Time* in 1986. Even when he didn't receive specific facts and figures from his undercover agents, their presence smoothed the way for a lot of deal making: "They lend beauty and fragrance to the surroundings."

Everywhere he went, Khashoggi was enveloped in a fantasy world of excitement and promise. Not surprisingly, his rumoured wealth was sufficient to buy him respect and deference from governments around the world. On October 1, 1985, he dropped into Toronto to spend a few hours celebrating his son Mohamed's twenty-second birthday and to draw attention to his investment plans in Canada. Attendees included Ontario's lieutenant-governor and his predecessor, a former premier, and an assortment of influential bankers and businessmen. Khashoggi left for Washington, D.C., before dessert, but not before letting everyone know that Canada's fate lay in the hands of his son Mohamed. "I really want to take some of these Canadian companies overseas and get them to work in countries like Egypt, Morocco,

Kenya," the young man said, hinting at immense opportunities. "There are a lot of places where Canada could blend in nicely."

Around the VSE, style has always counted more heavily than substance, and using that criteria, Khashoggi seemed like a dream come true. Although he never personally set foot in Vancouver, his reputation and charisma—plus a number of carefully worded press releases—were enough to shoot his stocks through the ceiling. His involvement in the VSE is easy to explain—he had desperate financial problems (most of them rooted in the recession that had slashed oil profits), exacerbated by years of poor management and ill-conceived expansion. The world oil market, which had begun to falter in the early 1980s, decimated his global investments, most particularly those in Saudi Arabia. He began stripping overseas assets for cash to keep the companies, especially those with royal partners, alive.

By 1985 there were unmistakable signs that Khasoggi's empire was in serious trouble. In April, President Jaafar Nimeiri of Sudan was deposed, Khashoggi was declared persona non grata and his oil concession cancelled. Also in 1985 the crew of his yacht blackmailed him into paying long overdue wages by threatening to sail around the Mediterranean festooned with giant signs of complaint. In September of that year *Fortune* published a devastating exposé of his problems. Further ignominies followed. Sixty servants at his huge headquarters estate in Marbella, Spain, on the Costa del Sol, staged a strike to collect $70,000 in back wages. The maids in his New York penthouse had also not been paid for months. Khashoggi's pilots had to file bizarre zigzag flight plans to avoid landing at airfields where he hadn't paid his fuel bills. Many hotels, which had once redecorated entire floors for a Khashoggi visit, refused to accept his patronage unless he paid in advance. In Salt Lake City, Khashoggi's development projects were stalled, less than a quarter of the way to completion, by a myriad of unpaid bills and lawsuits. Even his personal lawyer reportedly instituted a pay-as-you-go policy. From Cannes to Timbuktu, he was either hounded or avoided.

As Khashoggi's desperation grew, he became more accessible to the media, possibly in an attempt to paper over his problems. Previously, the excesses of his life had been widely known in broad outline, but the details were not, particularly those relating to his business. Then, in February 1985, he unexpectedly allowed ABC television's "Lifestyles of the Rich and Famous" to probe into his personal privacy and corporate deal making. The program's producers, who had been pursuing him for some time, were surprised. "At the time, we thought he agreed because of the increasing credibility of 'Lifestyles,' " one of the show's producers said. Not only did Khashoggi allow unfettered viewing of his many possessions, he even invited a production team to accompany him to Jordan to record a deal he was negotiating. The show obliged with a fawning, hour-long profile of the man and his money.

In 1986 Khashoggi's distress reached the crisis point. His normal sources of funding—banks, nonbank financial institutions and even old friends and partners—were no longer receptive. In desperation, he resurrected his role as an arms dealer in the ill-fated Iran arms-for-hostages exchange. Shortly afterwards, Khashoggi turned to the Vancouver Stock Exchange.

In June 1986, the first public evidence of Khashoggi's activity on the VSE surfaced with the announcement that he would join Skyhigh Resources Ltd.'s board of directors. Skyhigh also announced the acquisition of MIU Automation Inc. of Toronto, a firm with no revenue and assets consisting only of a software program under development. MIU was valued at $2.6 million by the international accounting firm Ernst & Whinney. Before the announcements, Skyhigh had traded sporadically in the 60 cent range with 1.7 million shares issued. From the middle of June to October 10, 1986, the stock price jumped to $13 a share, and suddenly there were 19.6 million shares outstanding. (The stock had been split four-for-one. As well, a number of private placements had been conducted.) The company's share value increased from $416,000 at the end of May to $255 million, on the strength of the purchase of a nonrevenue-producing asset and Khashoggi's name. In comparison, MacDonald Dettwiler and Associates of Vancouver, one of Canada's foremost high-tech research companies with long-term contracts and $21 million in annual revenue, had changed hands in 1984 for less than $6 million.

In the four weeks leading up to November 20, 1986, when Skyhigh jumped to $17 a share, with 33 million shares outstanding, another asset was added. Khashoggi, now listed as chairman of Skyhigh, was on both sides of the deal, selling Edgington Oil Company Inc., part of his financially troubled Triad America Corporation of Salt Lake City, to Skyhigh for $125 million U.S.. This time the asset had revenue of $780 million in 1985 and pretax profits of $17.3 million. Skyhigh's share value more than doubled to $612 million. When the dust settled, Khashoggi held approximately 8.7 million shares (some of them in escrow), with a paper worth of $147 million. If he exercised all his options, Khashoggi would have to pay less than $1 million for the shares. In the time span of little more than six months, Skyhigh shares had jumped from 60 cents each to $72, after a four-for-one split was taken into account.

On November 28, 1986, another VSE-listed company with links to Khashoggi, Tangent Oil and Gas Ltd., made headlines. Tangent announced a proposed purchase of Johnson Geneva, a company that had a joint-venture agreement with a subsidiary of Pan American Corporation to refurbish, at a cost of between $75 and $85 million, a communication satellite recovered from space by the space shuttle. Between January 1st and the end of November 1986, Tangent had traded only 7,000 shares at prices ranging between 10 and 20 cents, but during the three days after making the announcement, Tangent traded 700,000 shares at prices between $15 and $22. The total value of trading was around $14 million. Nearly 5 million of Tangent's 5.3 million outstanding shares had been purchased from an American company for 10 cents a share, or a total of $500,000. Among the identifiable purchasers of Tangent at 10 cents were Khashoggi himself (259,200 shares that soon had a paper value of $5.69 million), Peter Brown's holding company, MacLachlan Investment Corporation (102,800 shares worth $2.26 million), Channing Buckland, Brown's partner and vice-president of Canarim Investment Corporation Ltd. (99,200 shares worth $2.18 million), Clive Stockdale, Canarim's oil analyst (102,450 shares worth $2.25 million) and Intercan, the holding company that controls Canarim (58,700 shares worth $1.29 million). Associates of Khashoggi bought a further 259,000 shares, and the remainder went to a long list of mysterious and anonymous holding companies.

Khashoggi's VSE promotions were going swimmingly, and he was able to pump millions of dollars into his cash-poor enterprises. Then the unexpected intruded in December 1986 with the disclosure of Khashoggi's involvement as a middleman in the Iran arms scandal. The scandal deepened with the implication, since proven false, that somehow Khashoggi's VSE companies and/or his VSE associates were part of the arms deal funding. Journalists from all over North America were keenly interested in just what the VSE's involvement was, and the VSE itself suddenly began to take a closer look at Khashoggi's companies. Sporadic and short-lived trading halts were issued, but business largely went on as before, though the lustre of Khashoggi's name was somewhat tarnished.

On January 6, 1987, in the midst of the spreading U.S./Iranian arms embroglio, another Khashoggi company, Vault Explorations Inc., surfaced. This time the company's goal was none other than to find King Solomon's fabled mines:

> Gold may be the only commodity with real value within the next few years. It has long been known that perhaps the last great gold reserves are in the country of Mali in West Africa; it has been speculated that these are, in fact, the legendary King Solomon's Mines . . . [it is] a very large and extensive gold, diamond and other precious metal concession with absolutely enormous potential.

Never mind that the very existence of King Solomon's mines is hotly debated by academics or that those who credit the legend usually locate the mines in Zimbabwe.

Vault, which was first listed on the vse on November 26, 1986, at 35 cents a share, came equipped with the usual list of insiders who bought cheap shares. Khashoggi was to get 95 million shares from Vault in return for 48 per cent of his Mali American Mines Ltd. But the announcement of a quest for King Solomon's mines was too much even for the vse—especially now that Khashoggi's own legend was tainted—and the exchange halted trading in Vault.

Meanwhile, Tangent and Skyhigh were still trading heavily, though Tangent's proposed deal with Pan American was in limbo and Skyhigh's purchase of Edgington Oil was bogged down in a myriad of lawsuits, some of which claimed that the vse deal was an elaborate plan to spirit the company away from Khashoggi's ever-multiplying creditors.

As 1987 wore on, Khashoggi's name was mentioned less and less around the vse, and his companies retreated into the shells from which they had emerged. No one knows how much money was drained out of the exchange by the Khashoggi affair, but estimates range from $5 million to $50 million. The real cost was to the vse's reputation. International headlines portrayed it as a collection of dupes, rubes and rogues. Once again the exchange, and most particularly the investors, had been fleeced.

CHAPTER 18

Saving the Lamb

"It's open season to rape and pillage. If you don't drop someone, hog-tie them and haul them into the cop shop, you don't have a case. It's open season here." A HIGHLY SUCCESSFUL VSE BROKER, who also promotes his own companies by using nominees, or puppets, to circumvent VSE rules.

The question most often asked about the Vancouver Stock Exchange is "How the hell do they get away with it?" referring to the horde of promoters, brokers and insiders who treat the VSE like an open wallet. The answer has everything to do with ethics, fear and self-interest. The VSE has never been without standards, but the emphasis is often in the wrong place. Regardless of rules, regulations, enforcement and good intentions, them that brings in the money calls the shots.

Since the VSE opened in 1907, it has been at the mercy of high-flying fast talkers who bend the rules and the exchange anyway they like. Some do it within the law, others outside it. A few, like Morris Black, get caught. Most don't. And even the ones who do end up in court have taken their profits long before the law tracks them down.

The crux of the VSE's dilemma is that it is largely responsible for regulating itself. The exchange exists for the convenience of the forty-eight brokerage firms that own and control it. Not only must they police each other, but they must also weed out errant companies and promoters. It is, of course, these same companies and their promoters that generate the members' profits. To further complicate the problem, the brokers who own the exchange are the ones who, through the board of governors and executive committee, hire and fire the senior management, the very people responsible for carrying out the exchange's regulations.

The daily business of the exchange is conducted by employees who are diligent, dedicated and honest. At all levels there is a professionalism that compares favourably with any exchange in the world. Don Hudson, the VSE president, can be credited with this. He has assembled a smartly dressed, efficient bureaucracy that gets to work on time, opens the doors, moves paper all day long, reacts to events, strives to avoid controversy and turns out the lights at the end of the day. It's probably as good an administration as can be created under the constraints of money. Unfortunately the professionalism hides a growing lack of understanding of how things really work on the street. Those close to the industry are already aware of the problem. "They think they know what they're doing, but they don't know, and they don't know they don't know," says a VSE seat holder. Fewer and fewer people within the exchange have an intimate knowledge of the industry because the best and the brightest soon leave for more lucrative pastures. Exchange staff are paid penuriously compared to others in the industry. When told that the salary for a listing officer starts at $32,000, Ted Bence, a Vancouver securities lawyer, scoffs, saying that secretaries can earn as much.

Money is not the only issue. The VSE has long had a policy of hiring senior executives from outside the exchange, and no exchange president since Jack Van Luven has been promoted from within the ranks. The result is that the good junior people leave once they have accumulated enough experience to make them attractive elsewhere. The securities industry knows this, and the street raids the VSE unmercifully. Exchange employees are in considerable demand for their expertise and, in many cases, receive double their VSE pay compensation when they join a private firm.

The turnover of the best and the brightest hurts the VSE because it takes years for key staff to immerse themselves in the system deeply enough to sense when things are right and when they're not. There is more to knowing how the market works than memorizing the policy books. True understanding comes when the key people can read the little danger signs. It's knowing that when promoter A is hooked up with broker B using securities lawyer C, the game is afoot. It's being able to chart the intention of a promotion by reading between the lines of press releases. It's following trading patterns—not only price but also volume, insider trading and shorting—to develop a feeling for the timing of a promotion. It's knowing that the deal smells long before it becomes a public scandal.

If the VSE is not performing its policing duties as rigorously as it might, then logically the law enforcement agencies should take up the slack. Unfortunately, the superintendent of brokers and the RCMP, are poorly equipped for the battle. Aside from desire and intent, the good guys are simply out-manned, out-hustled, out-financed and often out-thought by the bad guys. And, even when they're on top of the problem, internecine squabbling frequently negates their best efforts.

When most people speak of the regulators or the cops in reference to the Vancouver Stock Exchange, they are talking about the superintendent of brokers. That office is a curious animal—derided by many, loved by few and peopled by an uneasy combination of ex-cops whose love affair with the job is tenacious and clock-watching bureaucrats far removed from the brutal realities of the street. Until 1978, the superintendent of brokers was under the jurisdiction of the provincial attorney general's department and had its headquarters in Victoria, even though that city's exchange had been closed since 1925. In 1978 the office moved to Vancouver and came under the control of the Ministry of Consumer and Corporate Affairs (now Finance and Corporate Relations). The SOB has always been pig in the middle, caught in the net of private industry, government, the police, the public and the VSE itself. The SOB is responsible for a massive and diverse territory that between 1978 and 1986 included real estate, insurance, mortgages and mortgage brokers, as well as securities. Today the SOB oversees commodities, investment contracts and securities.

Until the mid-1960s, the relationship between the superintendent of brokers and the securities industry was comfortable and familial. After the Windfall scandal, regulation took on new meaning as the lemminglike rush of promoters and mining brokers from Toronto found the regulators poorly armed to combat people who devoted themselves to outwitting the paper chasers. By 1971, the SOB office was completely overwhelmed. "At one stage I counted 236 open files," recalls Bob Scott, then in charge of investigations and commanding a staff of two. "A lot were very small, but some were big and would take hundreds of hours to clear. It was an impossible load. I kept sending memos to Irwin [then superintendent of brokers] and pestering him, trying to get more people. The investigators, older people with lots of experience and street smarts, used to say that as far as they were concerned the government would be quite happy to have monkeys sitting there except for the bad publicity they would get."

When Rupert Bullock, fresh from a five-year stint as head of the RCMP's commercial crime squad, market section, in Vancouver, took over as superintendent of brokers from Bill Irwin in 1980, he was appalled by the chaos. "We simply didn't have the resources to administer the security system. . . . [There was] no firm structure; the top six positions were open when I got there. There were morale problems, budget problems, no computerization." In August 1981, eight of the twenty-five positions, including most of the senior ones dealing exclusively with securities, were vacant. Additionally, eighteen of the sixty-four employees, including almost all the critically important filing clerks, were temporaries, so the staff turnover was horrendous. When Bullock took over, his office was handling four times as many filings as the Ontario Securities Commission and doing it with far fewer employees. Further, the office was processing 35,000 business licences a year; they were stored in shoeboxes on long tables and were sorted by hand.

The understaffing and confusion resulted in long delays for approval of prospectuses and statements of material facts. Applications would often sit for three or four weeks before getting into the system. When they did get into the system, thorough investigations were out of the question. If the SOB office had any doubts about the validity of engineering or geological results, they had to consult with the Department of Energy, Mines and Resources, which took another five or six weeks to respond, usually with a request for more information. Not surprisingly, with brokers, promoters and lawyers screaming about their livelihood, the SOB rarely asked for technical support from that department.

The screams from brokers and promoters continue today. "B.C. has made it very difficult at the superintendent's level to get anything through," promoter Bruce McDonald told Vancouver *Sun* reporter Peter O'Neil in December 1986, after announcing that he was moving ten of his VSE-listed companies to the Alberta Stock Exchange. "The time lags and bureaucracy there are just so long, by the time you get something through there, you forget why you were doing it." It is important to note that McDonald and the other promoters and brokers aren't complaining about the SOB's thoroughness, just the lack of speed.

When the SOB office does attempt to tighten up, the effort inevitably backfires with an increased workload. For example, in 1985, new securities regulations (announced in the aftermath of Black Friday) raised the minimum amount a company had to spend on exploration and development from $25,000 to $60,000, and raised the minimum price of founder's or "cheap" shares from 15 cents to 25 cents. Rupert Bullock made the announcement of the altered requirements on December 15, purposefully giving promoters only two weeks' notice. "With so many promoters, lawyers and accountants about to go on holidays, we thought there would be little time for them to file prospectuses under the old rules," he said. But a blizzard of paper hit the securities regulators. Sixty-seven prospectuses were filed that month, fifty of them during the last few days of the month. In comparison, only eleven prospectuses had been filed the preceding November, thirteen in October and sixteen in September. Bullock described the tactics as "underhanded." "Never in my wildest dreams did I expect so many in so few days. I was shocked at how quickly they could be put together and jammed in here."

Aside from manpower, the most severe problem facing the superintendent of brokers office is lack of clout. The authority to suspend companies and eventually delist them is an ominous weapon, but if a company does a good job of its paperwork, maintains statutory listing requirements, files annual reports, insider reports and financial statements, there is little the SOB can do. Had Beverlee Claydon, for example, filed her financial statements regularly, Ultra Glow might never have been suspended. The impotence of the SOB's office is well understood on the street. "Give me $100,000 and a good lawyer, and I can tie up the SOB's office until the next century," sneers a former VSE executive.

Beneath the SOB's lack of power lies the fact that regulating the VSE is far from a high priority politically. When Rupert Bullock left the SOB office in January 1986, having given the usual three months' notice, the position was left vacant for five months. For much of that time, a gag order was placed on SOB employees, forbidding them to talk to the media without first consulting the Ministry of Consumer and Corporate Affairs in Victoria. Somehow the order was interpreted to cover even minor enquiries from the public and the industry. As a result, the minister's office ended up fielding virtually every call placed to the SOB.

In 1981, Peter Stanley, a Vancouver accountant and a VSE public governor, was commissioned by the Ministry of Consumer and Corporate Affairs to study the SOB's office and its cousin, the investigations branch of the ministry. He pointed out that the superintendent of brokers' workload was four times higher than that of the Ontario Securities Commission, but that the OSC had thirty-one employees in investigations, whereas the SOB had only nine (and three of those positions were vacant). "The danger of a violent explosion in the securities industry in British Columbia is ever present while standards and requirements remain below those of New York, London and Toronto. If it comes it will be disastrous for the Ministry and the VSE," Stanley concluded.

The corporate investigations branch of the Ministry of Finance and Corporate Relations is an autonomous department responsible for investigating securities cases for the SOB, obviously a critical aspect of the regulatory process. Its chief is H. Alan "Al" Dilworth, a beefy man whose heavy presence betrays his policeman's background. At odds with the image of a veteran cop are his soft, Paul Newmanesque blue eyes, his two gold rings, gold watch and gold bracelet. But the ornamentation can't hide the fact that he has one of the sharpest minds on either side of the street. Dilworth has improved his office's position since 1980 with a total of twenty-three employees including three accountants and clerical staff. But in relative terms, he too has fallen further behind.

In 1985–86, Dilworth's department handled nearly 2,400 cases, of which 38 per cent were directly or indirectly related to securities. Because of the total caseload, he could carry out only two major investigations tied to the VSE: Ultra Glow and Black Friday. His branch also handled three other major cases, Victoria Mortgage and Trust, Holiday Condos and Innovative Supply Company Ltd. Over 7,000 hours were spent on Ultra Glow and Black Friday before they were ready to be forwarded to the attorney general's department to determine if there was sufficient grounds for laying charges. "You have to be damn sure that you can substantiate a charge before you invest that kind of time in an investigation," points out Dilworth. "The whole secret of the game is how to take out bad guys without hurting good guys." He calculates that his department's efforts have deprived the bad guys on the exchange of $235 million since 1983, but admits that he's really only scratching the surface.

Salary restrictions are eroding Dilworth's battle against the bad guys. In 1982, when he took over the investigations branch, his salary was a big jump over his pay as an RCMP staff sergeant. Today, the nearly $50,000 he earns is matched by the RCMP wage rates. In 1982, his investigators were mostly highly experienced ex-police officers. Today, his salary range for investigators—$27,600 to $32,400—makes it difficult for him to attract the educated, experienced, street-smart cops that he needs. Dilworth maintains that unschooled staffers need a minimum of three years just to learn how the speculative stock industry works before they can begin to be effective. A guy like Dilworth stays because he loves the job.

The overriding concern within the SOB office is the fact that the government is filling the top positions with administrators and managers. The replacement for Rupert Bullock, a career cop, was forty-eight-year-old Michael Ross, a man with a B.A. in commerce and an enormously varied background in finance and management but little experience in the securities field. Ross talked very tough at first: "If I find that our major purpose is being thwarted by people who are abusing the rules and procedures, I will take advantage of the discretion allowed in the legislation in order to make sure the market works. If I find that these people have been in trouble before, or even if we have suspicions about them, I will run them out of town." Any fear provoked by his words evaporated into sniggers when he announced to the media that he'd won a local songwriting contest. Ross left under a cloud early in February 1987, barely seven months after he was hired. At the centre of the controversy was his 1986 trip with Nelson Skalbania to the Superbowl as a guest of Denver Broncos owner Pat Bowlen, who paid for the plane tickets and accommodations. Both Bowlen and Skalbania are substantial investors in the VSE. Shortly after his departure, Ross was offering his services as a "musical consultant."

The first chairman of the B.C. Securities Commission, a position freshly defined by the 1986 Securities Act, was Jill Bodkin, a civil servant who'd most recently been deputy minister of Consumer and Corporate Affairs. The position of commission chairman is a key one in that it involves policy making for the securities industry and serves as a court of appeal for decisions made by the superintendent of brokers.

Like Ross, Bodkin had little or no direct experience in the securities industry.

In April 1987, in another one of those fantastic turns of events for which the Vancouver stock community is becoming notorious, Jill Bodkin resigned. She had lasted less than ten months in the position. Rumours abounded that Bodkin had been forced out of her job by powerful figures who had the ear of the Social Credit government. Bodkin herself made no comment. She was quickly replaced by Doug Hyndman, a thirty-six-year-old former assistant minister in the finance department. He too has no direct experience in the junior securities industry.

The B.C. government took one small step toward recognizing the importance of its securities watchdog by nearly doubling the salary of the superintendent of brokers to $100,000 in May 1987. However, the new SOB, thirty-four-year-old Neil de Gelder, a partner in the prestigious law firm of Ladner Downs, is yet another neophyte in the speculative securities game. "Quite frankly," said one VSE broker upon hearing of the appointment, "the less they know, the better for us."

Despite all the difficulties, the regulatory system would have some strength if the two key parties, the SOB and the VSE, were on good terms. But they're not, and haven't been for years. In January 1968, Superintendent of Brokers Bill Irwin was writing letters marked "Personal and Confidential" to the new VSE chairman of the board, George Tapp, to complain about the problem: "I don't mind telling you relations have deteriorated considerably between the Commission and the Exchange during the past year. I like to think that this development is not of my making." The letter also contains a handwritten P.S. from Irwin to Tapp: "I advise you destroy this after reading." In the 1970s, communication between the VSE and the SOB was so bad that when Thomas Dohm, Cyril White and Bob Scott were hired as successive presidents, they were all told that improving relations was almost as important as balancing the books.

Today, you don't have to go too far on the street before you come across a VSE member or employee willing to rain curses in the direction of the SOB. One former VSE executive complains that the SOB rarely informs the exchange's listings and compliance departments when a listed company is under suspicion, let alone being investigated: "The SOB had the [Beverlee] Claydon file for years. They were investigating her while the Ultra Glow listing was pending and didn't tell us." Other vse regulators say there is a great deal of confusion at the exchange over who is responsible for regulating what. "The vse is where things start, then the sob steps in," says Bill Calhoun, an ex-Mountie and a former vse compliance officer. "The sob likes to lay the blame back on the vse. It's always a fight between the two. The sob would send over garbage, saying they think it's a vse problem." On the other hand, sob employees privately complain about the vse's lack of backbone in dealing with suspect companies, promoters and brokers.

The rcmp are another regulatory force. In the early days they were seldom involved with vse business, because the vse avoided the police unless a situation threatened to roll out of control. During the first twenty-five years of its existence, the vse turned over only two letters of complaint by investors to the police. The problem the police have always faced, then and now, is one of complexity. The machinations of securities fraud demand an understanding of how the industry really works, as opposed to textbook explanations of the rules. This was one of the reasons why the rcmp formed a commercial crime squad in 1967.

Even with a battery of specialists, some of whom have spent three or four years educating themselves about the field, the business of catching stock market crooks is as tough a job as exists in police work. Market manipulation is, by its nature, complicated. Most stock schemes are complex and often subtle blends of legal, illegal and semilegal activities. Catching perpetrators is a long, costly and frustrating business. The Ivan Boesky/Dennis Levine insider trading scandal demonstrates this perfectly. In November 1986, Boesky paid $100 million in fines and pleaded guilty to one felony count after an sec insider trading investigation. An outcry erupted when the press discovered that he had been allowed to sell $400 million worth of stock before his trading privileges were suspended and before the charges were made public. The American sec, even with their crack squads, huge budget, state-of-the-art computer technology and reams of regulations, ultimately had to rely on an informer to break the case. But informers are traditionally difficult to come by on the vse, and the other alternative, wiretapping, is extremely expensive.

As hard as it is to prove a securities case in the U.S., a case involving the vse is a far tougher nut to crack. Even simple problems can become staggering obstacles. Name changes, consolidations and takeovers can turn an investigation into a quagmire. Of the 650 companies listed on the VSE in 1977, only 12 had been untouched by a name change, a merger or a delisting since 1965. In that period there were also 1,623 separate financings. By 1987 the number of companies listed had more than tripled to 2,000. The picture becomes even more complex when the approximately 10,000 directors of those companies are considered. "There could be donkeys listed on the board of directors and we wouldn't know about it," laments Al Dilworth of the difficulty in tracking insider trading.

Promoters complicate things further, especially since they don't always give themselves a position on the board. In fact, some promoters make a point of remaining as anonymous as possible. If anything goes wrong, it is extremely difficult to implicate persons who have no official position. One way to keep out of the limelight is to ensure they never directly own more than 10 per cent of a company, so they don't have to file insider trading reports. That's not to say they don't control more than 10 per cent. It is common practice for promoters to be shrouded by nominees, straw men and back-door agreements. Insider trading, by promoters and others, is one of the most difficult areas to regulate. Some police officials believe that only half of the insider trading on the VSE is ever reported, and it isn't uncommon for insiders to buy and sell VSE stocks through U.S. brokers to avoid making the required declarations. Without full knowledge of what the people with inside information are doing, investors and the police lose one of the most powerful means of evaluating trading patterns.

Despite the difficulties in tracking down securities violators, some of them do get caught. But even after a case is fully investigated and charges are laid, the problems don't end. Very few prosecutors are experienced in handling complex commercial crime cases, and the police find it hard to simplify stock manipulation sufficiently so that judges and juries can understand. One result of trying to de-complicate evidence is that the process sometimes makes the charges appear trivial.

The RCMP are having the same manpower problems as the rest of the regulators. The effectiveness of the commercial crime squad and the Co-ordinated Law Enforcement Unit in policing the securities industry has been eroded in the 1980s by the demands of international terrorism and other, higher profile crimes. "Let's face it," one long-time commercial crime officer says, "a bunch of guys in three-piece suits ripping each other off just doesn't bother people as much as crazies blowing up planes and raping little girls."

While the investigators and the executives of the SOB, the RCMP's commercial crime squad and CLEU are dedicated and intelligent people, the manipulators, con artists and thieves are working the VSE with sophistication and forethought. They've got a battery of lawyers, accountants and brokers to help them slide around the rules and cover their tracks. After all, if they come across a little wrinkle that flummoxes the cops, they stand to make millions with impunity. Also on their side is the fact that the techniques of manipulation and fraud are often so closely allied to honest trading that it is sometimes impossible to tell them apart. The experts themselves can't always agree on things like the definition of an insider or what constitutes a violation such as wash trading.

In the final analysis, the VSE itself should be the most important regulator. The exchange has all the powers it needs to eliminate the undesirable element, and it isn't constrained by the legal or governmental restrictions that bind the police and the SOB. It has the ultimate control over trading and listing. The exchange is also on the front lines; it sees the daily trading and has antennae reaching out to every aspect of the securities industry from the trading floor to the promoter community. But the VSE has steadfastly refused to make itself the dominant regulator. The reasons are simple. The first reason is fear: fear that business will be driven away to seek more accommodating quarters. "You can't squeeze too tightly or you will strangle initiative," is the common refrain. The VSE, however, has yet to test the validity of its long-held philosophy.

The second reason has to do with a basic lack of ethics at the heart of the industry. The unwritten code among some members of the VSE is: "If you can get away with it, then go ahead." This attitude is absorbed by young brokers early on: do nothing to impair the capital requirements of the firm, avoid anything criminal and if you get into trouble you are on your own. Young brokers quickly learn that if they don't toe the company line, they're soon history. More people per capita in B.C. take the securities course than anywhere else in Canada. For every employed broker, there are a hundred working as taxi drivers, telephone repairmen and cooks, waiting to take his place.

A little parable that elicits gales of knowing laughter from brokers perfectly illustrates the way too many view their clients. It's called "Five Ways to Get a Client":

1. You tout a hot stock to your client, get his money and then burn him.
2. You tell him, "Geez, you had a bad break, losing on your first try! It won't happen again, I promise." Take his money and burn him again.
3. "Geez, you've had terrible luck! Losing twice in a row. But I've got a real hot one that'll get all your money back." Take his money, burn him again.
4. "This has never happened to me before. I'm going to let you into a nice little deal that I've got my money into and that hardly anyone knows about, so keep it quiet." Take his money and burn him again.
5. "Christ! We all lost money on that one. You're the only client I've ever had that's had such bad luck. To make it up to you, I'm going to transfer your account to our biggest earner, Midas Jones. You'll make it up in no time." In turn, Midas turns a client over to you, with much the same story, then you burn them both five more times.

The lack of ethics at the foundation of the securities industry can also be seen in the way brokers behave towards each other. In the 1940s when John McGraw was king of the VSE, Cecil Stone recalls that brokers would put one over on their fellow members without a backward glance. "I remember one of the brokers had just recently underwritten a certain stock. He pulled me over and said you should buy some, and he told me how good it was. I went down on the floor, and here was his man selling all he could." Recently, a VSE member with a national firm caught an employee stealing $500,000 from his clients and the company. After forcing the man to repay the money, he unloaded him on a competitor, even providing a reference. No disciplinary hearings were held, and the police were not informed. Today he is vastly amused by the knowledge that the worm is boring into someone else's apple. There are many honourable people associated with the speculative market, people who view the VSE world with fascination and fondness, but too often brokers and promoters treat the VSE as their own personal money machine.

To all public appearances, the VSE is keeping pace with the new age and rapidly moving into an evermore glorious period of profitability and respectability. Proponents confidently declare it to be the leading venture capital market in the world. "Right now, you've got a market that's got growing European interest, a growing American interest every day and is balancing out itself from mining into the industrial sector," boasts Peter Brown. The figures make his comments seem understated. In 1986–87 both the VSE volume of 3.8 billion shares and their value of $5 billion set exchange records. Financings nearly doubled from $348 million in 1985 to $808 million in 1986–87. Expenditures were modest, and the exchange treasury chalked up a $5.5 million surplus. Best of all, the VSE's character appears to be changing with the global industrial trend. Once a repository of prospectors' dreams, the VSE is becoming a marketplace for microchips, cancer cures and technological wizardry. Less than a decade ago 97 per cent of the exchange's listings were resource companies. Today, more than 30 per cent are related to manufacturing, high technology or other nonresource-based enterprises.

As a result, the VSE is in the midst of a crisis, one that could prove its undoing: the phenomenal increase of nonresource stocks. The VSE is completely unprepared for these so-called industrials with assets ranging from supercomputers to new processes for hulling rice. The exchange has used a small body of outside experts, primarily geologists and engineers, to help evaluate properties and acquisitions by listed companies, but now it needs experts from a multitude of different fields to assess cosmetics, breakdance videos, fish farms, cattle ranches, computer software, medical equipment, massage franchises, kitty litter, miniature satellite receivers and a host of other schemes, some of which make the most cockeyed notions of Morris Black and Murray Pezim seem rational in comparison. "It used to be gold, then oil, now it's goddamn cancer cures," snorts Al Dilworth. Inevitably, early in 1987, a treatment for Acquired Immune Deficiency Syndrome (AIDS) surfaced on the VSE. It was an undisclosed natural process trumpeted by a company already involved with a herbal tea treatment for cancer. "We get these 'industrial companies' applying for a listing and we look them over, but we don't know what they are doing, our bosses don't know what they are doing, and so we have to rely on supposedly 'objective' letters of support and evaluation from the companies' own experts. We should be digging around a little to find up what they are up to, but who has the time?" shrugs one of the VSE's current listing officers.

The trickiest of the industrials are the concept stocks, which lend new dimensions to the term "speculative." These companies, usually with few assets and no revenue, exist on the strength of an idea. Sometimes the idea is as ethereal as the right to distribute a product, not yet developed let alone proven, in an unspecified market for an undetermined sum. The public company frequently purchases these rights from a private company owned by the same promoter who controls the public company. Often the area of interest is one so esoteric (like supercomputers) or controversial (like cancer cures) that even if experts could be hired to vet these claims, they wouldn't agree on the validity of the idea. To make things even more complicated, the companies associated with these concepts are typically located in several countries: money raised in Vancouver, scientists based at Harvard, publicists hired in Hollywood, warehouses rented in Arizona and markets planned in China.

Ed Fitch's breakdance empire was one of the many and fleeting concepts to pass through the vse recently. Fitch was a 28-year-old self-styled stock promoter who blew into town to live off the federal government's 1984 scientific research tax credit plan.* Outfitted with a Mercedes, a Victoria penthouse apartment, a California tan and a convincing line, he pulled hundreds of gullible investors, including scientists and academics, into his schemes. One of the funniest was his idea to teach breakdancing to the Chinese. In January 1985, he gained control of a vse shell, Golden Cadillac Resources Ltd., which was trading at 40 cents. The stock jumped to nearly $5 after Fitch announced that the company would be receiving unspecified royalties when a series of ten breakdance flip books were published in Hong Kong and distributed in China. After the stock reached its peak, the breakdance craze ended, and the vse halted trading. Fitch resigned from the company and is currently rumoured to be domiciled in Hong Kong.

The problem with this mass of new concept companies and industrials becomes apparent once you realize how high the stakes have become. It's bad enough that the vse can't properly evaluate the worth or validity of a company trading at $5. But when a Chopp Computers appears and shoots to $120 a share, tens of millions of dollars can be lost and made on a single company. This kind of money naturally attracts an increasingly slick and fast-moving international crowd, over whom it is impossible to exercise any real control. Local promoters

*This mercifully brief program allowed investors to channel money to individuals or companies. The recipients only had to promise to spend the money on scientific research, and the lender could then claim that amount as a tax credit. The system has cost the government over $2 billion not only in lost taxes but also in the time required to investigate the legion of abuses and audit the 1,800 companies that applied for the credit.

already spin the exchange on a merry chase, but at least they are usually known commodities who take some care not to foul their own nests too badly. But international financial wizards like Khashoggi are virtually impenetrable; their deals are cloaked in layers of companies spread around the globe and buttressed by a phalanx of sophisticated legal and entrepreneurial minds. Khashoggi used the vse because he was in deep financial trouble and his advisors told him it was a quick and safe way to raise some badly needed cash. By the time the vse was over the excitement of his presence and started to become suspicious, he was long gone. In the end, far from having its international image improved, the vse came off looking like a sucker.

The underlying problem facing the vse revolves around leadership. It is a befuddled bureaucracy drifting comfortably on its own momentum and is increasingly at the mercy of forces it believes it cannot control. The exchange has always been buffeted by circumstance and forced into change by external pressures. But it has adapted well, defusing crises, scrambling to capitalize on changing market trends and generally reacting to events as they happen. Part of this adaptability has been based on strong leaders who exercised great personal influence on a relatively small organization. However, the vse's most recent strong man, Peter Brown, who showed the rest of the exchange how to profit during changing times, is starting to lose his interest and effectiveness. No successor is waiting in the wings.

Brown is facing a far different exchange from the one he mastered in 1976. It's no longer as easy for him to dominate, nor is the much enlarged and far more bureaucratic exchange as malleable to his will. The bureaucratization of the vse coincides with Brown's declining interest. "I think we're at another level now ten years later [after the 1976 coup]," he said in 1986. "[The vse] needs to take the next step in maturity. And I don't know who's going to lead that. I'm not going to lead it, I want to get back to my own work. Someone else will have to come along." The last time the vse was without a strong man, from 1971 to 1976, was disastrous. The exchange was directionless, unprofitable and generally unable to cope.

Since 1981, the vse president has been the dignified, elegantly dressed and immaculately groomed Don Hudson. He is an extremely nice man and a consummate technical administrator. Hudson was born in 1930, graduated from the University of British Columbia in 1952, worked at cp Air from 1953 to 1964 and then joined Eaton's department stores as senior vice-president of the Pacific division. He is credited with turning the then-frumpy downtown Vancouver outlet into a Bloomingdale-like series of boutiques to cater to upscale Vancouverites with high fashion clothing and furniture. In 1981, he was appointed senior vice-president of the central division (Ontario, Saskatchewan and Manitoba) and moved east. Unhappy with living in Toronto and in conflict with a superior, he resigned. Within two weeks the VSE hired him to take over as president from Bob Scott, who was close to a nervous breakdown.

The VSE is a mid-sized company with only 280 employees. Yet, after five years, some middle-management employees claimed never to have spoken to Hudson, even though they shared the same fourth floor offices. His management style is to communicate almost exclusively through his six vice-presidents, some of whom in turn communicate predominantly through their secretaries. In 1986, a staff meeting was held to discuss continuing morale problems at the VSE. One of the recurring themes was Hudson's perceived aloofness. The next day, Hudson almost tackled an exchange employee whom he'd barely said hello to before and instigated a vigorous conversation about hobbies. There's a running joke between male and female employees on the VSE's fourth floor about the supposed advantage the men have over the women. The women say, only half in jest, that at least the men can see Hudson while they're urinating.

If Hudson is a little shy with his staff, he's downright elusive with the media, which he apparently views either with fear or distaste. It's an attitude that has settled deeply into the exchange, despite the fact that with a few notable exceptions the local media, especially recently, has been very evenhanded with the VSE. "I quit because I was tired of being attacked all the time," says the popular and effective former vice-president of listings, Doug Garrod, a man whom many pick to be president of the VSE one day. "You were always reacting. It was a battleground. . . . The media was part of the enemy, you were always defending yourself." As a result of this us-versus-them mentality, writing routine stories about the VSE can become a herculean task. Phone calls aren't returned, basic factual information commonly provided by other public and private business organizations is unavailable, and many employees, particularly senior ones, are downright hostile. "They act like they've got something to hide," says veteran journalist Paul Grescoe of his dealings with the exchange.

The attitude extends even to academe. "We've had several students try to study the VSE," bemoans John Herzog, chairman of Simon

Fraser University's finance department. "You can't do it even if you try to get very simple information. . . . They're not required [by law] to disclose, and they just won't reveal anything. You can talk to them 'til you're blue in the face." Herzog points to the experience of Sean Killam, a student in the finance department, as a typical case. Supported by phone calls and letters from Herzog and the dean of business, Killam attempted to do some basic research into the efficiency of the VSE. The exchange's lack of co-operation was impressive. First, they wouldn't waive the $2.50 per file viewing fee for his research. Finally, after months of pressure, they offered to provide a copy of the computer tape detailing all transactions for $10,000. "I think they expected me to bugger off and go away," says Killam. He did eventually bugger off, but not before he'd stubbornly invested thirty months of time and $5,000 in the project.

In spite of the us-versus-them attitude, or perhaps because of it, the VSE can engender fierce loyalty. "I loved working there," admits Garrod. "I would go in first thing in the morning and unlock the doors of the floor, watch the lights flood the board and I would say, 'What can I do for the old lady today?' " Except for this and a few other notable oases of passion, the VSE is a cheerless, unfriendly place where smiles are so infrequent you wonder if someone is recording every instance as a demerit for the personnel files.

The VSE is not a place for sentiment. The filing room is a crowded, windowless enclave, with negligible ventilation and the mosquito buzz of dozens of fluorescent tubes. Thousands of files in red and green folders line the walls from floor to ceiling. Few more boring or poorly paid jobs exist than that of a VSE filing clerk. Yet, the job is crucial. The complete histories of all VSE-listed companies are contained in this room: clerks spend their days endlessly inserting annual reports, statements of material facts, financial statements and press releases into the 5,000-plus folders, then retrieving the folders for public and internal VSE use. In 1986, one of the six clerks, a young woman who'd worked there for five years—and precious few in the whole organization have been there that long—resigned. Her last three weeks at work came and went with no sign of recognition or farewell from her colleagues or superiors. The day she left she quietly cried, hidden behind a bank of file cabinets.

The VSE's current direction and future promise is further hindered by the fact that the exchange has forgotten what its business is—selling stocks—and who its real customers are—the investing public.

When the Black Friday fiasco broke, the VSE maintained that, other than margined brokers, the only people hurt were West German investors. It was bad enough that the board didn't see West Germans, the VSE's oldest and most faithful investors, as being important, but it was incredible that the executive claimed to believe that no locals lost money. VSE board members even went so far as to suggest that the public was stupid to have invested in the VSE-listed stocks.

Criticism of the VSE by outsiders is met with a series of time-honoured defences. "The exchange is already too highly regulated, and besides, we tightened it up yesterday." "Stringent rules will drive away both investors and companies." "Risk is inherent in a venture capital market." "The exchange is merely an impartial marketplace, it cannot assume responsibility for the product it sells."

VSE apologists are quick to point out that no amount of regulation will remove all the bad apples from the exchange. They are right, to a point. Even the rigidly controlled New York Stock Exchange has scandals. But there are ways the VSE can improve its reputation without damaging its purpose. First of all, the VSE has to recognize a greater obligation to its investors and a greater responsibility for the companies it lists. The VSE staff, as it is currently structured and financed, is unequal to the task of investigating companies and individuals in any rigorous way. But the exchange, with a $5.5 million surplus in 1986–87, could well afford to create a special investigative squad with a mandate to examine closely suspicious people and companies. The VSE compliance and listing departments are in daily contact with the U.S. Securities and Exchange Commission, but they simply lack the time to give specific cases more than a cursory inspection if their pro formas are correct. A special investigative squad, which would cross all department boundaries. It could have tracked down Ultra Glow's mysterious inventory, for example. It could have learned that Adnan Khashoggi's much-vaunted empire was in ruins by the time he surfaced on the VSE.

No amount of regulation or investigation is going to halt all stock market abuses, but a knowledgeable investigative squad with superior research skills could cut down their incidence and serve as a deterrent to those who see the VSE as an open wallet. The exchange doesn't have to prove anyone "raped the Queen" in order to justify blackballing a promoter or refusing a listing. It is common practice at other exchanges, even if a company technically qualifies for a listing, to refuse the application if exchange officials don't like the people behind it.

Because the exchange does not have to prepare cases for prosecution or fulfill a narrowly defined government mandate, it is not restricted in its attempts to rout and scare off the crooks, whereas the superintendent of brokers and the RCMP are bound and gagged.

Halting a stock and suspending it from trading are problems in that investors' money is at stake. But, if a promotion is a scam, better to halt it at $3 on the way up than at the $30 peak. One of the most common arguments against halting trading on the way up is the damage that could be done to an innocent company. But during the eighteen months spent researching this book, no instance was ever pointed out to the authors of a legitimate company being harmed by a trading halt. Investors and brokers will still scream, but at least the exchange will be seen as trying to protect the investor and make their anguish less expensive.

Reforms will not work without a rebirth of ethics. The VSE exists in a bareknuckle world, and it never has been and never will be a paragon of rectitude. But the pendulum has shifted far too far to the philosophy of "What you can get away with is right." The average investor must come first because he or she is taking the real risks, and no mealy-mouthed philosophizing about the free-enterprise system can change that. The simple fact is that insiders and those who own the VSE are taking far fewer risks than the average investor. And thanks to their control and understanding of the rules, regulations and enforcement, they are being rewarded at levels the mooches, pooches and lambs can only dream about.

Afterword

The Vancouver Stock Exchange's historic boom, bust and clean-up cycle is still intact, but the time between each phase is shortening relentlessly. Events once spread over a decade are now compressed into a few years.

Since 1987 the VSE has staggered through numerous major scandals, including the worst debacles in its history. The first varied from a classic stock swindle only in its international cast of characters and the size of the haul. In this saga, which began back in 1984 but didn't end until 1990, stock promoters Ed Carter and David Ward teamed up to milk a Texas mutual fund of more than $26 million. They bribed Carl Lazzell, a portfolio manager employed by San Antonio's United Services Funds, with $1.4 million to buy shares of nineteen different VSE-listed companies that they controlled.

Screened by 150 nominee accounts, Carter and Ward funnelled most of Lazzell's purchases through Ed Carter's son, a Toronto broker with Richardson Greenshields of Canada. Since they and their associates owned most of the shares, which they'd earlier bought for pennies, Carter and Ward profited hugely as buying drove the stock prices up. Throughout 1984 and early 1985, when these transactions took place, Carter, in particular, was the toast of the exchange and widely heralded as the successor to

Murray Pezim, then in one of his periodic downturns.

Unbeknownst to its senior officers, the San Antonio mutual fund ended up controlling massive blocks of stock in seven VSE companies, even owning all the free trading shares of Tye Explorations, one of the Carter-Ward stable. The VSE somehow overlooked its own disclosure requirements and did not demand that the listed companies involved issue public statements about the fund's controlling positions.

The public was aghast at how effortlessly Carter and Ward manipulated trading and circumvented VSE rules. But more damning was how long they had been at it before the law moved in. Even worse, the regulators didn't pounce until Peter Brown, chairman of Canarim Investment Corporation, where the duo had lodged twenty-nine nominee accounts, informed them of the fund's "problem" in June 1985. The subsequent and secret "rescue operation" by Brown, with the knowledge of VSE vice-president Doug Garrod and superintendent of brokers Rupert Bullock, involved selling over 750,000 shares to Canarim, Carter and Ward. The shares were immediately resold to the unsuspecting public, providing what Brown quaintly termed "rescue profits."

Somehow, Brown, Bullock and Garrod forgot the Securities Act requirement that controlling shareholders must inform the public before selling any shares. So, while "rescue profits" were being made by insiders, even after regulators became aware of the scam, by the time the public found out four months later in October 1985, all hope of recouping their investment had evaporated as the stock prices nosedived.

For once, even VSE president Don Hudson seemed to understand that the exchange had been asleep at the switch. "I am quite prepared to make the general observation that the whole situation was a mess," he admitted to David Baines of the Vancouver *Sun* in April 1990. "In retrospect (it) was not handled very well by anybody. My overall view is that not very many people did very much right."

VSE mythology has it that though the exchange itself experiences scandals from time to time, the brokerage firms that own, run and profit from it are clean and do a good job of policing each other. Though often implicated in shady dealings over the years, brokerage houses and their owners have portrayed themselves as hapless victims of avaricious stock promoters. But the nex debacle showed that VSE seatholders could be bought and sold just as easily as shell companies. The characters behind First Vancouver Securities slithered into the VSE and set up a brokerage firm with a direct connection to former Phillipine president Ferdinand Marcos.

In January 1988 the post Carter-Ward clean-up measures were supposedly firmly in place. That month, First Vancouver purchased a VSE seat after what exchange officials later claimed was an exhaustive three-month investigation on three continents. George Delmas, a thirty-two-year-old stockbroker, became president and Philippine born Fausto Mabanta vice-president. The board of directors included Doug Garrod, a former VSE vice-president.

Nine months later, it took only a few phone calls to uncover the fact that First Vancouver was propped up by racketeering money, but throughout most of 1988 the VSE remained blissfully unaware of the firm's connections and real reason for existence. The exchange was apparently unconcerned that one of First Vancouver's major shareholders, Paradela Holding Corp., was owned by a Spaniard, Leandro Vazquez, who no one, including the board of directors, had ever talked to, let alone seen. And no questions were asked when, just days after First Vancouver opened for business, Paradels's share position jumped from 40 per cent to 75 per cent. The other major shareholder, Rio Grande Investment Corp., dropped to 10 per cent and Delmas, the president, transferred 11 of his 15 per cent share to Mabanta.

Rio Grande was just as mysterious as Paradela. The exchange never discovered what kind of business it was in or even where it was registered. VSE officials were satisfied with the knowledge that Tomas Zita of New Jersey, a relative of Mabanta's, owned the company.

As early as May, only five months after First Vancouver bought a seat, rumours chased up and down Howe Street that Ferdinand Marcos had money in the new firm. First Vancouver didn't work very hard to hide its connections. For example, cheques made out to the firm from National Sugar Trading Co., a well-known Marcos company, were cashed openly at a local bank.

Nonetheless, it wasn't until October, when the U.S. Supreme Court indicted Roberto Benedicto, a close associate of Marco's, on various racketeering charges and froze his assets, including Paradela, that the VSE tumbled to the obvious. Not only did Benedicto own Paradela, but he turned out to be Zita's uncle. Both had worked for National Sugar during Marco's reign.

First Vancouver's accounts were quietly transferred to West Coast Securities. No action was taken against anyone, and most of the participants are still active on the exchange. In the aftermath, a subdued superintendent of brokers, Neil de Gelder, noted, "If we would have known then what we know now, there is no way in the world we would have registered that firm to trade securities in this province." Exactly why they didn't know was never addressed.

The next catastrophe turned out to be not another promoter playing fast and loose with the market, but an unexpected one-two punch from two of the most prestigious and influential business magazines in the world: *Forbes* and *Barron's*. On May 15, 1989, *Barron's* published the "Saga of an Unrepentant Tout," documenting the tangled world of a VSE promoter. *Forbes* followed two weeks later with a story entitled "The Scam Capital of the World." "Vancouver has a serious garbage disposal problem," *Forbes* charged, "the garbage is the Vancouver Stock Exchange. It is polluting much of the civilized world." The publication dubbed the VSE "the longest standing joke in North America."

Exchange president Don Hudson and vice-chairman M.J. Reynolds peevishly complained that both articles neglected to mention "moves undertaken by the exchange to deal with the problems of the past." The *Forbes* piece, they claimed, was packed with "inaccuracies, rumours, innuendoes and exaggerations" though they neglected to offer any specifics. Not above a little innuendo themselves, the two men stated that the article was "so decidedly out of character with your magazine that one cannot help wonder at its motivation," presumably implying that the author, editor or publication owners had lost a packet on the VSE and were seeking revenge.

Having left *Barron's* and *Forbes* trembling from the force of these broadsides, Hudson and Reynolds turned their attention to the local media, which has been even-handed in the face of the VSE never-ending shenanigans. "It is dismaying to see the Vancouver business press jump on the bandwagon of recent publicity in the U.S. and, in a wholesale manner, adopt the extreme statements of the writers, who clearly show lack of understanding, little objectivity, and no balance," Hudson wrote in response to a Vancouver *Sun* editorial headlined "An Augean Stench from Howe Street."

A few days later, apparently intending to defend the VSE, B.C. Minister of Finance Mel Couvelier regenerated international coverage by referring to VSE operators as "scum" and "scumbags." At first Couvelier's comments seemed to be all inclusive. Later, he narrowed charges to those "violating" the "rules and regulations."

VSE investors have always had very short and forgiving memories, but even they couldn't ignore the barrage of international criticism coupled with two monumental scandals. The number of shares traded plummeted from 4.8 billion worth $6.65 billion in 1987 to 3.47 billion worth only $3.36 in 1988. The average price per share offered an even more depressing statistic as it sunk below $1 and hung there interminably.

Historically, a strong man has always appeared to save the VSE during troubled times. Unfortunately for the exchange, Peter Brown, the VSE's unquestioned leader for more than a decade, made good his promise to step back and "get back to my own work." While his company still profited from virtually every major financing and almost every trading flurry, he chose to sit on the sidelines as the exchange floundered. To some it seemed that Brown was trying to wash his hands of the VSE when he took Canarim to Toronto in 1987 and opened up a branch office there. After swallowing millions of dollars in start-up costs, employee contracts, advertising and Bay Street hoopla, Brown, in a previously, undreamt-of move, folded up his tent and sold out to Loewen, Ondaatje, McCutcheon Inc. in late 1989. Since then, Brown has worked as hard at disappearing from public view as he once did at making a name for himself.

Just when the VSE needed him most, the sixty-nine-year-old superstar promoter Murray Pezim wheezed into the picture. Back in 1987, he had created Prime Resources Group Inc. and shovelled into it fifty or so of the VSE companies he carries around with him like so many bangles. One of those companies, Calpine Resources Inc., had holdings in the Eskay Creek region, six hundred miles north of Vancouver, near the Alaska border.

In July 1989 Calpine struck gold, the real kind. When the news hit the street it touched off a classic trading frenzy. Clapine's share price shot up from $1 in May to $9.75 in September and Prime jumped from $1.60 to $5.75 in extremely heavy trading. Pezim is an old hand at the proximity play. As the major landholder in Eskay Creek, all his little companies with claims in the area doubled and tripled in value, no matter how remote their connection.

Pezim accounted for nearly 20 per cent of the VSE volume during those months as trading records were set. For awhile it seemed like old times. The number of shares traded zoomed from 261 million worth $222 million in July to nearly 600 million worth $667 million in August, and Howe Street celebrated the end of a long, bleak winter. Pezim, who had temporarily stopped calling himself "the Greatest," now answered to "the Legend."

When he's on a roll, Murray Pezim thinks he's invincible. Apparently forgetting his earlier disastrous incursions into sports promotion, he swooped in and bought the ailing BC Lions football team in September 1989 for $1.7 million and a $2-million letter of credit.

Typically, Pezim's triumphs begin unravelling almost the moment they are achieved. Thanks to such high jinks as forcing the team to sign aging NFL player Mark Gastineau, who Pezim had earlier tried to turn into a boxer, and rushing out on the field to kiss the foot of kicker Lou Passaglia, he turned the Lions into the laughing-stock of professional football. The team ended the year with a seven-eleven win-loss record and performed even more dismally in 1990 while losing millions.

At the same time as Pezim was toying with the Lions, in the fall of 1989 the B.C. Securities Commission began investigating his trading activities.

In March 1990 the commission announced hearings into charges that Pezim and his associates, John Ivany and Lawrence Page, had breached disclosure and insider trading regulations. It was the first time Pezim had ever been hauled in front of the Securities Commission and in response he threatened to quit the exchange forever, claiming that he'd lost $200 million during the course of the hearing.

Murray Pezim's roller-coaster continues to career through the VSE community, terrifying some that his presence might bring down the whole exchange and others that his absence would do the same. Like the compression of time between the boom, bust and clean-up phases of the VSE endless cycle, Pezim's ups and downs are closing in on each other.

No sooner had Pezim's hearing ended when another public relations nightmare erupted. In the summer of 1990 "PrimeTime Live," an ABC-TV investigative show, slipped a team of employees into Vancouver. The ABC provocateurs posed as a New York investment club and approached a number of VSE promoters and brokers, who they filmed with hidden cameras. Word of the program leaked out and the VSE's index plunged to nineteen consecutive all-time lows, bottoming out just before the program was aired.

"PrimeTime Live" showed brokers offering to manipulate stock prices down to oblige the phoney investors and promoters purveying insider information and making patently false claims about their companies. The reporters then whipsawed VSE president Don Hudson by interviewing him while he watched the videotapes. It was a brutal confrontation which left Hudson baffled, sputtering and no doubt wishing he was back selling socks.

Once again, the VSE claimed the outsiders had "a predetermined agenda" and steadfastly maintained that new computers and fresh regulations had "cleaned up" the exchange.

As usual, the VSE missed the point. The simple fact is that the scandals that reached the public eye are only a small portion of the dozens bubbling below the surface at any given time. Everyone expects "wrongdoing" to happen from time to time, but they also expect the exchange to catch a few of the wrongdoers *before* the widows and orphans are fleeced. All of the recent scandals have been exposed by accident or by a tip-off, and well after the fact.

The VSE remains far more concerned about its image than its product — seemingly unaware of the connection between the two. Increasingly, the investing public realizes that skulduggery is deeply rooted and that "moves undertaken to clean up the problems of the past" only occur when trading volume and value drops dramatically. Invariably, this spirit of reform magically disappears in the next bull market.

The exchange must begin to make changes that aren't just cosmetic, and to realize that the protection of investors, not promoters and brokerage firms, is its most important job. Otherwise, one day the lambs *will* go away, and no amount of image scouring will bring them back.

VSE Annual Trading Volume, Value and Financing

Date	Volume	Value	Financing
1908	367,441	136,440	Figures not
1909	847,665	290,683	recorded
1910	1,829,716	673,342	until 1968
1911	2,030,012	531,065	
1912 to 1914 Figures not available			
1925	24,309,208	890,304	
1926	17,335,987	1,883,107	
1927	21,317,577	5,176,895	
1928	87,228,965	28,563,543	
1929	143,023,643	133,525,733	
1930	9,926,050	3,240,694	
1931	16,653,912	2,753,266	
1932	16,643,358	2,490,758	
1933	88,258,610	28,915,200	
1934	92,136,287	32,434,025	
1935	47,208,890	14,567,081	
1936	99,168,178	26,702,524	
1937	120,699,523	33,497,284	
1938	29,646,047	10,147,392	
1939	21,134,233	8,879,484	
1940	9,026,025	3,136,250	
1941	4,700,832	1,939,404	
1942	3,498,475	1,261,547	
1943	7,374,616	2,384,066	
1944	11,036,061	3,336,234	
1945	27,623,778	9,532,559	

Date	Volume	Value	Financing
1946	22,231,062	12,584,759	
1947	19,962,470	9,926,288	
1948	24,208,687	20,678,293	
1949	16,061,899	17,282,262	
1950	35,108,170	37,534,806	
1951	51,264,920	56,178,188	
1952	36,219,714	40,206,591	
1953	27,530,239	25,369,442	
1954	32,891,615	34,805,113	
1955	49,278,885	61,181,507	
1956	53,784,370	62,393,430	
1957	34,632,868	51,511,109	
1958	31,509,555	48,730,433	
1959	31,680,758	58,111,930	
1960	21,262,921	40,468,040	
1961	89,139,175	115,626,390	
1962	104,793,372	113,276,594	
1963	100,907,384	125,692,533	
1964	263,289,883	219,784,049	
1965	300,502,360	302,201,821	
1966	303,930,085	319,017,975	
1967	351,800,663	337,617,964	
1968	502,214,258	633,311,634	28,988,000
1969	755,727,906	1,147,735,011	46,136,000
1970	518,779,497	454,367,618	18,517,249
1971	606,552,554	488,440,880	18,631,285
1972	906,053,892	784,102,576	31,019,275
1973	592,744,506	483,271,028	26,685,938
1974	557,821,210	464,168,806	24,000,000 estimate
1975	189,842,741	314,500,793	50,593,893
1976	453,919,213	328,311,707	24,689,371
1977	544,433,103	395,075,357	25,128,102
1978	596,925,641	610,514,353	40,284,825
1979	912,866,503	1,467,111,101	104,608,835
1980	1,718,109,539	4,419,598,703	217,754,962
1981	1,574,389,477	3,859,215,887	217,657,244
1982	1,445,363,447	1,559,041,562	50,444,803
1983	3,116,891,756	3,962,958,082	204,575,654
1984	2,263,627,902	2,233,110,456	205,061,048
1985	2,752,966,088	2,718,838,474	348,058,913
1986	3,493,491,647	4,484,519,571	705,134,825
1987	4,795,142,725	6,650,299,602	1,342,824,033
1988	3,473,220,715	3,257,513,049	1,037,778,892
1989	3,982,816,680	3,821,461,428	642,336,529
1990 (First half)	2,180,000,000	2,220,000,000	262,800,000

Stock Exchanges in
British Columbia

Between 1877 and 1910 at least fifteen stock exchanges were formed in British Columbia. Despite the rather suspect intentions of most of these, the first B.C. stock exchange was one of the best planned and least self-serving of all. The British Columbia Mining Stock Board was incorporated in 1877 in Victoria, and its founding officers were a noteworthy lot including the Honourable George A. Walkem (premier of B.C. from 1874 to 1876 and from 1878 to 1882), realtor H. F. Heisterman, Dr. J. S. Helmcken, R. B. McMicking of early light and power fame, John Robson (premier of B.C. from 1889 to 1892) and pioneer druggist Thomas Shadbolt. They took the trouble to incorporate, to gather working capital and to purchase a building. Nonetheless, like its successors, the B.C. Mining Stock Board faded quickly from sight, and no records exist of its demise.

The first exchange to open in Vancouver, the Vancouver Exchange, began trading in 1894 with ten members, including H. Abbott, a superintendent with the CPR, C. D. Rand and Charles Loewen. All the stocks were hydraulic properties, companies that explored for gold by dredging river bottoms. The most significant discovery these listings boasted was the recovery of a single English sovereign, apparently dropped overboard from a passing riverboat, at the Van Winkle bar on the Fraser River. When interest in hydraulic gold operations evaporated a year later, the exchange closed. Rand and Loewen weren't discouraged, and they did come back for a second chance.

In 1897 a small notice in the Victoria *Colonist*, listing new arrivals to the city and the date of the latest strawberry social, included mention of a new

Victoria stock exchange. It was managed by F. H. Blashfield and enjoyed direct telegraphic communication with many financial centres including Chicago and New York. The next year, Vancouver newcomer Grant S. Taggart aimed high when he formed his own exchange, which was to be operated as a branch of the New York Stock Exchange. It opened for business, at the then-unheard-of hour of 7 A.M., in his offices on Hastings Street in Vancouver. There are no records of the fate of Blashfield's or Taggart's exchanges.

During the Rossland gold rush of 1898, two stock exchanges were formed there, ostensibly to grubstake the flood of prospectors who rolled into the tiny community greedy, eager and penniless. The Rossland Stock Exchange of B.C. and the Rossland Exchange were actually created by Toronto brokers. Two may seem excessive for a one-street town, but in those days Rossland was growing with frightening speed. One of the big discoveries was the Le Roi gold mine, which opened in 1899. (The mine was situated just on the outskirts of Rossland, now a pleasant little ski town—probably best known as Nancy Greene's home—and bedroom community servicing the giant Cominco smelter at Trail, forty miles down the road.) In four years Rossland changed from a mountain-dominated tract of forest with neither river, train track nor other transportation route to recommend it, into a thriving centre requiring forty-two saloons, four breweries, two distilleries and an unknown number of bawdy houses to service its 7,000 residents. Between its discovery and shutdown in 1930, the Le Roi mine produced six million tons of ore, which yielded $165 million—worth billions in today's dollars. The two exchanges lasted out the gold rush. The RSE's charter expired in 1908, but there are no records of the RE's last days.

Two more exchanges, in Stewart in 1897 and in Prince Rupert in 1904, were hastily put together in response to the short-lived mining frenzy that centred on the nearby Portland Canal district at the turn of the century. These backwoods exchanges largely fed on the brief but heady influx of prospectors, promoters and remittance men who followed strikes from one stretch of bush to another. They were, in the main, grubstaking enterprises often started by the local grocer, blacksmith, hotel proprietor, saloonkeeper or whoever else had money to risk on a man, a mule and a shovel.

By 1899, Vancouver had jumped into the stock exchange derby again as a group of mining brokers gathered in the city to consider opening yet another one, "In reaction to the excessive difficulty we brokers suffer from not having people and bankers with the inclination to finance our worthy activity." Nothing came of that meeting, mainly because gold fever had peaked and passed. In 1903, the Standard Stock Exchange Ltd. was incorporated in Vancouver. Local mining brokers were sorely disappointed to learn the new exchange was steering far clear of their business, choosing to deal only in New York stocks and bonds and Chicago grain. The Standard Stock Exchange closed its doors almost immediately, but momentum was building to form a permanent exchange.

The next exchange popped up in 1905, hard on the coattails of the not-yet-forgotten gold rushes. It was called the Victoria Stock Exchange Ltd., and its founders R. P. Rithet, E. Crow, T. B. Hall, A. C. Flumerfelt and E. G. Prior were noted community leaders, many of whose names would end up gracing Victoria street signs. There were a few years of activity in a room supplied by the Victoria Board of Trade, but these men did not reckon on the work involved in running an exchange, beyond the raising of their initial $2500 in capital. One by one the founders drifted off to other things. The charter lapsed, but was revived again in 1911, when the city's business and mining elite eyed the increasingly active Vancouver Stock Exchange across the Strait of Georgia and realized what they were missing.

A second Vancouver Stock Exchange set up shop in 1910 heedless of the vse's claim to the name. The vse management committee sent out a flurry of indignant letters to lawyers and the legislature protesting the intruder, only to be terribly embarrassed when they discovered that the rival exchange had rented rooms in the newly erected Exchange Building (a separate corporation), which listed two vse members as its directors. The Pacific Coast Stock Exchange also shouldered into Vancouver that year and, unlike the second Vancouver Stock Exchange, actually conducted some business. Two vse seat holders, H. Lockwood and J. S. B. O'Brian, listed themselves as pcse members.

The vse, which had little enough business of its own until 1910, that year found itself the target of suitors. Two exchanges, the Prince Rupert Stock and Mining Exchange (incorporated in 1904 but dormant until 1910) and its competitor, the Prince Rupert Stockbrokers Association (founded in 1909), both wrote to the vse asking for affiliation to the exclusion of the other.

Among all of these only the vse flourished. It was men like A. N. Wolverton, C. D. Rand, Alvo von Alvensleben and Johnny Jukes who drove the exchange away from a reliance on gold rushes and into a rich pasture of ever-willing lambs.

Note on Sources

This book is not intended to be a definitive academic history of the Vancouver Stock Exchange. Nonetheless, during the eighteen months of research and writing, every effort was made to use original documentation as the basis for the historical information: VSE ledgers, minutes, public and private correspondence, diaries, past members' scrapbooks, court records, memorabilia and government documents. The staffs of the Vancouver and Victoria archives, the Provincial Archives of British Columbia, the Vancouver Public Library and the University of British Columbia Library were particularly helpful in this aspect. Where possible, we conducted personal interviews to highlight and illustrate key moments in the exchange's history. Unfortunately, the exchange itself has no records prior to 1965, and those before the late 1970s are sketchy at best. The only substantial historical collection exists in the provincial archives and roughly covers the period 1907 to the mid-1950s. Figures relating to trading were taken from VSE official documents when available, although in the early years these contained some discrepancies.

The chapters covering recent times are the result of literally hundreds of hours of personal and telephone interviews, and in some cases, lengthy correspondence. As well, we made a research trip to the Montreal and Toronto exchanges and interviewed members of the junior stock and corporate communities in those cities.

We would like to credit the reporting of Brian Powers, Der Hoi-Yin and Peter O'Neil, all of the Vancouver *Sun,* and Allan Robinson of the *Globe and Mail* for uncovering many of the facts contained in the section on "New Cinch: Salting an Assay" in Chapter 15.

Finding out anything someone doesn't want you to know is always a laborious exercise, particularly so in this case. There is a subtle and often not

so subtle undercurrent of fear and secrecy around the VSE that demands
anonymity of sources both within the exchange and in the stock community
at large. There is a great deal of money involved on the VSE and those making it are often less than pleased to have anyone poking into their affairs. One
source was so frightened about being quoted that initially he would contact us
only via telegrams sent to a post office box, with our questions and his answers being vetted by his lawyer. After months of fencing he agreed to talk
but only over the phone. He had good reason to be cautious. A few years earlier, the VSE promoter he'd been working with had told an associate to "get
out of town or else." Apparently the man wasn't fast enough. The next day
the former associate was in hospital with four bullets in his stomach.

On a less sinister level, many within the industry are afraid to be quoted or
even interviewed, regardless of whether or not they have anything critical to
say. They worry about being ostracized or fired. The same anxieties exist in
the brokerage community, where even the most honest and forthcoming are
afraid of having their activities laid bare. As one broker put it, "I may abhor
everything the VSE stands for, but I look after my clients and myself. Get that
straight."

As a result of these attitudes, information about companies listed on the
VSE was often hard to come by. The facts behind the Beverlee Claydon chapter alone took three solid months to uncover, entailing over a hundred separate interviews, thousands of dollars in telephone calls in Canada and to the
U.S., and the sifting of thousands of pieces of documentation.

While there has only been one book ever written about the VSE, the exchange and the people around it are mentioned in several publications.

The Traders by Sandy Ross (Collins, 1984)
The Vancouver Stock Exchange by Frank Keane (Chinook Communications
  Inc., 1981)
Golden Giant by Matthew Hart (Douglas & McIntyre, 1985)
The Acquisitors by Peter C. Newman (Seal Books, 1981)

Other useful published material includes:
Gentlemen Emigrants by Patrick A. Dunae (Douglas & McIntyre, 1981)
The Mine Finders by George Lonn (Pitt Publishing Co., 1966)
The Discoverers ed. Monica R. Hanula (Pitt Publishing Co., 1982)
Swindle! by Roger Croft (Gage Publishing, 1975)
Trading by Susan Goldenberg (Harcourt Brace Jovanovich, 1986)
Under Protective Surveillance by Marlis Flemming (McClelland and Stewart,
  1976)
The Stock Exchange Story by Alan Jenkins (Heinemann, 1973)
The Kingdom by Robert Lacey (Avon Books, 1981)
The Arms Bazaar by Anthony Sampson (Viking, 1975)
Canadian Mining Speculation by T. H. Mitchell (George J. McLeod Ltd.,
  1957)

Index

Printed in Canada